Putting Inequality in Context

Rising income inequality has been highlighted as one of the largest challenges facing the United States. This increasing disparity between rich and poor affects civic participation, and political representation. Although the wealthy can and do often exert more political influence, prevailing over a disempowered ordinary citizenry, this is not always the case. To fix the problem of political inequality, it is important to understand exactly how class divisions manifest themselves in political outcomes, and what factors serve to enhance, or depress, inequalities in political voice. Thus *Putting Inequality in Context* focuses attention on the ways in which citizens and legislators actually experience inequality in their daily lives.

Ellis argues that citizens'—and legislators'—view of class politics are not driven by abstract statistics or aggregate trends, but by lived experience in particular communities. Some of that experience is formally political, but, on an informal basis, citizens learn a great deal about their own position in the broader socioeconomic spectrum, and about the social norms that govern how class intersects with day-to-day life. These contextual factors are also important for policymakers, since most legislators do not represent "the public" at large, but specific constituencies within particular geographic areas.

Focusing on differences across U.S. congressional districts, Ellis argues that individuals' political behavior cannot be separated from their environment, and shows how income's role in political processes is affected by the contexts in which citizens and legislators act and interact. Political inequality exists in the aggregate, but it does not exist everywhere. It is, rather, a function of specific contextual arrangements that serve to depress the political influence of the poor. Identifying and understanding these factors is a crucial step in thinking about what sorts of reforms might be especially helpful in enhancing equality of political voice.

Christopher Ellis is Associate Professor of Political Science at Bucknell University.

PUTTING INEQUALITY IN CONTEXT

Class, Public Opinion,
and Representation in the United States

Christopher Ellis

University of Michigan Press
Ann Arbor

Published in the United States of America by the
University of Michigan Press
Printed and bound by CPI Group (UK) Ltd, Croydon, CR0 4YY

2020 2019 2018 2017 4 3 2 1

A CIP catalog record for this book is available from the British Library.

Library of Congress Cataloging-in-Publication Data

Names: Ellis, Christopher, 1978– author.
Title: Putting inequality in context : class, public opinion, and representation in the United States / Christopher Ellis.
Description: Ann Arbor : University of Michigan Press, [2017] | Includes bibliographical references and index.
Identifiers: LCCN 2017003531 | ISBN 9780472130498 (hardcover : acid-free paper) | ISBN 9780472123124 (e-book)
Subjects: LCSH: Equality—United States. | Political participation—United States. | United States—Social conditions. | United States—Economic conditions. | United States—Politics and government.
Classification: LCC JC575 .E45 2017 | DDC 306.20973—dc23
LC record available at https://lccn.loc.gov/2017003531

Contents

Contents

Acknowledgments

This book could not have been written without intellectual and personal support from a number of different people. Much of the impetus for this book began in a now decade-old series of conversations in an American Politics graduate seminar at the University of North Carolina. Joe Ura was an especially prominent member of those discussions, and from them began a productive series of collaborations with him from which this book builds (and, occasionally, challenges).

Numerous coauthors and friends have made comments on various parts of this project that have greatly improved the arguments made in this book and the papers and presentations that preceded it. Michael MacKuen, Christopher Faricy, Peter Enns, Patrick Wohlfarth, Christopher Wlezien, Scott Meinke, and Marco Steenbergen, as well as participants at the UNC American Politics Research Group seminar, have been especially helpful in challenging me to produce a more refined and focused book. Janine Glathar in Bucknell's Department of Information Technology deserves special recognition for having the patience to help me through learning the rudimentary GIS skills necessary to produce the maps in this book. I also wish to thank both Melody Herr and Meredith Norwich at the University of Michigan Press for a review process that was prompt, thorough, and professional. The manuscript is much stronger as a result.

As with all of my work, I owe a special debt of gratitude to Jim Stimson, whose constant counsel and wisdom helped to steer me in the right path as an academic, and whose unwavering support and encouragement played a pivotal role in keeping me in this profession in the first place. Jim's work has fundamentally shaped how we think about public opinion and representation in American politics, and I couldn't be prouder to have worked with him as a student, collaborator, and friend.

Finally, thanks as always goes to Carrie, for sticking with me, picking me up when I fell, and always helping to remind me of what's important. The best times, I promise, are still to come. And to Connor and Charlotte, you are the best things that could have ever happened to me, and have made my life better in every possible way. I will do everything I can to return the favor.

Tables

Figures

ONE

Thinking about Political Inequality

In 2013, the Birmingham, Alabama suburb of Gardendale began the process of disassociating itself from the Jefferson County school district, of which it had been a part. Residents did so in order to form their own school district, comprised only of students who live within the town boundary. Officials of Gardendale (which is 88 percent white and has a median income roughly twice that of the state average) voted to raise property taxes to finance development of this new district—which they expect will offer educational opportunities far more enriching than those provided by the Jefferson County schools (where more than half of the students enrolled qualify for federal free or reduced lunch subsidies). Gardendale's efforts are part of what the *Nation* (2014) refers to as a "new secessionist movement," in which wealthy towns or communities (largely, but by no means exclusively, in the South) within larger, mixed-income school districts vote to establish their own, well-funded, districts.

Many of these sorts of efforts have occurred in Alabama, where funding inequities across high- and low-income districts are among the greatest in the country. With very little state revenue earmarked to compensate for the low property tax bases of economically struggling areas, Alabama's high-poverty districts receive, on average, nearly $1,000 less per pupil than do its districts with very little poverty (Baker, Sciarra, and Farrie 2015). Alabama's aggregate performance on standard educational metrics has been improving in recent years, but its low-income students still achieve at rates well below the national average (Annie Casey Foundation 2014). Though the state has commissioned a study to determine whether there are ways to target additional resources to high-poverty districts, or districts with large numbers of at-risk students, large-scale efforts to do so would almost certainly require an amendment to the state Constitution (Lyman 2014).

Minnesota, meanwhile, has been moving in the other direction. In 2013, the state legislature approved several changes in state law that are designed to funnel additional state resources to low-income districts. Such "Location Equity Revenue" (Walseth 2013) is meant to compensate for both the challenges of educating academically disadvantaged students and for the lower revenue bases of lower-income districts. It adds to an already progressive school funding formula that, on average, provides high-poverty districts roughly 30 percent more per pupil than low-poverty ones. The educational performance of Minnesota's low-income students—while still lagging well behind that of their high-income peers—ranks among the best in the country (Annie Casey Foundation 2014).

The politics behind these stories are complex: embedded in them are views on ideology, history and tradition, the value of education, and myriad other things. Given where they took place, they also say something about the enduring importance of race in American politics.[1] But they are also a story of how different areas of the United States have responded to the country's growing divergence of incomes. As Piketty and Saez (2014) and many others have shown, nearly all economic gains over the past half century have been captured by a fairly small slice of the population. As a result, income and wealth in the United States are as unequally distributed as they have been in nearly a century. This inequality is in many ways the defining story of American politics over the past several decades, one President Barack Obama has called the "defining challenge of our time."

But while income inequality has increased nationally, the ways in which citizens experience it is not the same everywhere. Poor children in both Alabama and Minnesota face challenges. For some, these challenges are exacerbated by race, family status, or other factors. But the context in which they live matters, too. All else equal, poor children—or wealthy children—growing up in certain areas have different experiences, and different opportunities, than others. These differences are not just limited to educational experience. Wealthier people, on average, enjoy greater social and community resources, and closer ties to the policy-making processes that affect them, than do the poor. But the contexts in which they live also say a great deal about the environments in which they are socialized, the opportunities and resources that they are offered, the milieu in which their civic and political discourse happens, and the ways in which they interact with their political and economic officials. Class matters in the United

States. But the ways in which it matters for both civic participation, and political representation, depends on the context in which it is experienced.

Inequality and American Democracy

This is a book about class politics in the United States. More to the point, it is a book about inequality in political power across income lines. Income inequality is, by essentially any measure, rising. There are also similar divergences in economic security and opportunity: wealthy citizens have become not only wealthier but also more insulated from market risk and job instability relative to the poor (Hacker 2006). Social mobility—the ability to move up or down on the income spectrum over the course of one's lifetime—has declined as well (Aaronsen and Mazumder 2008). Even increases in life span over the past 50 years have been enjoyed only by those in the top portion of the income distribution (Cohen, Preston, and Crimmins 2011).

While these facts in and of themselves may be cause for alarm, political science has made a strong case that economic inequality also is strongly connected to inequalities in political voice. Rising economic inequality, in other words, is largely a political construct, both a function of and a cause of a political system that allows people to use their economic means to get what they want from democratic processes. The notion that the health of a democracy could be jeopardized by the relationship between money and political power is, of course, not a new concern. And so long as political participation (and more broadly, freedom of speech) remains voluntary and relatively unregulated, wealthier people will have advantages in the political processes that the poor do not share. Political participation is a resource-based activity, and wealthy citizens generally have more political resources than the poor (Rosenstone and Hansen 1993).

But the notion that growing economic inequality may translate to significant disparities in political influence is a troubling phenomenon, given that a key virtue of successful democratic systems is their ability to largely separate economic power from political power (Walzer 1983). The equal consideration of all citizens is, as Verba (2003) states, "one of the bedrock principles in a democracy." A flurry of recent research has empirically investigated the connections between economic inequality and political influence, and the findings have been troubling. We have learned that inequality leads to a lower sense of political efficacy among the poor (Uslaner and Brown 2005), and a greater ability for wealthy people to set the political agenda and draft candidates that they prefer (Hacker and Pierson 2011). Some have also posited that economic inequalities have exacerbated differences in political engagement and participation (e.g., Solt 2008).

Most problematically, we have seen evidence that the political system privileges the interests of the wealthy over the poor (e.g., Bartels 2008; Gilens 2012; Flavin 2012; Ellis 2013). When policymakers have a choice to represent the views of the poor or the views of the wealthy, they by and large choose the views of the wealthy. The result is that rising inequality—abetted, to be sure, by other structural changes in global economic and technological forces—is not only tolerated but exacerbated by a political system that ignores the interests of the poor.

Inequalities in policy representation, in other words, seem to be the norm rather than the exception. And despite all this, lower-income citizens have generally not responded to growing inequality with stronger and louder demands for redistribution. Even though the United States has higher levels of inequality than nearly every other established democracy, Americans generally have lower levels of class consciousness than most other nations (Lipset and Marks 2000). On many major policy issues, the views of wealthy and poor citizens are more similar than they are different. By many accounts, this lack of class consciousness is born from the simple notion that citizens are either unable or unwilling to connect their preferences with the policies that are best for their own needs and values (Frank 2005; Bartels 2008). And at least according to some measures, high levels of inequality seems to *decrease* demands for redistribution—perhaps especially among wealthy citizens (who might be thought to benefit from such inequality) but also from the poor as well (Enns et al. 2014). The aggregate picture, one might surmise from this work, is bleak: one where "oligarchy" (Winters and Page 2009) reigns, the wealthy have significant power to turn their economic self-interest into established public policy, and ordinary citizens are too powerless or too disengaged to do anything about it.

But the story of income inequality and political influence is more complicated than this. There are some contexts—both in the United States and elsewhere—in which lower-income people have mobilized to be a potent political force (Hill, Leighley, and Hinton-Andersson 1995; Jackson, Brown, and Wright 1998), or where laws exist to enhance the political clout of the poor (Flavin 2015a). There are places where a robust political discussion revolving around class and redistribution exists, or where wealthy and poor citizens seem to be responding rationally to changes in the political environment around them (Soroka and Wlezien 2008). And there are contexts in which lower-income citizens do get what they want from elected officials (Ellis 2013; Rigby and Wright 2013). While political inequality seems to be the norm in American politics, it is far from clear that it is a universal, or at all necessary, outgrowth of the country's basic political and economic systems.

For reasons both theoretical (what do we know about how citizens and legislators think and behave in an era of rising inequality?) and substantive (if political inequality is a problem, how might we go about fixing it?), it is important to understand exactly how class divisions manifest themselves in political outcomes, and what factors serve to enhance, or depress, inequalities in political voice. This book takes a step in that direction, by focusing attention on the ways in which citizens and legislators actually experience inequality in their daily lives.

National Inequality, Local Experiences

Income inequality is a national issue with national consequences. But we know that citizens are largely unaware or uninterested in these sorts of national trends (Lawrence and Sides 2014). And even for citizens who are aware of them, the economic inequalities and class divisions that are reflected in national statistics may be a poor reflection on the ways in which these factors manifest themselves in citizens' regular experiences. Some communities are more equal than others. Some are wealthier than others. Some provide more educational and social resources than others. Some are more economically segregated than others, while some provide more opportunities to see and interact with different sorts of people than others.

The general argument in this book is that it is these sorts of local factors that provide a basis for how citizens—and legislators—connect income inequality to their attitudes and behaviors. Thinking about "rising inequality" solely as a national phenomenon misses a good deal about how that inequality is experienced and lived in diverse ways in diverse types of communities. As a result, while inequality is increasing more or less everywhere, the way that that inequality—and class politics more generally—manifests itself in political behavior will differ in predictable and meaningful ways based on political context.

The main point of what is to come is simple: citizens'—and legislators'—view of class politics is not driven by abstract statistics or aggregate trends, but by lived experience in particular communities. Whether or not "all politics is local," it stands to reason that the ways in which citizens think about inequality, and about their class position more generally, is driven by the immediate environment in which those things are experienced.

Citizens learn much that can inform their views about their own economic position and class politics more generally from the context in which they live. Some of these experiences are formally political, or the result of political processes—debates between friends, neighbors, or local politicians regarding property tax rates or public assistance, or the educational and communal resources to which citizens have access. But most of them are not. In the course of regular interactions with people and environments, citizens learn a great deal about their own position in the broader socioeconomic spectrum, and about the social norms that govern how class intersects with day-to-day life. Are the people around me mostly richer than me, or mostly poorer than me? Do I regularly interact with people who look different from me, or not? Are these interactions, in the main, positive or negative? Do I receive messages—through the media, or through conservations with friends and acquaintances—that the poor are lazy or responsible for their own fate, or that the wealthy are simple beneficiaries of luck and circumstance? Do people like me care about politics? Are they politically active? Do they feel as if they can make a difference? Does it appear that people like me have a real chance to get ahead in life? These sorts of interactions—what Baybeck and McClurg (2005) call the "slow drip of everyday life"—are integral in shaping how citizens think about class, inequality, and political life.

To a great extent, the same sorts of contextual factors are important for policymakers, too. Broader changes in the political and economic climate may be increasing the pressures for policymakers of all stripes to cater more strongly to the interests of the wealthy. But most legislators do not represent "the public" at large, nor are they ultimately accountable to the interests of specific pressure groups. Rather, they represent specific constituencies within particular geographic areas. We know that legislators do not see their constituencies as a simple undifferentiated mass, but as a number of separate subconstituencies, each with different views, motivations, and usefulness to the legislator's career and policy goals (Fenno 1978). The composition of these subconstituencies, their relative power and numbers, and the political resources at their disposal, vary in substantial ways across areas of the country. These factors, in turn, affect who policymakers hear from and, in turn, who they represent (Miler 2010).

Context and Class Politics

In the book, I develop a general model of how local context affects class politics in the United States. I use it to explore two central questions. First, how does context affect the way in which rich and poor make sense of political life? Second, how does context affect how rich and poor are represented by policymakers?

Most theoretical discussions and empirical models in this book seek to explain the choices of individuals, whether ordinary citizens or legislators. What factors affect whether a citizen is likely to vote? Or to hold "liberal" or "conservative" views on redistributive issues? What factors affect how well, or how equally, a legislator represents his or her constituents? There is a rich tradition of scholarship of the sort under consideration here, studying the behavior of both public opinion and legislator choice with respect to these sorts of questions from an individual-level, micro perspective.

But following from the excellent work of Robert Huckfeldt, this book argues that "political opinions and behavior of individuals cannot be explained apart from the environments in which they occur" (1986, 1). With that perspective in mind, the book will work to understand how income's role in political processes—in shaping both how citizens think and act, and how legislators represent their constituents—is affected by the contexts in which citizens and legislators act and interact.

The book will focus on U.S. congressional districts as the contextual unit of interest. As I outline in more detail in chapter 2, congressional districts are assumed to be formal political boundaries that provide a useful, if imperfect, approximation of the context in which citizens experience political life. They also serve as a critical nexus of representation between citizens and the federal government. Finally, their geographical, socioeconomic, and demographic composition varies starkly across areas of the country. They thus provide a uniquely valuable way to understand contextual differences in both public opinion and representation.

The rest of the book proceeds as follows. Chapter 2 reviews what we know about the role of contextual factors in political choices, and introduces a general model of how context affects the landscape of class politics in the United States. This model builds from and integrates insights from many different disciplines to understand the contextual factors—both formal and informal—that shape how both citizens and legislators think and act. The rest of the book works to apply aspects of this model to issues pertinent to the study of class politics and political inequality in the United States.

Chapter 3 and 4 explore the role of context in shaping the behavior of ordinary citizens. Chapter 3 addresses the issue of equality in political participation. We know that wealthier citizens participate in politics at greater rates than poorer ones: political participation is a resource-based activity, and wealthier individuals generally possess more political resources than poorer ones. But particularly for the poor, the ways these resources are developed and translated into politically meaningful activity is affected by both informal (e.g., social norms) and formal (e.g., institutional structures and laws) attributes of the areas in which citizens live.

Chapter 4 deals with class differences in public opinion. Building from chapter 2, this chapter offers a model of "activated class awareness" that works to understand where we should expect opinions on political issues to divide strongly along class lines, and where the opinions of rich and poor should remain roughly similar to one another.

Chapters 5 through 8 turn to the issue of political representation. Chapter 5 outlines the concept of "dyadic representation," and makes the case that inequalities in political representation are real and significant. Importantly, it also makes the case that simple aggregate explanations for why inequalities across income lines persist—that wealthy people donate and vote more than the poor, or are more likely to belong to privileged demographic groups—tell only a limited part of the story.

Chapter 6 explores the impact of contextual factors on representational equality, showing that a persistent representational bias in the aggregate masks significant differences in representational inequality across congressional districts, and arguing that these differences can be explained by differences in how visible, and how relevant, poor citizens are to their representatives. Chapter 7 turns the focus to representational inequality over time, highlighting the fact that many of the contextual factors that we would expect to increase the size of the representational gap between rich and poor are becoming more prominent over time. Accordingly, representational inequality is growing over time as well. Finally, chapter 8 offers some broader analyses of democratic accountability and representation, and offers some ways to use what we have learned to think about remediating political inequality.

The implications of the findings are diverse, and the effects of context on behavior are not always linear or straightforward. But the general message is simple: contextual factors—in particular, the resources that a community offers to its lower-income citizens, and the visibility that such citizens have to their elected representatives—can serve either to enhance the political voice of the poor or to take it away. Political inequality exists in the aggregate, but it does not exist everywhere. It is, rather, a function of specific contextual arrangements that serve to depress the political influence of the poor. Identifying and understanding these factors is a crucial step in thinking about what sorts of reforms might be especially helpful in enhancing equality of political voice.

TWO

Context and Inequality in American Politics

The economic gap between rich and poor is an enduring and deeply important feature of American politics. Its steady increase over time has been identified as a cause or consequence of nearly every other major economic, political, or sociodemographic shift in American politics over the past 40 years—changes in immigration patterns, changes in educational and public health outcomes, and increasing party polarization, to name just a few (Wilkinson and Pickett 2006; McCarty, Poole, and Rosenthal 2006; Berube 2014; Bonica et al. 2015). But how does this growing income gap map onto the choices that ordinary citizens make—how, in other words, does one's income position affect how one thinks about politics? And how do these effects translate into the sorts of actions that representatives take?

There is, of course, a wealth of national-level data documenting growing income inequality, and documenting differences in the lived experiences of the rich, poor, and middle class. These data often form the starting point for scholarly and media-driven conversations about income disparities in the United States. But citizens are, generally speaking, not terribly well informed when it comes to national economic conditions, or even their own standing in the country's broader class structure (Vanneman and Pampel 1977; Gorman 2000). This lack of understanding of one's economic "place" is often cited as an argument for why class interests do not neatly map onto political conflict in the United States: If citizens cannot understand basic facts about economic inequality and their own social status, then how can they connect their own interests to politics in a meaningful way?

Citizens, are, however, somewhat better at identifying economic and social conditions in the communities in which they live (Newman, Johnston, and Lown 2015), and use local conditions as a way to inform their estimates about national conditions (Ansolabahere, Meredith, and Snowberg 2014; Hansford and Gomez 2015): citizens' evaluations of what is going on in the nation are driven largely by their evaluations and perceptions of what is going on immediately around them. Further, it is these experiences with, and concerns about, local conditions that ultimately informs how citizens translate economic evaluations into political choices (Cho and Gimpel 2009; Rogers 2014). When understanding how economic divisions map onto political attitudes and behaviors, in other words, focusing on what is happening in the nation at large might matter considerably less than focusing on what is happening in the particular contexts in which citizens live, work, and interact.

The goal of this chapter is to offer a contextual explanation of how economic differences manifest themselves in political choices. The general argument is that neither citizens nor legislators view income inequality in abstract, nation-centric ways, but rather through experiences in their communities, districts, and social environments. The ways that citizens experience both income inequality and their own economic position in society is driven not by national trends or statistics, nor by a comparison of how one is doing compared to "Americans" broadly defined. It is, rather, driven by how they see themselves, and how they perceive economic divisions, in the environment around them. I expect that these "lived experiences" to matter to how wealthy and poor citizens make political choices and make the decision to participate in political life. They should also matter to the ways in which legislators view their rich and poor constituents, and the ways in which they choose to represent (or not represent) their interests in policymaking.

Why Does Context Matter?

The rationale for a context-driven model of political behavior is simple: people do not live or make decisions in isolation, but rather as social beings embedded in particular environments. Myriad individual-level attributes—family socialization, personality, race and ethnicity, gender, economic self-interest, and religious beliefs, to name just a few—have obviously important effects on political behavior. But we also know that people who are demographically similar, but live in different places, often make starkly different political choices. How one's personal attributes map to specific choices is at least a part a function of contextual experience.

Contextual effects on behavior—defined broadly by Huckfeldt (1986) as "environmental influences that arise through social interaction with the environment" are rooted in myriad personal experiences—with the laws and customs of a given area, in formal and informal social interactions with people, and in observations of how people conduct themselves. Together, such factors provide an important way of teaching citizens how to think about the political world, and their place in it. The importance of the role of context has been borne out in a number of studies of political behavior in both the United States and elsewhere, and among both masses and political elites. Political attitudes and political behaviors are spatially clustered: all else equal, people who live near one another hold more similar political attitudes, and participate in politics at more similar rates, than would be expected when considering sociodemographic characteristics alone (e.g., Berelson, Lazarsfeld, and McPhee 1954; Huckfeldt and Sprague 1992; Gimpel and Schuknecht 2004; Dalton and Anderson 2011).

In some cases, context is important because of the laws and institutional arrangements it imposes on people. We know, for example, that electoral rules affect both the number and type of political choices offered to citizens, and how citizens respond to such choices.[1] These factors, in turn, affect citizens' decisions about who to vote for, the decision to participate in politics at all, and even attitudes toward the fairness and efficacy of the political system itself (e.g., Jackman 1987; Janda 1993; Blais 2006; Dalton 2008). Put simply, contexts matter because they provide a vehicle for social learning, a means of gathering information about the rules and norms under which political conflict is structured, and for forming the social networks that serve as a basis for political understanding (e.g., Mutz 2002; McClurg 2003).

Contexts also matter because of their psychological effects on citizens. The environment in which one is embedded shapes citizens' beliefs and values and how they view particular political or social interactions. Discussions narrowly related to politics matter, of course, as the political information that citizens use to make decisions (as well as the deeper political orientations that citizens use to evaluate that information) are distilled and obtained through social networks and opinion leaders within a political context (Huckfeldt, Johnson, and Sprague 2004; Walsh 2004, 2015).[2]

But perhaps most important, context matters because of the importance of the regular, low-intensity, nonpolitical experiences, interactions, and occurrences that citizens experience every day (Cho and Rudolph 2008). Even for apolitical individuals with few close social ties in a given community, basic interactions with people around them in the course of doing mundane tasks—shopping for groceries, walking in their neighborhoods, commuting to work—have deeply important consequences for shaping one's perceptions of the broader social world (Huckfeldt 1986). Regular interactions with people in one's physical environment, regardless of whether such interactions are particularly memorable, or explicitly political, are integral in forming social reference groups, views of what sorts of social behavior or views are considered "normal" or "acceptable," and beliefs as to what sorts of values, traits, and personal attributes are considered desirable (e.g., Hitlin 2003; Vauclair and Fischer 2011). These interactions need not be overt, or even consciously remembered, to exert a strong influence on one's views of social norms and community values: subtle and secondary cues (e.g., such as how yards are groomed, the cars that people drive, how people interact with workers in the course of obtaining services) all send messages that can have political implications. What we might think of as "bedrock" individual-level political and social values, in other words, are strongly contextually influenced.[3]

Contextual factors also matter to the choices of policymakers, not just ordinary citizens. There is, of course, a well-established literature on the role of political institutions in shaping policymaker behavior and legislative outcomes: we know that different rules governing the concentration of power, the processes through which legislation is enacted, the number of veto points in legislative process, and the like, affect the outcomes that a political system produces independent of both citizen and legislator preferences (e.g., Krehbiel 2010; Alesina and Glaeser 2003).[4] These outcomes, in turn, affect both how citizens perceive that they are represented by the political system, and the actual distance between citizens' views and the view of those that represent them (Miller and Listhaug 1990).

And while policymakers certainly have on average more informed and stable belief structures and policy positions than most citizens, legislators face many of the same decision-making challenges—having many competing considerations and pressures to reconcile, and having limited time and information to understand all of them perfectly—as citizens do (Kingdon 1989). Contextual factors—the strength of particular interest organizations or industries, the economic and social compositions of their constituencies, and even the geographic structure of their districts—affect who legislators hear from, how they perceive their constituents, and how they reconcile competing demands on their time, resources, and votes (Hall 1996). Both the manner and the environment in which legislators receive information, in other words, matters to how they use that information to make choices (Miler 2010).

Contexts, or Collections of Individuals?

Of course, we might be concerned whether contexts themselves have an impact above and beyond the individual-level attributes of people that live in them. This issue is especially pertinent given that people can, and often do, "self-select" into geographic areas that fit their personal experiences and values (Bishop 2009). People who work in the technology industry, or who are evangelical Christians, or care deeply about the environment, will, all else equal, prefer to live around other technology professionals, evangelicals, or environmentalists, respectively. So it is clearly the case that much of what we see as contextual differences in American politics are simply aggregations of the attitudes and behaviors of people who live in different places. And contextual differences can have a self-reinforcing capacity as well: areas with particular cultures attract people from other places who share the dominant values of that area (Nall 2015).

But at the same time, a significant body of research illustrates that differences between geographic areas are more than compositional: they influence behavior as well. Cultural differences bind people to local laws, customs, and cultures into which they are socialized (Axelrod 1997; Gimpel and Schuknecht 2004). The environment in which one lives encourages particular norms of behavior and thinking that affect the worldviews of people within those environments, even among people who are not otherwise predisposed to share those norms.

And formal policies and policies matter as well: as Pierson (1993) and others have documented, policies created in particular locations matter not just because of their intended and immediate effects but because their presence also encourages particular interpretations of the social world, and of government-citizen relations. Laws legitimate certain ways of thinking, and delegitimate others (Noelle-Neumann 1993). Places are aggregations of individuals, but also shared social spaces that shape, and reshape, values, beliefs, and behaviors.

Income and the Mechanisms of Contextual Influence

The goal of this book is to understand contextual differences in how income differences matter to political outcomes—both in how citizens approach the political world and in how elected officials respond to those citizens. There is no shortage of reasons to think that the environments in which citizens and legislators find themselves affect how class differences translate into political outcomes. In this section, I outline some of the mechanisms, both formal and informal, that I expect matter to how contextual differences become relevant to understanding the political divides between rich and poor.

Reference Group Formation

As we have discussed, some of the most important aspects of contextual influence on behavior are the regular, informal interactions that citizens have in their communities and surrounding areas. They need not be explicitly political or even particularly social—the life that one sees around one on the road, in the gas station, at the supermarket, or at church matters in large part because they shape citizens' social reference groups, and citizens' basis for social comparison with others. Put simply, even these simple and forgettable experiences, because they happen regularly enough, are integral because they provide a cumulatively strong influence on how people view themselves in comparison to others.[5] If someone works or is looking for work in a context near where they live, these sorts of interactions are buttressed by more structured tasks that also illustrate ways in which income and class manifest themselves in social behavior.

These sorts of interactions are important in shaping how people view their own economic position, and their relative level of economic success, in relation to others. They also matter in shaping how people view the degree of both connection and discord between people of different economic classes. Do I "fit in" economically with the people around me, or do I stand out? Do I have regular interactions with people who are different than me, or not? Does it appear that it is easy for someone to get ahead, or are peoples' economic fates more or less static? Do wealthier citizens seem to view poor citizens with sympathy? With condescension? Again, how citizens answer these sorts of questions is in part contextually based. An area in which wealthy and poor citizens live in separate, highly economically segregated enclaves is very likely to engender a different view of class politics than an area where rich and poor live near one another and interact—at least informally—regularly.

Political Culture

We know that the political cultures—defined broadly here as the general sets of communal values that shape political behavior—differ in meaningful ways across areas of the country. These cultures create differing sets of expectations, diffused throughout the citizenry in a given area, of what sorts of values and beliefs are prioritized and cherished. These differences are perhaps most obvious when it comes to religious and "cultural" matters. Debates over (for example) the ways that concepts such as evolution and "intelligent design" should be taught in public schools are dramatically different in various areas of the country, and reflect enduring differences in how citizens in different areas view the relationship between religious belief and scientific inquiry. Both proponents and opponents of teaching religious-based theories of creation know that these debates matter because the content of school curricula reflects, in a fairly fundamental ways, the values that will be used to assimilate citizens to a particular way of thinking about the social world.[6] They also make a strong statement about the values that adults within a given community are expected to hold. Even if these values are not universally shared, they serve as basis for understanding what is within the bounds of acceptable belief and behavior, and as a groundwork for structuring social interaction (Beyer and Liston 1996).

In much the same way, cultures matter in shaping how people view the current economic playing field and, in turn, matter to how people think about inequality and political issues pertaining to the divide between rich and poor. Are concepts such as "meritocracy" prized and valued, or are there reasons to think that economic success and failure are often out of an individual's control? Are the rich to be viewed with admiration for working hard, taking risks, and succeeding, or to be viewed with scorn for benefiting from an unlevel playing field? Is poverty primarily a function of individual failings, or structural factors? The ways in which citizens answer questions such as these differ across various areas of the country (Hopkins 2009). We should expect these differences to be integral to how citizens of all income levels view their own economic position and the positions of others, and approach political issues related to the politics of income differences.

Shared Norms of Behavior

The idea that people who live near one another might act similarly is not unique to politics: people who share space also tend to share similar patterns of conduct in all sorts of realms (Crenson 1983). But this tendency for contextually based norms of behavior is particularly relevant in the political realm, given the strong social component to the decision to participate in political life. Through regular formal and informal interactions, citizens learn the "prevailing norms" (Cho and Rudolph 2008, 276) of their social network, and tend to structure their own behavior accordingly.

Again, people tend to take informal cues from their social environments about what the norms of citizenship and participation are generally, and what they are for people of similar social position more specifically. Is voting, for example, perceived as something that everyone does, or is it something that takes a specific effort and commitment? Is it normal for people to know and care about politics? Do people like me tend to speak up and get involved in political life, or is political conversation limited to those who are more educated, wealthy, or connected than me? Does it appear that participation from people like me will make a difference?

Distribution of and Access to Resources

Context also matters because it affects access to resources—both economic and political—that citizens have. In some cases, the presence or absence of these resources is simply a matter of what sorts of individuals live in a given area. Areas with large concentrations of wealthy people, for example, tend to have higher quality public schools and public services than areas with large concentrations of poorer people (Massey 1996; Sampson 2003). These resources, in turn, have meaningful effects on the opportunities and outcomes of citizens that live in these contexts. Living in well-resourced and well-networked areas is associated with a wide variety of positive outcomes, from social capital (Kawachi et al. 1997) to health (Yen and Kaplan 1999) to educational success (Stewart, Stewart, and Simons 2007). These effects, in turn, affect how citizens perceive their neighborhoods and their political systems. And we also know that these benefits tend to extend to people who live in these areas regardless of their own personal economic standing: poor children who attend schools with large concentrations of wealthy students, for example, tend to fare better on a wide variety of educational metrics than poor children who attend schools with large concentrations of poorer students (Roosa et al. 2003; Leventhal and Brooks-Gunn 2000).

The logic here extends to politics as well: citizens who live in well-resourced and well-networked areas should have greater opportunities for meaningful political participation, and should hold different attitudes toward the functioning of the political system, than citizens who live in less-well-resourced areas. This is in large part due to the stronger social infrastructures of these communities, and the resources that they tend to provide in support of meaningful political engagement. But it is also due to the greater attention paid to these communities by policymakers and political candidates. Parties and candidates concentrate their mobilization efforts on communities with significant political and social resources, for example, simply because they know that these sorts of efforts are more likely to be successful in attracting new participants (Brady, Schlozman, and Verba 1999).[7]

Laws and Institutional Structures

Finally, we know that contexts matter because they shape the rules under which political discourse and political engagement is conducted. In the United States, the laws that govern political debate and political participation, the transparency of the political process, and the like vary across the country in ways that have meaningful consequences. Governments structure choices and incentives for citizens, and these incentives, in turn, affect behavior. The ease or difficulty with which citizens can register to vote or cast a ballot, the requirements that citizens must meet to receive means-tested government aid, the availability of resources to train for or look for work, and so on all matter to how citizens view and participate in the political world.

These sorts of laws matter because of their direct effects: making voting comparably difficult will depress voter turnout, and will likely affect certain kinds of citizens more than others. But they also matter because of their feedback effects (Pierson 1993): the effects that they have on shaping how citizens view the relationship between themselves, their communities, and government. As a simple example, some American states place significant restrictions on how low-income citizens can use government benefit money (restricting withdrawal of such benefits to a particular dollar amount per day, or prohibiting them from being used in certain places or on certain "luxury" food items). These laws are not passed at random: they exist because elected policymakers in a given context want them. But such laws do not just affect the fairly specific issue of benefit withdrawal, but also encourage a particular interpretation of how to view beneficiaries of means-tested aid—that they are not trustworthy, that they need paternalistic supervision, and so on—that contexts without such laws do not.

Context and Class Politics: A General Model

The above discussion suggests a multifaceted role for political context in shaping how income differences map onto political conflict. In this section,

I outline four general ways in which these contextual factors may become politically relevant. This discussion will serve as a foundation for the more general exploration of these sorts of contextual influences in the remaining chapters of the book.

First, the presence or absence of specific contextual characteristics ***can prime income as a relevant dividing line in political conflict.*** Clearly, in a society where most government actions focus on issues of redistribution, regulation, and "who gets what" (Stimson 1999; Kelly 2009), one's personal income is certainly a factor that can be deeply relevant to forming political opinions. Several prominent economic models of political attitudes, for example, begin by assuming that rich and poor have different preferences for what government should or should not do (Meltzer and Richard 1981). But self-interest is far from the only thing that drives policy opinions, and, generally speaking, class differences in opinions on many highly salient issues are often minimal. On many important policy matters, in other words, the views of rich and poor simply are not that different from one another (Enns and Kellstedt 2008; Soroka and Wlezien 2008; Ura and Ellis 2008), as other factors—religious values, ideology, prejudice, and the like—take precedence over material interest when forming policy views (Sears and Funk 1990; Page and Shapiro 1992).

The degree to which material self-interest is connected to policy positions is driven, in large part, by two general factors: the relative salience of one's class position to one's political identity, and the ease with which citizens can connect their own material interests to specific policy positions. I argue here that the degree to which both of these conditions are met is a function, at least in part, of the environment in which one lives.

When it comes to the salience of class to political life, for example, is it the case that one's immediate environment provides for regular opportunities to interact with people who are from a different economic position? Are such interactions likely to be positive (in that they improve, or at least humanize) perceptions of people who are in a different economic situation, or negative? Do they foster a sense of cooperation or competition with others, or an opportunity to develop class consciousness?[8]

Do the dominant cultural messages in an area suggest that income differences are a natural and perhaps desirable aspect of economic life, or suggest that they are problems that need to be remedied? All of these sorts of factors are important in understanding how someone maps class interests to policy views. A wealthy citizen who rarely needs to interact with other nonwealthy people, and who lives in an area that supports the idea that wealth disparities are justified, is likely to think about one's wealth differently than someone who lives in an area where interactions with less well-off citizens are common and wealth is something that is to be viewed with suspicion.

Second, context can either ***enhance or mitigate participatory inequalities between rich and poor.*** Most models of political participation argue that the decision to participate is driven by political resources: people with more political resources participate more than those with less. These factors help to explain why wealthy people tend to participate in politics more than the poor: wealthy people simply have more resources—skills, time, social contacts, and the like—that they can use to devote to political participation. But the degree to which someone possesses political resources, and the ways in which they can use them to get involved in politics, is at least in part context-dependent. This is especially true for lower-income citizens, who do not have access to many of the sorts of things that make participation by the wealthy more likely.

We know, for example, that being mobilized to participate is critical to determining whether citizens actually participate: as Rosenstone and Hansen (1993) put it, a dominant reason for citizens' nonparticipation is simply that "nobody asked." For strategic reasons, mobilization efforts usually are concentrated among the resource-rich. But does a given area also have organizations with a vested interest in educating and mobilizing lower-income citizens? Or are such citizens comparably ignored in the political process? Does the political system in an area make participation comparably difficult (thus increasing the likelihood that resource-poor citizens will not be able to pay the costs of participation) or easy? More broadly speaking, does the political and economic context in a given area make someone feel as if their participation *could* make a difference?[9] If contextual factors depress feelings of political efficacy, then we should expect them to depress political participation as well—and that these effects will be concentrated most strongly among the resource-poor.

Third, I expect that contextual factors affect the relative ***political visibility of rich and poor.*** In some cases, visibility is literal: certain types of contextual and geographic arrangements render the lifestyles of wealthy and poor essentially disconnected from one another, with the consequence that wealthy citizens rarely if ever need to see lower-income citizens if they choose not to (Fallows 2000). This economic segregation is known to have significant effects on class politics and policy outcomes (Franko and Livingston 2015).

Visibility here can also refer to the degree to which citizens' views are perceived, and perceived as important, by the people that represent them. Policymakers have neither the time nor the ability to form a perfect perception of what their district and its various subconstituencies want and value: a policymaker's view of what his or her district "is" is based on the constituents that are most immediately salient and visible to them (Miler 2010). Who elected officials hear from, in other words, matters. Because wealthy citizens are more likely to participate in politics and be important to elected officials for other reasons, this often means that a policymakers' perception of what his or her constituency wants is biased toward the views of his or her wealthy constituents. But, again, context can affect these perceptions in fairly fundamental ways. Contexts where poorer citizens are deeply involved in the political process, comprise an electorally valuable mass of constituents, or have organizations that are mobilized to advocate on behalf of their interests, for example, will present a very different picture of what a "constituency" looks like to policymakers than contexts where the poor are silent, and there are few who advocate on their behalf.

Finally, and perhaps most important, context can affect the ***relative political influence of rich and poor***. As discussed in chapter 1, there is a significant body of evidence that policymakers are much more likely to cater to the views of the wealthy when creating policy. Though the precise explanations for this phenomenon vary, the common thread running through them is simple: policymakers need money, and wealthy citizens and groups meet that need—in exchange, of course, for outsized influence. There is certainly a good deal of truth to this statement, as a general statement. But the reality behind unequal representation is more complex: strategic policymakers do not simply represent "the wealthy" as a matter of course, but represent the interests of those who are most likely to fulfill the goals they wish to achieve (Mayhew 2004; Jusko 2008).

Different sorts of policymakers have different constituencies, different external pressures, and different sorts of goals. In some contexts, these factors are entirely consistent with the unequal representation story. But in others, they are not. Some policymakers, in other words, represent constituencies in which ignoring the views of the poor is likely to have significant negative consequences—either because the votes of poorer citizens are critical to getting reelected, or because organizations that mobilize on behalf of the poor are politically powerful. Others can pay less attention to the poor with little potential for repercussions. In contexts where taking the views of the poor into account is of significant concern to policymakers, the poor will be better represented.

Thinking about Political Equality

How does all of this bear on the central substantive theme of political equality across income lines? Perhaps simplistically, political representation in the United States can be thought of through both its "demand side" (What are citizens asking for from government? How loudly are they asking for it, and who is doing most of the speaking?) and its "supply side" (How attuned are elected officials to the wants and needs of citizens? What incentives do they have to represent the will of their constituencies—or subsets of their constituencies—above and beyond other pressures they might have?). The argument to be made in the subsequent chapters is that contexts can affect, sometimes strongly, both sides of this representation equation. They can affect from whom legislators are hearing, and the content of the messages that they are hearing. They can also affect the incentives that legislators have to privilege certain citizens' views over others when making policy decisions.

When it comes to political equality, the core message that this book will drive home is simple: context matters because it affects how strongly the material and other interests of less well-off citizens are made visible and relevant to policymakers. Political equality, in other words, is likely to be enhanced in contexts where policymakers can see and hear what nonrich citizens want and need from government, and in contexts where the concerns of such citizens are instrumental to other concerns (such as securing reelection) that policymakers wish to achieve.

Studying the Role of Context using U.S. House Districts

The subsequent chapters will explore these themes, highlighting how aspects from the contexts in which citizens and policymakers interact matter to both public opinion and political representation. To be sure, the argument is not that context is the only, or even the most important, aspect of citizen or legislator behavior. We cannot take a wealthy, ideologically sophisticated person from a conservative, rural place, for example, drop them in a liberal and densely populated one, and expect their political attitudes to change dramatically. Similarly, one cannot take a poor citizen from an impoverished community, drop them into a wealthy one with high-quality political and social resources, and expect them to be as well equipped to take advantage of those resources as the wealthy people around them. One's own resources, predispositions, and proclivities are too important. But this book will illustrate that contexts do matter, and matter in important ways that have deeply important consequences for understanding political inequality in the United States.

The contextual unit of analysis in this book will be the United States congressional district. The U.S. House of Representatives, with 435 districts that vary in myriad politically relevant ways, provides an ideal opportunity to explore how contextual experiences inform both how rich and poor think about politics, and how members of Congress (MCs) represent those views in policy action. The assumption that motivates the book is that differences in both the sociodemographic composition and political cultures of these districts affect the experiences that both citizens and legislators have within them.

Certainly, there are limitations to an analysis which uses the congressional district as a unit of analysis. Other, more granular aspects of place—such as the neighborhood (Huckfeldt 1986), county (Newman, Johnston, and Lown 2015), precinct (Gay 2001), or zip code (Pacheco 2008)[10]—perhaps do a better, or at least different, job of capturing the "lived experience" that is so critical to understanding why context matters. It is easier to avoid interacting with people from parts of a congressional district than it is to avoid interacting with parts of a neighborhood.[11]

And in a broader sense, political boundaries of any sort (whether district, county, zip code, or something else) are in a sense arbitrary, and not a flawless proxy for the experiences that all citizens within those boundaries share. Cultures or customs that are common to a particular culture do not necessarily sort themselves neatly into bounded political units, particularly when those units are geographically large or irregularly shaped. Particularly in heavily gerrymandered districts that stretch a long geographic distance, people may often have more in common with those who live in very close geographic proximity to them—even though these people may reside in a different district, or even a different state—than people who live in the very wealthy suburbs that exist in the northern part of the district. So it is important to take these limitations into account: geographic boundaries provide a convenient, though not ideal, way to understand the shared environment in which citizens live.[12]

But after acknowledging these limitations, there is still a good deal that we can learn about how context affects both citizens and lawmakers through the use of congressional districts. Political boundaries such as congressional districts matter for a number of reasons: they affect the choices available to citizens, the representatives they hear from and have access to, and (since congressional districts are confined within states) many of the policies that affect the taxes they pay, the services they receive, and the laws to which they are bound (Fenno 1978; Flavin 2015b). We have long known that political boundaries are vital in sending signals as to what a particular community is like and the sorts of people that it caters to (Tiebout 1956), and that the rules and norms that are shaped by political boundaries help inform citizens about what their roles are, and what is expected from them (Soss and Jacobs 2009; Hacker, Mettler, and Pinderhughes 2005).

Congressional districts are also integral to the study of political representation: the relationship between constituents and their MCs is one of the most foundational aspects of the American political system. MCs provide both targeted federal dollars, and hours of constituency service, to support projects and concerns that benefit those who reside in particular districts, and citizens (and policymakers) tend to see their specific MCs as the voice of a particular constituency's interests in the broader federal government (Parker and Davidson 1979; Fenno 2006). This relationship matters for how citizens view the political system: those who approve of the job that their Congress member is doing are also more likely, all else equal, to feel more positively about the broader political system as well (Grill 2007).

The congressional district is also critical to the study of opinion-policy linkages: the relationships between MCs and their constituents are the focus of large bodies of research on representation generally (e.g., Miller and Stokes 1963; Erikson 1978; Bartels 1991; Griffin 2013; Sullivan and Uslaner 1978; Burden 2007) and biases in representation more specifically (e.g., Griffin and Newman 2005, 2008; Griffin and Flavin 2007; Carnes 2013; Grumbach 2015). Knowing how well citizens are represented by their particular MCs, in other words, is integral to our understanding of how well representative democracy is functioning.

And importantly to the analysis here, congressional districts in the United States vary in a wide variety of fairly fundamental ways. Figures 2.1–2.6 provide an illustration of this, using data from a variety of sources to map congressional districts in the United States on several factors that are important to the arguments in this book: income inequality (as measured by a pre-tax-and-transfer Gini coefficient); median household income; population density (as measured by persons per square mile); the percentage of citizens that reside in a union household; the percentage of citizens who voted for Barack Obama in the 2012 Presidential election; and the percentage of citizens who view religion as "very important" to their daily lives.

Some of these factors are correlated with one another: table 2.1 dis-

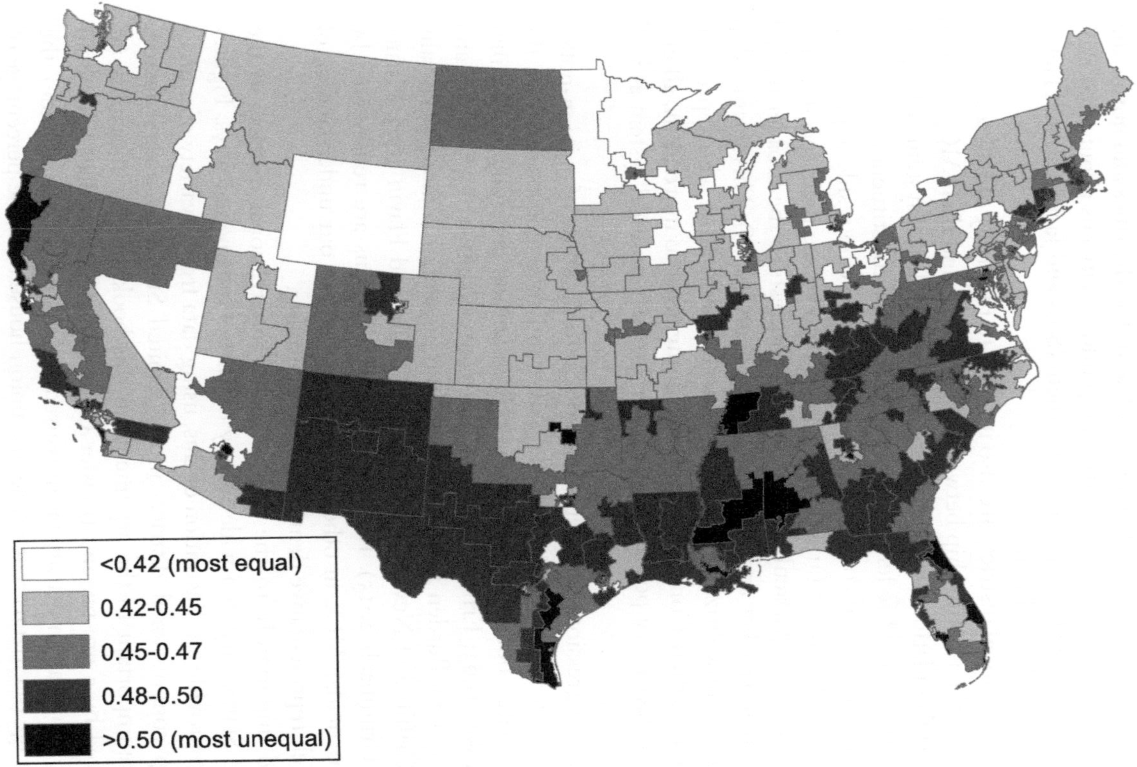

Fig. 2.1. Gini Coefficient, by Congressional District
Source: 2012–14 American Communities Survey.

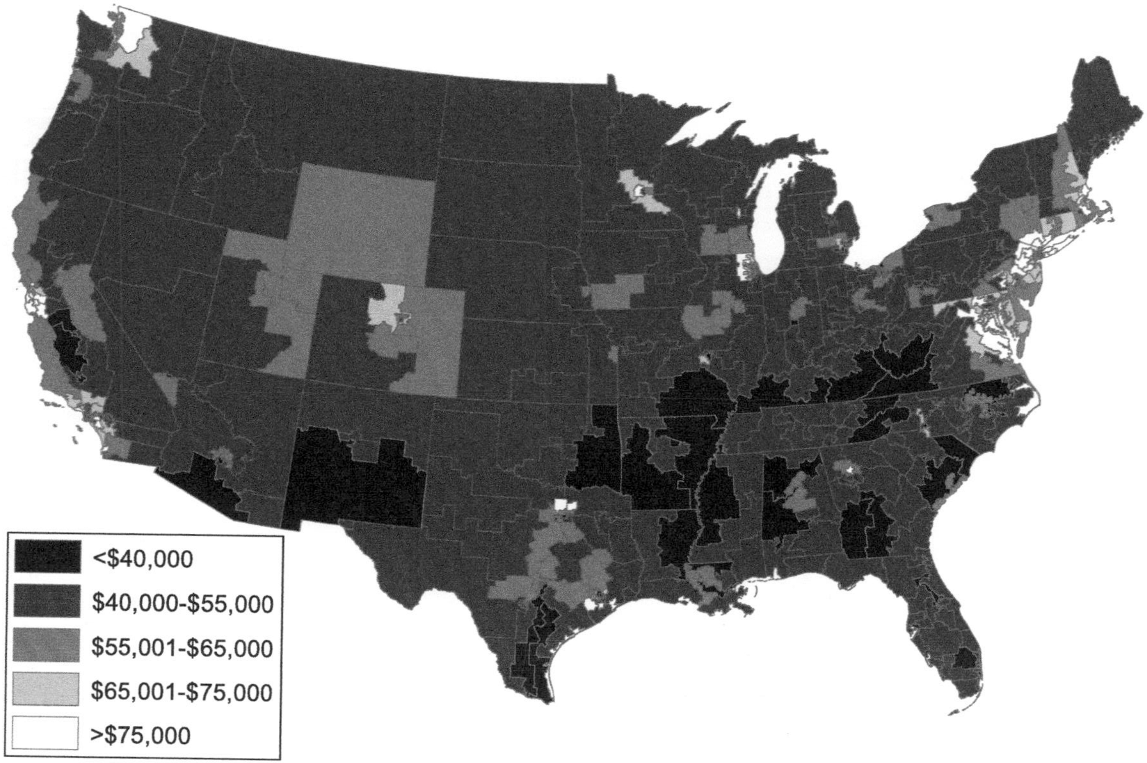

Fig. 2.2. Median Household Income, by Congressional District
Source: 2012–14 American Communities Survey.

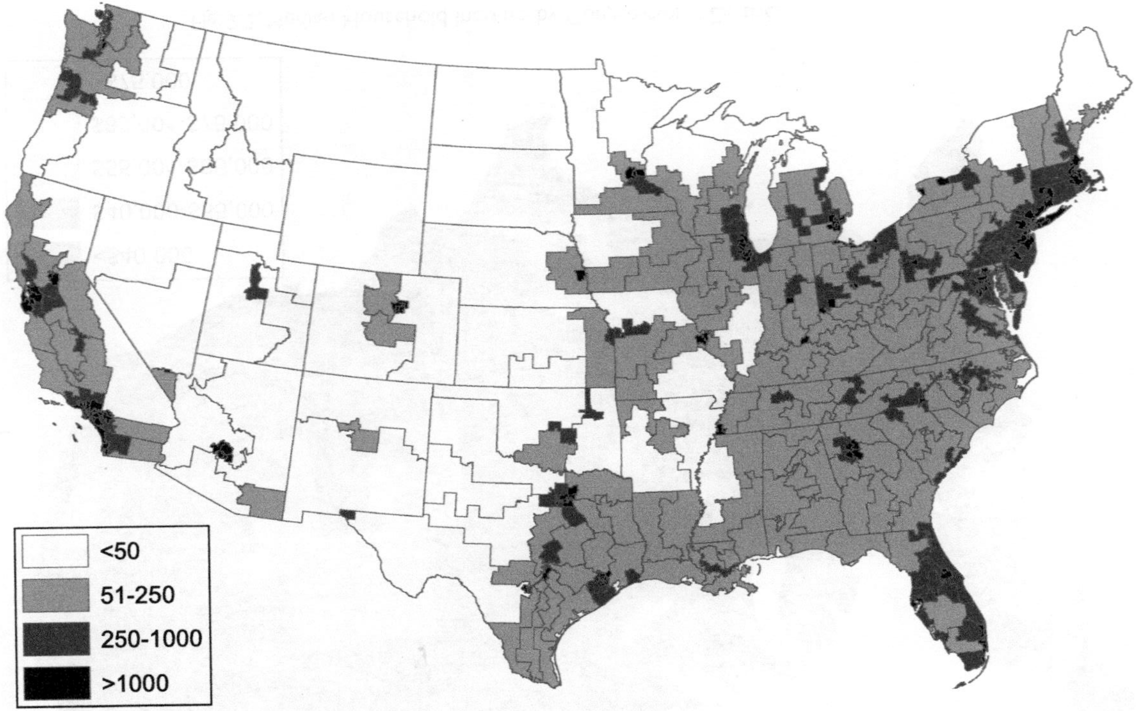

Fig. 2.3. Population Density (persons per square mile), by Congressional District

Source: 2012–14 American Communities Survey.

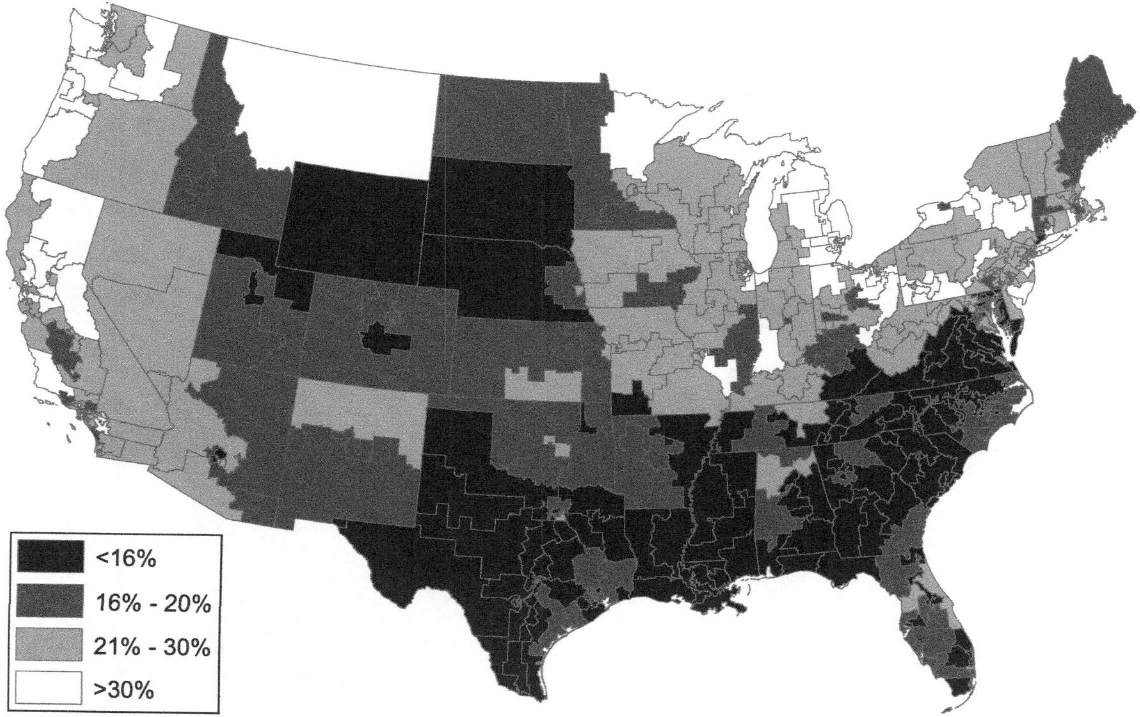

Fig. 2.4. Union Households, by Congressional District
Source: 2012–14 American Communities Survey.

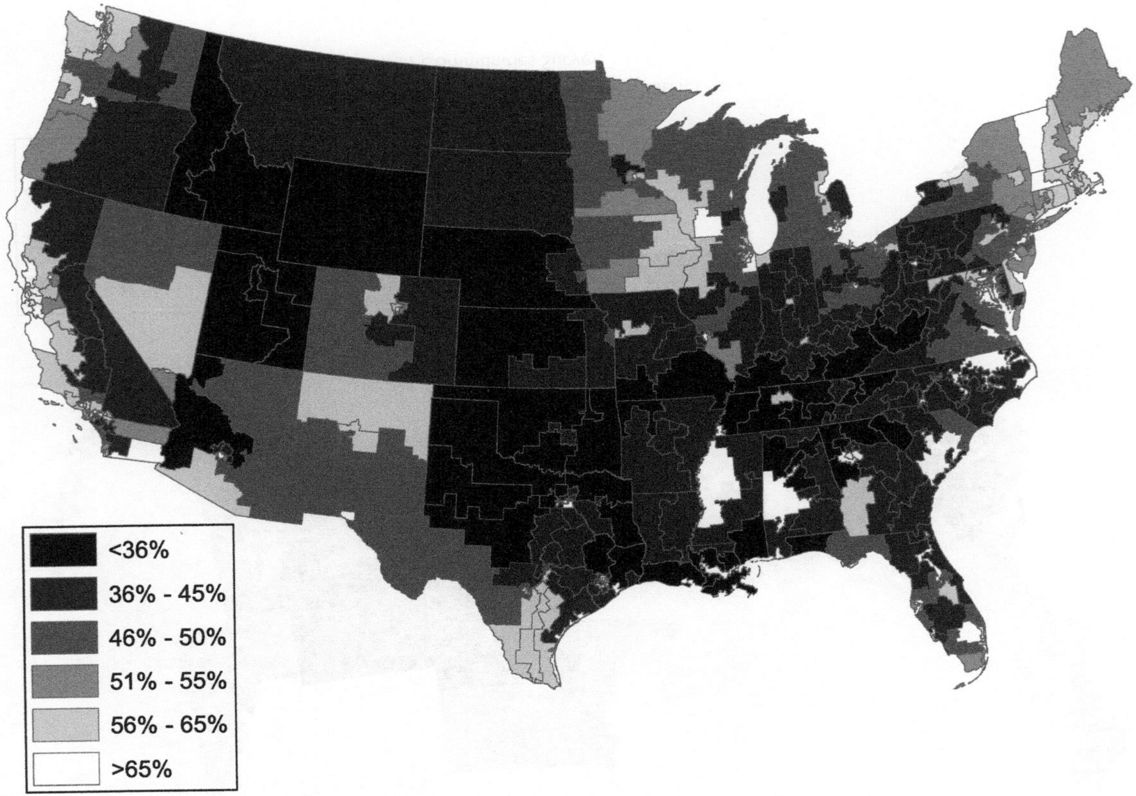

Fig. 2.5. Obama Percent of 2012 Presidential Vote, by Congressional District
Source: New York Times Elections Database: http://elections.nytimes.com

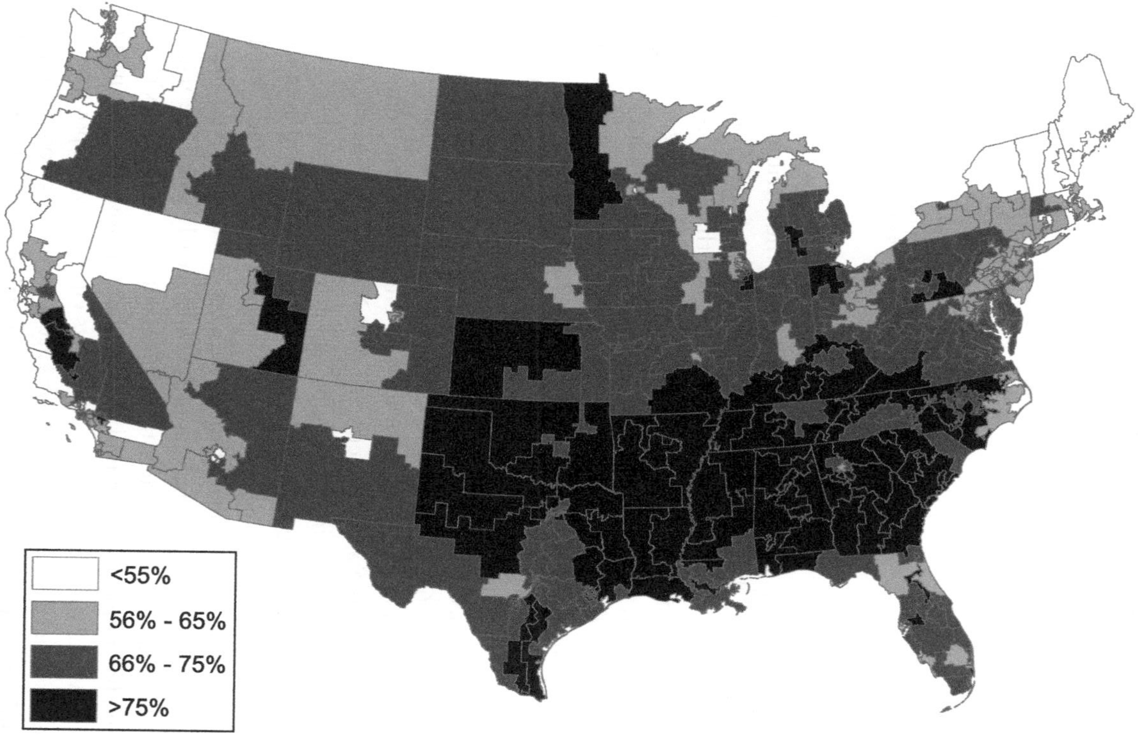

Fig. 2.6. Percentage Who View Religion as Important, by Congressional District
Source: 2014 Cooperative Congressional Election Study.

TABLE 2.1. First-Order Correlations between District-Level Contextual Attributes

	Gini Coefficient	Median Income	Population Density	Union Households	Religious Importance	2012 Obama %
Gini Coefficient	1.00					
Median Income	–0.15	1.00				
Population Density	0.38	0.00	1.00			
Union Households	–0.16	0.20	0.14	1.00		
Religious Importance	–0.06	–0.46	–0.15	–0.42	1.00	
2012 Obama %	0.33	0.01	0.48	0.27	–0.34	1.00

Source: Data from the 2012–2014 American Communities Survey (Gini, Median Income, and Population Density), the 2014 Cooperative Congressional Election Study (Religious Importance and Unionization), and the *New York Times* Election Database (Obama Vote Share).

plays the simple first-order correlations between the attributes mapped in the above figures. Districts that have high levels of citizen religiosity, for example, are also more likely to be Republican than districts that are less religious. Democratic districts also tend to be densely populated (and, interestingly, have comparably higher levels of income inequality). But each of these six factors, as well as many others, are to some degree independent from one another, making the experiences that occur in each congressional district on some level independent from one another.

At the extremes, differences across districts are especially stark: the most equal district (MN-6, encompassing exurban and rural areas northwest of Minneapolis) among those I will study has a Gini coefficient comparable or lower to those of Sweden, Denmark, and Norway: the most unequal district (PA-2, encompassing "main line" suburbs of Philadelphia, as well as majority-minority aspects of Philadelphia city) has a Gini coefficient comparable to the developing economies of Namibia, Haiti, and Zambia.[13] The wealthiest congressional district (VA-10, encompassing suburban Washington, DC) has a median family income nearly twice the national average and a poverty rate of less than 6 percent. The poorest (NY-16, in the Bronx) has a median household income that is below any nation in the developed world; more than 40 percent of its citizens live in poverty. Several congressional districts in New York City have over 25,000 persons per square mile; roughly 25 percent of congressional districts have fewer than 100 persons per square mile.

But even outside these extremes, every congressional district differs in meaningful ways—on the dimensions shown in these figures, but also in their racial and ethnic compositions, in the industries and sectors on which they rely for economic activity, in the commuting patterns of their citizens, in what their political cultures are like, in what their schools teach, and so on—that are important to how citizens experience political and social life. In what is to come, we will work to understand the impact of these factors on how citizens of different income levels think and act politically, and how their legislators represent their views through policymaking. We begin in chapter 3 with the study of political participation and participatory equality.

THREE

Context and Political Participation

In many ways, the defining story of participatory democracy in the United States since the founding has been an expansion of participation rights to larger and more diverse groups of citizens. Once largely the domain of only certain politically protected classes, legal restrictions on voting and other forms of political engagement have been lifted, and, with few exceptions, there are few formal laws barring adults (at least those who have not been convicted of a felony) from participating in politics either through voting or through other means.

But as Verba, Schlozman, and Brady's (1995) classic work on civic engagement pointed out, an equal *right* to participate is not that same as an equal *capacity* to participate. And it has been long known that the participatory public—those citizens who vote, protest, volunteer for political causes, or donate to political campaigns—is at best an imperfect reflection of the general public. In particular, nearly all forms of political participation have an upper class bias—no matter the form of political activity, wealthy citizens are almost always more likely to be politically engaged than poorer ones. This participatory bias has several clear consequences for how American democracy functions, and the sorts of political outcomes it produces.

More equal levels of participation may produce different electoral outcomes, either in terms of who is elected to office or in terms of the policy positions that candidates adopt in order to secure a majority of the electorate. Evidence is mixed on whether universal or higher levels of turnout would lead to frequent or substantial changes in who wins and loses elections (Citrin, Schickler, and Sides 2003; Hansford and Gomez 2010), though candidates that had to appeal to an electorate more heavily comprised of lower-income voters would likely have strategic incentives to tailor their platforms to the interests of such voters than they currently do (Lijphart 1997).

In addition, policymakers might rationally pay more attention to the concerns of those who get involved in politics than the concerns of those who do not (Griffin and Newman 2005). The representation of citizen interests by policymakers is driven in part by the threat of electoral sanction—the desire of policymakers to not lose the support of those who have the ability to vote them out of office. As V. O. Key (1949) puts it, "The blunt truth is that politicians and officials are under no compulsion to pay much heed to classes and groups of citizens that do not vote." An electorate composed more strongly of higher-income citizens is one that is likely to exhibit a bias toward representing the views of higher-income citizens in policymaking activity (Hill and Leighley 1992).[1]

Finally, unequal levels of participation speak more broadly to concerns about the legitimacy of the political system itself: myriad theorists have argued that a well-functioning democratic system values both high and equal levels of political participation not necessarily—or at least not only—because of any precise effect on policy outcomes, but for its own sake (see Schattschneider 1960). Put simply, healthy democracies have engaged citizens, and healthy democracies include the voices of all types of citizens.

A considerable body of research has examined the reasons for participatory biases across income lines. It reaches the clear and intuitive conclusion that poor citizens are simply less able, for a variety of reasons, to both shoulder the burdens of participation and to derive benefits from participation. This chapter reinforces that conclusion, but also offers a model of contextual participatory inequality, one that also takes into account the environment in which one lives. The general argument is that context affects the political resources that citizens have available to them, and also affects the degree to which citizens can pay the costs and receive benefits from participation. Some of these contextual factors apply universally: political systems that make voting difficult, or that offer citizens few differentiated choices, tend to have lower levels of voter turnout than those where voting is easy and the choices are stark (Dalton 2008; Brockington 2009).

But some of these factors apply differentially to rich and poor: particular kinds of social norms, institutional rules, or other factors affect the political decisions of rich and poor in distinct ways. In the aggregate, the presence or absence of these factors leads to either larger or smaller participation gaps across income lines. It is this topic—how contextual factors affect participatory inequalities between rich and poor—that is the focus of this chapter.

Why Do the Poor Participate Less Than the Wealthy?

The individual-level decision to get involved in political life is one of the most studied topics in political science. Clearly, there are an enormous number of factors that affect the likelihood that an individual will choose to vote or participate in other ways (see Smets and van Ham 2013 for a meta-analysis of the research on this topic). Some of these factors, such as age, are relatively uncorrelated with income. But most explanations of political participation, whether driven by an understanding of precise costs and benefits (e.g., Downs 1957), resources (Verba, Schlozman, and Brady 1995), mobilization (Rosenstone and Hansen 1993), or other social-psychological factors (Plutzer 2002; Stoker and Jennings 1995), point to a calculus of participation that make it less likely that lower-income citizens will get involved in politics.

Poor citizens, in general, face more practical costs to participation. Lower levels of income tend to raise the opportunity costs of political participation (Rosenstone 1982), as the time, money, or sacrifice of income that it may require to get to the polls or participate in other ways tend to place heavier burdens on citizens with less money or less stable and flexible jobs.

They also generally have lower levels of political resources: the money, educational experiences, unstructured time, and civic skills that citizens can marshal to get involved in politics in meaningful ways (Brady, Verba, and Schlozman 1993; Nie, Junn, and Stehlik-Barry 1996). Poor citizens are also less likely to have the large and diverse social networks that emphasize the importance of political participation, and tend to have less tangible ties to communities—as exhibited by characteristics such as homeownership—that lead people to both participate in civic affairs and believe that their participation matters (Wolfinger and Rosenstone 1980; Highton and Wolfinger 2001; Form and Huber 1971).

Finally, poor citizens are less likely to be contacted by candidates, parties, or interest groups to encourage their participation. Some groups—labor unions or religious organizations, for example—work to mobilize working-class citizens (Claassen and Povtak 2010; Leighley and Nagler 2007). But most political organizations tend to focus their mobilization efforts on groups of citizens that—largely because of patterns of past participation or high levels of political resources—are disproportionately likely to respond to mobilization efforts. If, in part, people do not participate in politics because "nobody asked" (Rosenstone and Hansen 1993), poor citizens are simply less likely to have been asked.

Broadly speaking, these explanations of participatory inequality across income lines emphasize a number of things—tangible costs, personal resources, the importance of mobilization—that together explain much of the individual-level motivation to participate. But the degree to which citizens are affected by each of these factors are not formed in a vacuum, and the way that they are marshaled in support of various forms of political participation does not take place in a vacuum. The role that such individual-level factors play in the participation decision, in other words, is moderated by the context in which such resources are both developed and used.

Income and Participation in Context

This line of thinking illustrates several ways in which context can differentially affect wealthy and poor citizens. First, context can differentially affect the degree to which citizens *can pay the costs* of participation. Context affects some of the more tangible and identifiable factors that affect the costs and benefits of participation: all else equal, contexts where formal participation is legally or practically harder tend to have lower levels of citizen participation than contexts where participation is comparably easier (Hershey 2009). Since practical barriers to participation (free time during voting hours, transportation to the polls, and the like) are typically more of a burden for poorer rather than wealthier citizens, when citizens live in contexts where participation is tangibly harder or more costly we might expect that the burdens of these higher costs will be more likely to affect the participation of the poor. They are less able to have the resources necessary to bear such costs.

In addition, context can differentially affect the *perceived benefits* of participation. Personal mobilization, for example, matters to how citizens perceive the stakes of elections and how strongly they derive psychological benefits from participation (Rosenstone and Hansen 1993). Areas where political groups work hard to mobilize the poor will be more likely to confer such benefits on poorer citizens than areas where the poor are largely ignored.

Finally, context can affect *social norms* of participation in a way that differentially affects rich and poor. We know that norms of political participation are strongly socially constructed: both explicit forms of social interaction and implicit, less formally structured social cues generate strong environmental norms of participation or nonparticipation (Leighley 1990; Cho and Rudolph 2008; Christakis and Fowler 2009). One's immediate context, in other words, sends strong cues as to whether getting involved in politics is a normal thing to do: all else equal, those who live in contexts where engagement is the norm are more likely to feel politically efficacious, and as a result more likely to become engaged themselves.[2] Citizens who live in contexts without strong norms of political participation will be less likely to develop the formal skills and informal "habits of mind" (Soder 1996) that are associated with greater levels of participation than otherwise identical citizens who live in contexts where high levels of political engagement are the norm. These sorts of social norms matter for all citizens, but are likely to be disproportionately important for poorer ones, who for a variety of reasons are less likely to be socialized into a family environment that emphasizes regular participation (Plutzer 2002).

Together, these points lead us to expect that citizens who are in situations where the tangible costs of participation are relatively high, the social benefits of participation are relatively low, or the likelihood of being mobilized to participate are relatively low, would have lower levels of political participation than low-cost, high-benefit areas. Since poor citizens are the ones least likely to be able to pay the costs of participation, and the least likely to have the political resources to engage in the political system in the absence of strong motivations to do so, these sorts of contextual burdens would have a greater impact on the participation of the poor than that of the wealthy. We thus would expect that participation gaps between rich and poor will be greater in some contexts than in others, as some contexts provide poor citizens greater opportunities to overcome their general disadvantages in political resources than others. Below, I detail several factors that shed light on how context might matter to the decisions of rich and poor citizens to participate in politics.

Contextual Wealth

Sociologists have long pointed out that the disadvantages that come from living in poverty oneself are compounded by living in an area that is mired in poverty. Problems that are often associated with lower levels of income at the individual level (residential instability, unemployment, health problems, and the like) compound themselves at the neighborhood level. Numerous studies of things such as educational success and health outcomes bear this out: poor citizens tend to fare worse than wealthy ones regardless of where they live, but poor citizens who live in relatively high status areas (and can take advantage of the higher-quality schools, safer neighborhoods, public services, and systems of social support that such areas are more likely to offer) tend to fare better than poor citizens who live in low-income areas (Brooks-Gunn 1997; Wilson 2012; Tate 2008; Sampson 2003).

There are a number of reasons to think that a similar dynamic is at work when it comes to political participation: poor citizens who live in higher-income areas will be more likely to get involved in politics than poor citizens who live in low-income areas. Political parties' mobilization efforts, for example, are concentrated in high-income areas, where the likelihood of reaching a large pool of political participants is the strongest (Huckfeldt and Sprague 1992; Leighley 1990). Many of these mobilization efforts, of course, are designed to reach a larger pool of upper-income voters that are especially likely to get involved. But this sort of mobilization makes it likely that even lower-income citizens in such areas are more likely to be contacted than similar citizens in areas that parties tend to ignore (Rosenstone and Hansen 1993).

Similarly, higher status areas tend to have stronger social norms of participation, and participation in political affairs is more likely to be seen as a regular feature of civic life (Alex-Assensoh 1998).[3] Both poor and wealthy citizens living in contexts where participation is the norm, and where parties are more likely to invest in efforts to reach potential participants, are more likely to have strong social incentives to get involved in politics than they would elsewhere. But these extra incentives are apt to be particularly important for poor citizens, who are, all else equal, less endowed with the sorts of individual-level resources that make participation more likely. High concentrations of poverty, in other words, serve to diminish both interest in and capacity for political engagement.

Whether by choice or necessity, citizens do tend to live around citizens that have similar levels of income. But income-based residential segregation is not *so* extreme that, at least at the congressional district level, there are not significant numbers of citizens living in areas where their incomes are substantially larger (or smaller) than the average. Individual wealth and contextual wealth, in other words, are not proxies for one another. Figure 3.1 uses data from the 2014 Cooperative Congressional Election Study (CCES) data to display the distribution of household incomes in the wealthiest and poorest 25 percent of congressional districts. The wealthiest districts have a median household income of at least $61,500 per year, while the poorest districts have a median income of less than $44,700 per year.

The results show the obvious: there are, on average, more wealthy citizens in wealthy districts. But they also still show a significant distribution

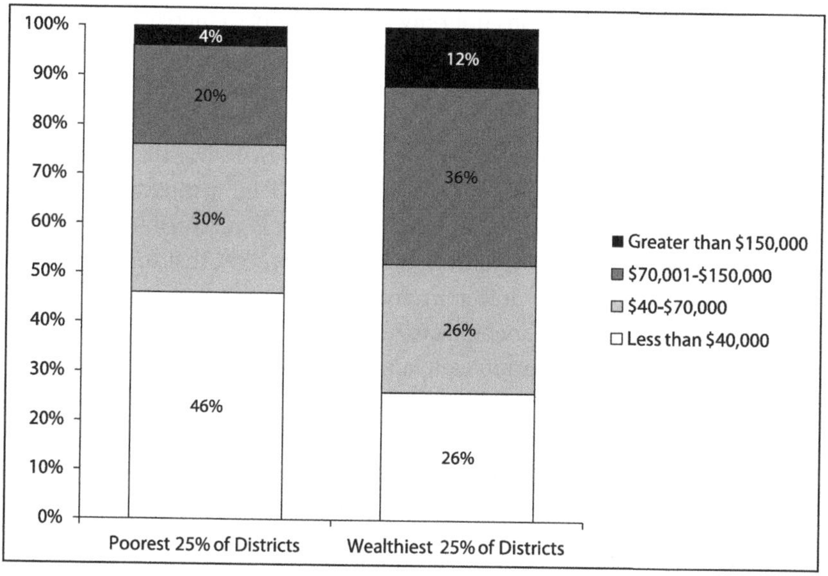

Fig. 3.1. Distribution of Incomes in "Rich" and "Poor" Districts
Source: 2014 Cooperative Congressional Election Study.

of incomes within these districts. There seem to be more poor citizens living in areas that are on average wealthy than there are wealthy citizens living in areas that are on average poor.[4] But the clear message is that large numbers of citizens are living in areas with people that have incomes far different than their own. It is for these citizens—particularly poorer ones in wealthier areas—that contextual effects might be particularly important. We thus would expect that participation gaps between rich and poor would be greater in low-wealth contexts than in high-wealth ones.

Unionization

As we have discussed, people are more likely to get involved in politics when they receive information or other things that help to reduce the costs of participation, or when they are mobilized to get involved. There exist myriad political organizations that serve these sorts of functions for wealthier groups and interests, as well as some organizations (such as the AARP, for example) which are interested in mobilizing citizens regardless of income. But there exist few influential interest groups explicitly interested in mobilizing lower income citizens. One significant exception to this is organized labor: unions not only invest efforts to increase the political engagement of their members but also serve as a significant source of mobilization and political information for lower-income citizens as well (Radcliff and Davis 2000).

Unions work to mobilize members, in other words, but they also work to mobilize nonmembers that they perceive will be sympathetic to the same sorts of causes as the unions themselves. It is reasonable to expect, consistent with the work of Leighley and Nagler (2007), that income biases in participation should be lower in areas with a strong organized labor presence, given that lower-income citizens in such areas will be more likely to be the target of mobilization campaigns (or other sorts of participation-encouraging activities, such as information regarding where to find polling places or transportation to the polls or political rallies) than in areas where unions have a weaker presence. We thus would expect that participation gaps between rich and poor will be greater in low-unionization contexts than in high-unionization ones.

Income Inequality

Perhaps the most researched contextual influence on political participation is that of income inequality. Theories on how inequality should impact political participation, however, are mixed, generating a number of competing hypotheses regarding the role of contextual inequality in shaping political participation. One might expect that inequality will depress political engagement among all sorts of citizens, regardless of income (Goodin and Dryzek 1980). The rationale for this is simple: research has shown that income inequality decreases citizens' senses of civic obligation, civic responsibility, and interpersonal trust (Alesina and La Ferrara 2002), and also decreases citizens' connections to the political process (Lancee and Van de Werfhorst 2012). These factors combine to decrease the political efficacy that is critical to wanting to pay the costs of political participation. Others, however, have argued the reverse: that inequality should increase political participation among all sorts of citizens, because inequality heightens the importance of class conflict and increases perceived competition for scarce social resources (Brady 2004).

Still others have asserted that the effect of inequality on participation is conditional on income, either heightening or mitigating income biases in participation. The relative power theory of politics offered by Schattschneider (1960) suggests that inequality should decrease political participation, but do so primarily among poor citizens (see also Solt 2008). The argument here is that high levels of inequality cause issues that are important to the poor to be marginalized in the public agenda. These feelings of marginalization lead to a decreased sense of political efficacy among the poor, and their participation suffers as a result.

And, finally, some argue that high levels of inequality may well serve to increase levels of political participation among the poor, as inequality leads to a heightened demand for redistributive policy (Meltzer and Richard 1981). The high levels of contention and conflict that high inequality brings raise the perceived status of policy outcomes: economically diverse areas have more people pursuing conflicting goals, and heightened levels of political interest and engagement than more equal, more homogenous ones (Burns 1992; Oliver 1999; Kelleher and Lowery 2004, 2009). Evidence on this point has been mixed: recent large-*N* studies by Solt (2008, 2010) point to a possible depressing effect of inequality on participation, but others find different or more nuanced effects (Uslaner and Brown 2005; Galbraith and Hale 2008).

Laws and Institutional Barriers

Finally, we might consider possible policy-based factors that would differentially affect the participation of rich and poor citizens. States vary considerably in the demands that they place on citizens wishing to cast a vote. In some cases, these efforts work to make voting more convenient for citizens, either by making voter registration automatic or comparably easy, by encouraging the use of mail- or absentee-voting for those who cannot make it to polling places, or by encouraging early voting. In other cases, these efforts work to make casting a vote harder, usually by requiring citizens to present some form of identification (usually a photo ID) at the polls prior to being able to cast a ballot.

The Brennan Center for Justice at New York University maintains a comprehensive record of state ballot-access laws, and has classified them into four groups, which can be categorized in rough order ranging from least restrictive (no form of identification is needed nor requested in order to vote) to most restrictive (a photo identification is required to vote) Figure 3.2 shows a map of these categories in 2012: we can see that these restrictions vary substantially across states.[5]

The expected effects of making voting more convenient are mixed: though there are good theoretical reasons to think that such efforts would increase voter turnout among the poor and other groups who may not be as easily able to vote at an appointed place and time, some research sug-

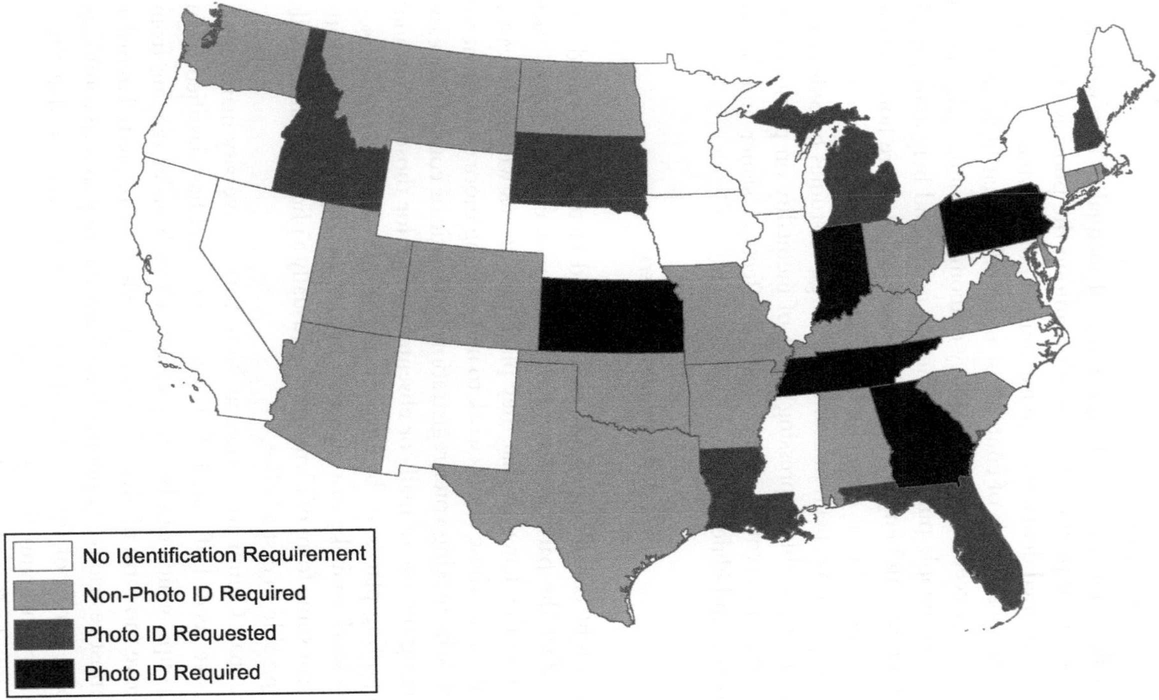

Fig. 3.2. Voter Identification Laws by State, 2012
Source: Brennan Center for Justice, New York University.

gests that such incentives actually increase voter turnout among groups (the wealthy, the educated, the highly politically engaged) that are already disproportionately likely to vote (Berinsky, Burns, and Traugott 2001).

When it comes to identification-based restrictions, though, the expected effects are clear: such restrictions will disproportionately decrease turnout among the poor, primarily because poorer citizens are less likely to already have a photo identification (such as a driver's license or a passport) that they have obtained for other reasons (see also Wolfinger and Rosenstone 1980; Mitchell and Wlezien 1995). Obtaining a photo identification for the primary purpose of voting is a time-consuming and often costly process that, for many, does not seem worth the trouble. Even if an identification is theoretically available for minimal cost, such restrictions can send more subtle cues to citizens regarding the types of citizens that *should* be voting. These perceptions serve to increase alienation among citizens for whom paying such costs are an extra burden (Piven and Cloward 2000). We thus should expect that at least when it comes to voting, participation gaps between rich and poor should be greater in contexts with stringent requirements for casting a ballot than in contexts with less stringent ones.

Measuring Political Activity

To examine the relationships between income, social context, and political participation, I turn to data from recent CCES surveys.[6] The analyses to come will explore voting in national elections, and engagement in politics that goes beyond regular voting. All recent versions of the CCES asked respondents if they voted in the general election closest to the survey being conducted. It also asked three questions regarding participation in the most recent national election: whether respondents attended political rallies or meetings, advertised their support for a particular cause or candidate, and worked (in either a paid or volunteer capacity) for a political cause or candidate.

Of course, all measures of participation that rely on survey data are potentially problematic because they rely on citizens' self-reported participation in political activities. And, for social desirability reasons, citizens tend to overstate their levels of participation to survey researchers. This has the obvious effect of overstating the aggregate levels of participation in politics (in the 2012 CCES, for example, self-reported turnout in the Obama-Romney presidential election approached 90 percent). It also has the more subtle effect of overstating levels of participation more strongly among particular political groups: overreporting participation is neither uniform nor random, but is rather most likely to happen among citizens who have internalized strong social norms of political participation (Sigelman 1982; Belli, Traugott, and Beckmann 2001). Citizens that are most likely to participate to begin with, in other words, are more likely to also say that they participated when they did not. In practice, this means, among other things, that higher income citizens are more likely to overreport than lower income citizens (Franko 2015).

There is little we can do about this phenomenon when it comes to political activity. But when it comes to voting, the 2010 and 2012 CCES surveys employed a novel strategy to validate self-reports of voting using data from Catalist, a private-sector political research firm that maintains vote history lists for citizens nationwide (see Ansolabahere and Hersh 2012 for details of the validation process). Individual-level identifiers allow respondents to CCES surveys to be matched to data from the Catalist voter files: the upshot is that we can compare what citizens *reported* about voting in the most recent election to what state voter record files (which are in the public domain in every state but Virginia) say about whether they *actually* voted in that election. This allows for independent validation of voting records for both the 2010 and 2012 elections.

Table 3.1 compares respondents' self-reports of voting in the 2010 and 2012 general elections to their actual record of voting according to the Catalist data. The data shows that misstating one's voting record is fairly common, and misstatements occur almost exclusively in one direction: virtually no one reports not voting when they in fact did, but a good number

TABLE 3.1. Differences between Self-Reported and Validated Voting

	Validated as Voting		Validated as Not Voting	
Voting and Validated Voting in 2012				
Reported Voting	31,095	(99%)	3,549	(64%)
Reported Not Voting	154	(1%)	1,970	(36%)
Total	31,249	(100%)	5,519	(100%)
Voting and Validated Voting in 2010				
Reported Voting	28,843	(99%)	7,891	(54%)
Reported Not Voting	151	(1%)	6,810	(46%)
Total	28,994	(100%)	14,701	(100%)

Source: 2010 and 2012 Cooperative Congressional Election Studies.

of citizens report voting when they did not.[7] The data also tell us that, consistent with prior research, overreporting is most common among upper income citizens: in 2012, for example, nearly 80 percent of top-tercile nonvoters, but only around 50 percent of bottom-tercile nonvoters, incorrectly reported voting in the 2012 CCES.

Given the high and nonrandom misreporting of voting, then, I employ a validated voting measure for the 2010 and 2012 elections: my measure of voting for these years is simply coded "1" if a respondent is recorded as having voted according to the Catalist voter registration files (regardless of whether a respondent reported voting or not), and "0" if they are recorded as having not voted. Vote validation is not available for the 2014 CCES, so I instead rely on self-reported voting for this year.

Table 3.2 displays measures of (self-reported) political activism and (validated) voting in the 2010 and 2012 general elections across income terciles in the United States, as well as self-reported measures of both voting and activism in 2014.[8] These data confirm a wealth of previous research showing significant income biases in participation across income lines. In general, inequalities in participation are smallest for activities that place comparably few demands on participants (such as voting), and larger for activities that require more in the way of resources or higher levels of interest in politics (such as working for a campaign).

The tables focus on the income tercile level, but as income dispari-

TABLE 3.2. Political Activism by Income Level

	Bottom Tercile	Middle Tercile	Top Tercile
Voter Turnout, 2010	53%	65%	72%
Voter Turnout, 2012	72%	82%	87%
(Self-Reported) Voter Turnout, 2014	60%	74%	83%
Attended Political Meeting, 2010	14%	21%	28%
Attended Political Meeting, 2012	9%	15%	21%
Attended Political Meeting, 2014	8%	12%	17%
Displayed Political Sign, 2010	19%	27%	31%
Displayed Political Sign, 2012	17%	25%	32%
Displayed Political Sign, 2014	10%	14%	19%
Worked for Campaign/Party, 2010	7%	11%	15%
Worked for Campaign/Party, 2012	6%	10%	13%
Worked for Campaign/Party, 2014	4%	6%	9%
Donated Money, 2010	20%	32%	46%
Donated Money, 2012	17%	30%	47%
Donated Money, 2014	10%	18%	32%

Source: 2010, 2012, and 2014 Cooperative Congressional Election Studies.

ties become greater, differences in participation become larger. In 2012, for example, citizens in households who earn over $100,000 per year are 1.4 times more likely to vote, more than twice as likely to have attended a political meeting or displayed a political sign, and nearly three times as likely to have worked for a political campaign than citizens in households that earn less than $30,000 per year. Participation levels were generally higher in the 2012 presidential election than in the 2010 or 2014 congressional ones, and income gaps were modestly lower in this election as well, confirming the notion that presidential elections are high-salience events that are disproportionately likely to attract "peripheral" participants, or those with low levels of political resources.[9]

Context, Income, and Participation

We now turn to the task of modeling contextual influences on participation. To do so, I estimate separate sets of models predicting whether a respondent *voted in the election* most proximate to their survey (as measured by the validated vote variable discussed above) and a respondents' level of *political activism* (as measured by a 0–3 scale, where 3 indicates that they engaged in all three political acts listed above—attending a political meeting, advertising support for a candidate, and working for a campaign—while "0" indicates that they did not engage in any of these activities. I estimate separate models for the 2010, 2012, and 2014 elections.

These models include both individual- and contextual-level predictors. Income is measured using responses to a question asking citizens for their household income: the CCES collapses responses to this question into 14 categories.[10] In addition to income, individual predictors are measures of factors that are commonly associated with political participation: a respondent's *race*, *age*, *level of formal education*, and dummies for whether they are *married* or a *homeowner*.[11]

Contextual predictors are measures of the concepts discussed above. *District median income* is taken from the 2012–14 three-year release of American Communities Survey, *income inequality* is measured via the district-level Gini coefficient (also using 2012–14 American Communities Survey data). *Union strength* is a measure, derived from CCES responses, of the percentage of citizens in a district that reside in a union household. *Voter ID laws* is a measure of how stringent identification laws are in a particular state. It is simply a 0–3 scale composed of the categories of voter-identification laws displayed in figure 3.2: 0 indicates the least restrictive voting environment, and 3 indicates the most restrictive environment.[12] The models interact income with each contextual predictor: significant positive interactions will suggest that the impact of income on participation is strengthened when values of the contextual predictor are high, while significant negative interactions suggests that high levels of the contextual predictor will serve to weaken the relationship between income and participation.

The results for these models (mixed effects logistic regression models for voter turnout, and mixed effects regression models for political activity) are presented in tables 3.3 and 3.4: table 3.3 reports results for voter turnout, while table 3.4 reports results for activism.[13] Before looking at contextual factors, the results first show the importance of individual-level factors to participation. The direct effect of income on participation is significant and positive in all models: regardless of context, wealthier people tend to get involved at higher rates than poorer ones. And with the exception of marital status, each of the individual-level predictors is a significant and highly powerful predictor of participation across models: being white, more highly educated, older, and a homeowner all significantly increase the likelihood of both voting and participating in politics. These findings again

TABLE 3.3. Voter Turnout as a Function of Individual and Contextual Attributes

Dependent Variables: Validated Voting (2010, 2012); Self-Reported Voting (2014)			
	2010	2012	2014
Income	0.13* (0.04)	0.32* (0.07)	0.32* (0.06)
Race (white)	0.50* (0.02)	0.11* (0.03)	0.18* (0.03)
Education (highest degree earned)	0.12* (0.01)	0.23* (0.01)	0.38* (0.01)
Married	0.04* (0.02)	-0.05 (0.03)	-0.03 (0.03)
Homeowner	0.46* (0.03)	0.34* (0.03)	0.45* (0.03)
Age	0.044* (0.001)	0.029* (0.001)	0.045* (0.001)
District Inequality	0.15 (0.82)	2.35* (0.86)	2.56* (0.84)
District Median Income (thousands)	0.72* (0.21)	0.23 (0.22)	0.06 (0.20)
District Percent Union	1.61* (0.50)	0.39 (0.33)	0.73* (0.33)
Voter ID Laws	-0.09* (0.03)	-0.08* (0.03)	-0.12* (0.03)
Income * District Inequality	-0.07 (0.09)	-0.61* (0.13)	-0.43* (0.12)
Income * District Median Income	-0.63* (0.24)	-0.54* (0.31)	-0.76* (0.27)
Income * District Percent Union	-0.12* (0.06)	0.04 (0.05)	-0.11*(0.05)
Income * Voter ID Laws	-0.009 (0.031)	0.017* (0.004)	0.015* (0.00)
N	47,298	39,415	43,390

Note: Table entries are logistic regression coefficients (standard errors are in parentheses). * $p < .05$

reinforce the notion that participation decisions are closely connected to the individual-level possession of political resources.

The results also show a meaningful contextual component to participation: participation is generally more common in high-income areas, in areas where elections are more likely to be close, in areas with a significant presence of organized labor, and in areas with stringent voter-ID requirements. Importantly, there is also evidence that contextual factors can mitigate the relationship between income and participation. The strongest and most consistent finding when it comes to these sorts of interactive relationships is that for median income. While both rich and poor tend to participate more in high-income areas, in all three years the negative interaction between income and district wealth indicates that the effect of income on participation is weaker in high-wealth than in low-wealth contexts: as a result, participation gaps between rich and poor *citizens* are smaller in wealthy contexts than they are in poorer contexts.

As an illustration of this, figure 3.3 considers the expected difference in voting probability for low-income (in roughly the 10th percentile of the income distribution, with a household income of between $10,000 and $20,000 per year) and high-income (in roughly the 90th percentile of the

TABLE 3.4. Political Activism as a Function of Individual and Contextual Attributes

	Dependent variable: self-reported political activism		
	2010	2012	2014
Income	0.07* (0.02)	0.05* (0.02)	0.04* (0.02)
Race (white)	0.06 *(0.01)	-0.01 (0.01)	0.00 (0.01)
Education (highest degree earned)	0.08* (0.00)	0.10* (0.00)	0.10* (0.00)
Married	0.04* (0.01)	-0.00 (0.01)	-0.01 (0.01)
Homeowner	0.11* (0.01)	0.08* (0.01)	0.08* (0.01)
Age	0.076* (0.003)	0.062* (0.003)	0.007* (0.001)
District Inequality	0.44 (0.34)	-0.18 (0.28)	-0.07 (0.27)
District Median Income (thousands)	0.09 (0.09)	-0.73 (0.70)	-1.19 (0.61)
District Percent Union	0.29 (0.21)	0.21 (0.11)	0.11 (0.14)
Voter ID Laws	-0.09 (0.11)	-0.01 (0.01)	-0.01 (0.01)
Income * District Inequality	-0.06 (0.04)	-0.04 (0.04)	-0.01 (0.04)
Income * District Median Income	-0.29* (0.09)	-0.25* (0.09)	-0.10 (0.08)
Income * District Percent Union	-0.04* (0.02)	-0.05 (0.15)	0.11 (0.15)
Income * Voter ID Laws	0.001 (0.02)	0.002 (0.01)	0.00 (0.01)
N	40,879	38,922	43,390

Note: Table entries are multilevel regression coefficients (standard errors are in parentheses). * $p < .05$

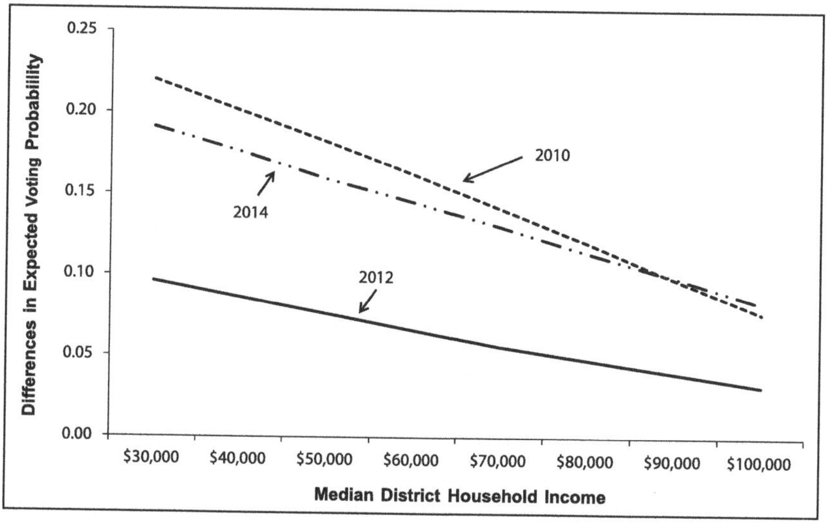

Fig. 3.3. Difference in Voting Probability between High- and Low-Income Citizens, as a Function of District Median Income

income distribution, with a household income of between $120,000 and $150,000 per year) citizens as a function of district wealth.[14] In low wealth contexts, wealthier citizens are expected to vote at a much higher rate that the poor: the expected turnout gap is roughly 10 percent in the presidential election year of 2012, and around 20 points in the two off-year elections. In high wealth contexts, gaps in participation are much smaller (and tend toward zero in the presidential election year of 2012).

Importantly, the smaller size in the turnout gap in high-income areas does not occur because wealthier people participate less (recall that the direct effect of district median income in table 3.3 was significant and positive for all three years). Expected voter turnout for our 90th percentile citizen remains roughly constant regardless of context: in 2012, for example, the probability of voting for our 90th percentile citizen was expected to be 0.78 in the poorest context, and 0.77 in the wealthiest context—a non-significant difference. Instead, these gaps are reduced because of a significantly greater propensity to vote among the poor—in 2012, the expected turnout rate our 10th percentile participant in the wealthiest context was 0.74, compared to 0.67 in the poorest context. We see perhaps even starker effects in the off-year elections: while the 90th percentile citizens were roughly equally likely to vote regardless of where they lived, the 10th percentile citizens were roughly 17 percent more likely to vote in 2010, and more than 20 percent more likely to vote in 2014, in the wealthiest as opposed to the poorest districts.

Wealthy citizens, in other words, are likely to vote regardless of where they live. Poor citizens, however, are much more likely to get involved in wealthier contexts: contexts where the social norms tend to encourage participation, and political parties and candidates are more likely to seek to mobilize large groups of voters. The finding that turnout gaps are greater in poorer contexts conforms with the argument that *individual* poverty is a significantly greater impediment to participation in a *high-poverty context*. Substantively, this provides support for the point that low-income citizens are doubly disadvantaged by living in low-status areas: such areas do not provide the social incentives to get involved that might be particularly important for citizens with lower levels of individual political resources.[15]

We also see that in the 2012 and 2014 (but not the 2010) election cycles, voter identification laws have significant and substantively important effects on turnout equality: the significant positive coefficient between income and voter ID laws means that the more stringent the requirement to cast a legal ballot, the greater the effect of income on turnout. Figure 3.4 illustrates these effects for these three election cycles, showing the expected gaps in participation between the 90th and 10th percentile citizens as a function of identification requirements. In states where no identification is required for casting a ballot, the difference in expected turnout probability between a "high income" and "low income" citizen is expected to be roughly 2 points in 2012 and 10 points in 2014. In states with the strictest identification requirement, those same differences are expected to be 8 points and 19 points, respectively.[16] (Voter identification laws have, as might be expected, no effect on equality in political activism: identification laws of this sort pertain only to voting, not to other forms of political activity). And again, these lower turnout gaps in low-requirement areas are due mainly to more participation among the poor, not less participation among the rich.

The explanation for why voter-ID requirements have become more important in recent years is fairly straightforward: the national debate over voter identification requirements increased markedly in salience since the 2010 election, and several states have passed more stringent identification requirements during this time (see Hasen 2012).[17] More important, the increased national debate over these laws have led in some cases to increased enforcement of these laws (many of which were enforced inconsistently or sporadically in some states), so that even states with existing laws may be seeing them more regularly applied.

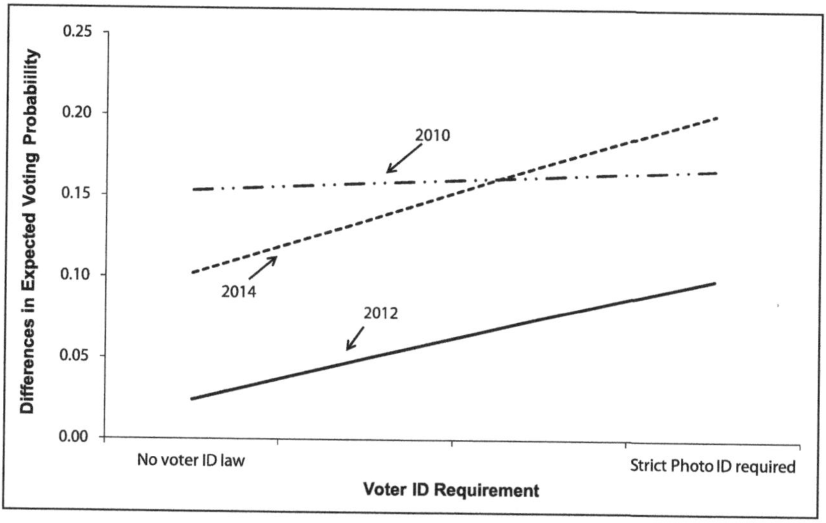

Fig. 3.4. Difference in Voting Probability between High- and Low-Income Citizens, as a Function of State Voter ID Requirement

We also see evidence, at least in two of the three election cycles (2010 and 2014), that the presence of strong labor unions—a key mobilizing agent for the poor—tends to reduce participation gaps across income lines. Labor unions do not equalize participation by depressing the participation of the wealthy—as with district wealth, high levels of union density are associated with higher levels of political participation generally speaking, perhaps a function of the fact that unions tend to heighten the salience of conflict over resources and political power (Kerrissey and Shofer 2013). Rather, they equalize participation by enhancing the participation of the poor.[18]

There is weaker evidence that union density matters in 2012: high levels of unionization are weakly associated with more equal voter turnout, but not associated with more equal levels of political activism. It appears, then, that union density is more important to participatory inequality midterm elections than in general ones. I cannot test exactly why this appears to be the case, though it may well be the case that in the absence of the high salience and substantial media coverage of a presidential election, mobilization becomes a more important factor in getting people to vote. The fact that voter turnout across income lines is, in general, more equal in presidential than congressional years seems to support the notion that contextual factors such as the presence of strong mobilizing agents may play a stronger role in getting low-income voters to the polls in off-year elections.

The findings for contextual inequality are weaker and more mixed. Inequality has no effect on political activism in any of the three years. But in 2012 and 2014, high levels of inequality seem to modestly depress the relationship between income and turnout: voter turnout, in other words, is more *equal* in contexts where incomes are highly *unequal*. This finding fits nicely with the Brady (2004) conception of inequality as heightening the salience of conflict over political resources, but contradicts a good bit of comparative work on the relationships between inequality and participation, which suggests that inequality depresses political activity, particularly among the poor.

These comparative findings are not necessarily directly comparable to the U.S. case: most studies that show a strong relationship between inequality and participation rely on cross-national comparisons of countries that are more dissimilar than are congressional districts in terms of political culture, overall wealth, and basic institutional resources (though see Solt 2010 for a study of American state elections). At a minimum, though, at least in the United States, it appears that the presence of significant material differences across citizens within a given context at least has the potential to stimulate political participation.

Conclusions

This chapter has highlighted the role that contextual factors play in shaping the decisions of citizens—particularly lower-income citizens—to participate in politics. To be sure, political participation is still primarily a decision made by individuals, driven by a rough understanding of the costs and benefits of participation, as well as a consideration of the resources that citizens have to devote to participation. But these findings also show the importance of contextual influences in shaping how individuals view the costs and benefits of participation, as well as the degree to which citizens are able to pay these costs or reap these benefits.

In general, this chapter has identified a number of factors—unionization, low concentrations of poverty, and less stringent identification requirements—that might help to mitigate gaps in participation between rich and poor. But it is important to note that in nearly all cases, these gaps are mitigated by *increasing* the likelihood that lower-income citizens will get involved in politics, not by *decreasing* the likelihood that wealthier citizens will get involved. At least when it comes to the forms of political activity identified here, political participation is not a zero-sum game: there are contextual factors that are especially important in enhancing the participation of the poor, but these factors also, at least to some extent, tend to enhance (or at least not detract from) the participation of the wealthy as well.

The most important of these factors to increasing participation among poorer citizens is the role of strong contextual norms of participation in given communities and contexts (see Huckfeldt 1979; Leighley 1990). When it comes to political participation—as well as many other aspects of civic life—poor citizens who live in wealthy areas tend to be significantly more likely than poor citizens to get involved in politics. Poor citizens in both types of contexts face the same sorts of individual-level obstacles—a lack of time, money, transportation, or other resources, as well as a lower likelihood of having been socialized into habits of participation—that make less well-off citizens less likely to get involved in general.

But high-status communities, in all likelihood, provide implicit social incentives for getting involved that communities where political alienation is the norm do not. They also attract mobilizing agents—parties, candidates, and the like—that target citizens for participation explicitly. Social networks matter when it comes to political activity, in other words, and poorer citizens living in well-off contexts are at least exposed to the sorts of networks that foster participation. While important to political participation, these findings can also be interpreted more broadly as speaking to the corrosive role that economic segregation and highly concentrated poverty play in shaping opportunities and outcomes for the poor.

To some extent, this reasoning also helps to shed light on the findings regarding income inequality. Scholars of municipal participation have long argued that when social class divisions are embedded in physical political boundaries, political participation is less likely (Burns 1992). Large urban municipalities with many competing interests foster conflict and debate and increase levels of civic engagement, while small, homogenous ones make conflict over resources (and thus civic engagement) less common (Rusk 1995). This type of work has focused mainly on engagement in local politics, but can be applied more broadly as well: more political conflict, in general, should lead to more participation. Perhaps that is what is happening with income inequality, too: high levels of inequality increase perceived conflict over resources, and stimulate political participation as a result.

We should not push this line of reasoning too far: the results here regarding income inequality were weak and somewhat inconsistent, and stand at odds with at least some recent work in the field. So although more work remains to be done, it is possible that inequality highlights the salience of political conflict between rich and poor in a way that serves as a mobilizing agent for poorer citizens. Whether this leads to a greater likelihood of poor citizens actually getting what they want from representatives, of course, is a different story: with greater inequalities come greater disparities in other sorts of political resources that might matter to how policymakers think and act. We will take up this question in chapters 5 and 6.

We have also seen that institutional barriers to voting have the expected (and perhaps intended) effects: they decrease voter turnout, particularly among citizens that have the most difficulty paying the costs of overcoming these barriers. These sorts of laws pose some tangible obstacles to citizens, but also perhaps pose some psychological ones as well: government policies can send meaningful cues to citizens about the types of characteristics that are required or desired in order to participate in civic life (Mettler and Soss 2004).

This analysis, of course, does not provide an exhaustive list of all of the contextual influences on participation. There is some evidence here, for example, that a strong labor union presence reduces participation biases across income lines, as labor unions seek to mobilize lower income voters that might otherwise be ignored by other parties or candidates. Unions were highlighted here as a particularly important form of mobilization, but we can certainly imagine other factors—particular kinds of religious organizations, for example—that might also be relevant to mobilizing the poor. The important point from this chapter is that the mobilization of the poor matters: unions can provide this sort of mobilization, but it is easy to imagine it coming from other places as well.

So far we have seen that context matters in shaping both how rich and poor decide to get involved in politics. Of course, how they are getting involved, and what views they are voicing when they do get involved, are separate matters. In the next chapter, we thus work to understand not only how rich and poor are participating in politics, but also the factors that shape the opinions that they are voicing when they do.

FOUR

Class Politics and American Public Opinion

The importance of material self-interest to one's views on what government should do or not do is central to classic understandings of politics in a variety of disciplines. Political theorists have long discussed the notion of politics as, at least in large part, a struggle between people and groups of different economic means. Sociologists have discussed enduring "democratic class struggle" (Anderson and Davison 1943) of politics in a wide variety of guises. And models of political behavior in the economics literature (e.g., Meltzer and Richard 1981) assume that rich and poor differ fundamentally in their policy views: such models take as a starting point that the poor should want more redistribution, while the rich want less.

But at the same time, it is clear that material self-interest is not always, or even usually, the most important predictor of policy views. Myriad other factors—party loyalty, religious beliefs, core values, and prejudices, to name just a few—also serve as powerful influences on citizens' policy views: economic self-interest alone explains relatively little of the variation in what citizens believe (Citrin and Green 1990; Sears and Funk 1990). Despite the clear importance of class interests to politics, in other words, it is not unreasonable to think that, on many salient issues, even those with strong distributive implications, there will be little daylight between the political views of the wealthy and the poor.

Many popular notions of American class politics (e.g., Frank 2005; Bageant 2008) have infused the notion of cross-class similarity in political views with normative implications: poor citizens, for example, think similarly to the rich in part because they have perhaps been "duped" into doing so. The question of whether a society more politically divided along class lines would be desirable or preferable to the current one goes well beyond the scope of this book. But even above these sorts of assertions, the notion that rich and poor might hold similar views is deeply important to the issue of political representation: if the wealthy and the poor are asking for essentially the same thing from government, then it would be functionally impossible for policymakers to represent the preferences of one group over the other, even if they wanted to (Soroka and Wlezien 2008).

In this chapter, I work to understand the factors that affect how strongly material interest, as measured by income, matters to political conflict. Put more directly, what factors cause rich and poor to want markedly different things from government, and what factors cause them to want many of the same things? I advance a model of *activated economic self-interest*, arguing that the degree to which the rich and the poor will differ in what they want from government depends, at least in part, on the degree to which the context in which they live primes class interest to be a relevant political concern.

Given the content and stakes of most political debates, in other words, one's income nearly always *could* play a significant role in shaping one's policy views. But the degree to which income actually *does* matter is dependent on whether one's immediate context leads one to align material self-interest with policy views. Context matters because it can serve to make citizens aware of income disparities, affect whether such citizens believe that such disparities are due to luck or differences in work ethic, and even affect how the rich and the poor view each other as people.

After showing that there is significant cross-district variance in how different the views of the rich and the poor are from one another, the chapter proceeds to identify and test several explanations for why the rich and the poor sometimes hold similar attitudes, and why they sometimes hold attitudes that are different from one another. I find that explanations for rich-poor opinion differences are rooted in both cultural factors (that is, the degree to which the dominant political messages in a given context either highlight or downplay the role of self-interest in political attitudes) and factors that affect how citizens experience their own economic standing, and compare their standing to others.

"American Exceptionalism" and Class Politics

While material self-interest is not a perfect predictor of political beliefs anywhere in the world, the connections between income and policy views are perhaps weaker in the United States than they are elsewhere. The United States stands nearly alone among industrial societies in lacking a strong labor or working-class party (Sombart 1976), and the relationship between income, party affiliation, and vote choice remains weaker than it is in most other Western democracies (Evans 2000; Lipset and Marks 2000; Svallfors 2006).

Why is class seemingly less salient in the United States than it is elsewhere? One could point to the unique historical experience of the United States: the availability of "free" land that allowed for expanded opportunities for social and economic mobility (Benabou and Tirole 2011), or the absence of historical feudal arrangements that led Americans to be born without the institutionalized class structures that give rise to strong class consciousness (Lipset and Marks 2000). Others note the relative affluence of the early United States compared to its Western counterparts (Sombart 1976), or the many waves of immigration (and the racial and ethnic conflicts that they engendered) that served to periodically disrupt class divisions and align the political system along other cleavages (Davis 2000).

The absence of strong class awareness may also be, in part, a religious construct: the Calvinist ethos of the early United States instilled a set of religious values whereby hard work was the key to salvation, idleness was a sign of spiritual bankruptcy, and salvation was the ultimate responsibility of the individual (Weber 1930). This doctrinal belief was thought to provide the basis for a strongly individualist political ethic, even among lower-class citizens.[1] Scholars also point to the importance of the U.S. electoral system: in particular, the "winner-take all" model of election that discouraged the formation of parties that cater explicitly to particular class interests (see Alesina and Glaeser 2004).

There remains considerable discussion over the relative importance of these factors, but the general argument is that these factors combine to affect how Americans of all income levels view both the causes of wealth disparities and the appeal of government remedies to ameliorate such disparities. Americans, in general, view individual agency as being considerably more important to economic success than do their European counterparts; are much more likely to believe that differences in effort, rather than luck, are responsible for differences in incomes; and are more likely to believe that anyone can get ahead if they work hard enough (Oorschot and Halman 2000). This belief in what might (simplistically) be called "meritocracy" is widely shared, even among the poor (Hochshild 1981).

In general, then, the cultural and historical background of the United States, and its role in shaping views on the power of hard work (Oorschot and Halman 2000), the deservingness of the rich (McCall 2013), and whether the poor should be viewed with compassion or disdain (Piston 2014), have provided important influences on how Americans think, combining to make the United States a less class-conscious society relative to most of its European counterparts, and one where the role of income in political debate is suppressed relative to other cleavages.

But despite the general evidence for this "American exceptionalism" (Lipset 1997) thesis of class conflict, it is a mistake to say that income and class are unimportant to American political conflict. Despite the occasional popular pronouncement that income divides have taken a back seat to "cultural" conflict over issues such as abortion or gay marriage, evidence persists that Americans know and care about income inequality (Page and Jacobs 2009), and can clearly identify one political party as being more strongly in the interests of the poor than the other (Nicholson and Segura 2011). The relationship between income and voting behavior remains strong and, by some accounts, is becoming stronger (Stonecash 2000; Bartels 2008). So while it is clearly wrong to simply *assume* that rich and poor want different things, in other words, the idea that "class is dead" to American politics is overstated as well.

Income and Opinion in American Politics

Do the wealthy and the poor differ substantially in their political views? This section provides a broad look at this subject, pulling data from a variety of large-*N* national surveys to look at income differences across a wide variety of questions with policy content. These questions are meant to encompass a wide variety of political views, from views on specific bills on which Congress actually voted, to more general political priorities (i.e., whether government should "spend more" or "spend less" in a particular domain), to even more expansive views on the proper role of government in citizens' lives. For expository purposes, I divide these questions into two categories: those where opinion differences between the top and bottom income terciles is greater than 10 percentage points (table 4.1), and those where differences across terciles is less than 10 percentage points (table 4.2).

TABLE 4.1. Issues with "Large" Differences in Opinions across Income Lines

	Source	Bottom Tercile	Middle Tercile	Top Tercile	Top-Bottom Difference
Percent who want to decrease spending on welfare	CCES (2014)	27%	42%	46%	19%
Percent who favor limits on foreign imports	ANES (2012)	73%	71%	56%	17%
Percent agreeing with "government should guarantee every citizen enough to eat and a place to sleep"	Pew Values (2012)	65%	50%	48%	17%
Percent who want to increase government spending on child care	GSS (2014)	62%	58%	47%	15%
Percent who believe that Wall Street hurts the economy more than it helps	Pew Polarization (2014)	48%	37%	33%	15%
Percent agreeing with "Freedom of speech should not extend to groups that are sympathetic to terrorists"	Pew Values (2012)	54%	45%	41%	14%
Percent who support a government-run system of health insurance	Annenberg (2012)	54%	48%	41%	13%
Percent who agree that the government should do more to help the needy, even if it increases the debt	Pew Polarization (2014)	50%	38%	38%	12%
Percent wanting to increase spending on public health	CCES (2014)	56%	48%	46%	10%

Sources: 2012 American National Election Study; 2012 Annenberg Election Survey; 2014 Cooperative Congressional Election Study; 2014 General Social Survey; 2012 Pew Research Center American Values Survey; 2014 Pew Research Center Polarization Survey.

Responses to these questions show reasonably consistent, yet generally modest, differences between those of higher and lower income levels. The questions on which we see the largest income differences are, as one might expect, those that directly address redistribution or the income divide between rich and poor. Perhaps the largest divide between the top and bottom terciles is with respect to the role of financial institutions: bottom tercile citizens are much more likely than the rich to view Wall Street

TABLE 4.2. Issues with "Small" Differences in Opinions across Income Lines

	Source	Bottom Tercile	Middle Tercile	Top Tercile	Top-Bottom Difference
Percent who support EPA efforts to regulate carbon emissions	CCES (2014)	73%	69%	66%	7%
Percent who identify as ideologically "conservative"	CCES (2014)	37%	41%	43%	6%
Percent who support gay marriage	CCES (2014)	58%	58%	64%	6%
Percent who believe that abortion should always be legal	CCES (2014)	60%	59%	63%	3%
Percent wanting to increase spending on education	CCES (2014)	63%	62%	61%	2%
Percent who support background checks on all gun purchases	CCES (2014)	89%	88%	87%	2%
Percent who would grant legal status to undocumented immigrants with jobs	CCES (2014)	48%	48%	50%	2%
Percent who support laws protecting gays and lesbians from job discrimination	ANES (2012)	75%	75%	77%	2%
Percent who wish to repeal the Affordable Care Act	CCES (2014)	49%	52%	50%	1%
Percent who think that the United States is too supportive of Israel	ANES (2012)	25%	26%	26%	1%
Percent who favor the Common Core educational standards	Pew Polarization (2014)	47%	43%	48%	1%
Percent agreeing with "the best way to insure peace is through military strength"	Pew Values (2012)	55%	55%	54%	1%

Sources: 2012 American National Election Study; 2014 Cooperative Congressional Election Study; 2012 Pew Research Center American Values Survey; 2014 Pew Research Center Polarization Survey.

as hurting the American economy, and to oppose "bailouts" or other assistance to financial institutions. Lower-income people are also more supportive of redistributive spending, and more likely to feel that government should help the needy. They are also generally more skeptical of free trade and trade agreements than the wealthy.[2]

These differences speak to the presence of at least some meaningful class divides in American politics: where self-interest motivations are present, the views of rich and poor differ in predictable ways. It is important to keep such differences in perspective, however: it is exceedingly rare for any issue to divide the top and bottom terciles by as much as 20 percentage points (a magnitude of division that is the norm when it comes to, for example, differences in the views of Democrats and Republicans). Even where differences are reasonably large, it is common for the *majority* preference of all income terciles to be the same. Though lower income citizens are generally both more pro–welfare spending and pro–minimum wage increase than the wealthy, for example, both top- and bottom-tercile citizens generally oppose an increase in welfare spending, and desire a higher minimum wage, for example. In addition, the *rank order* of preferences on each of these issues across income lines is relatively constant: top-, middle-, and bottom tercile citizens generally seem to agree on the policies on this list that are most preferred and least preferred, even if they differ in their relative levels of support for them (see also Enns 2015).

We see less meaningful differences between rich and poor on issues where we might think of the government's role as broadly distributive: regulating or spending money to improve the quality of transportation infrastructure, fight crime, or protect the environment, for example.[3] Rich and poor tend to differ the least when it comes to matters such as gun control, foreign policy, or immigration—all issues that lack a clear redistributive component. There is also little difference between rich and poor when it comes to the abstract matter of ideological self-placement. And wealthy citizens, owing in large part to higher levels of education, tend to be modestly more liberal than the poor when it comes to "cultural" matters such as abortion or gay marriage.

Figures 4.1–4.4 provides a more detailed look at income differences in opinion, displaying opinions on four high-profile questions asked of respondents in the 2014 Cooperative Congressional Election Study—ideological self-placement, Congress's vote to repeal the Affordable Care Act (ACA), welfare spending, and whether gay couples should be allowed to marry legally—segmented across the 14 income categories. Somewhat larger differences between the wealthiest and poorest citizens emerge

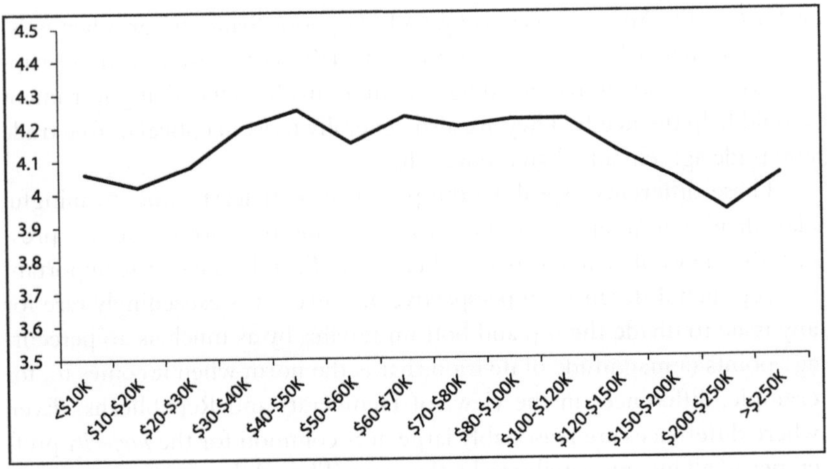

Fig. 4.1. Ideological Self-Placement, by Household Income

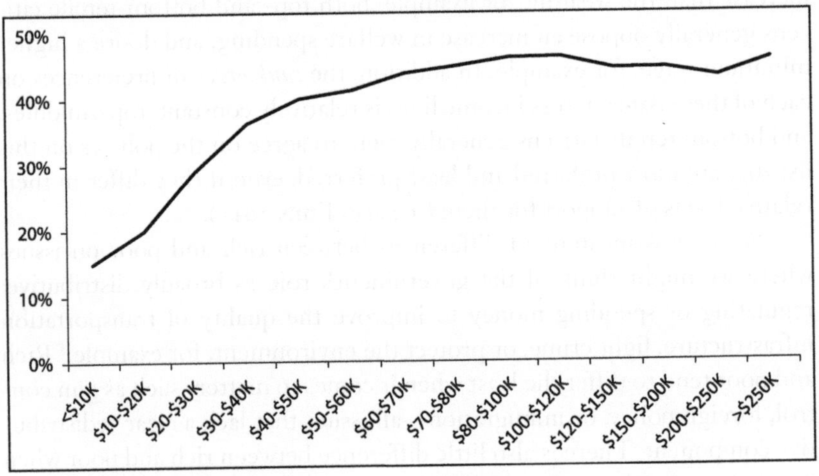

Fig. 4.2. Percent Who Want to Spend Less on Welfare, by Household Income

when it comes to welfare spending (poor citizens tend to be less opposed to it) and gay marriage (poorer citizens are less supportive). But, again, the differences here are relatively modest and not consistent across all issues.

Context and Opinion in American Politics

While opinions on salient issues vary modestly (and somewhat inconsistently) across income level, we see very clear differences in opinion across

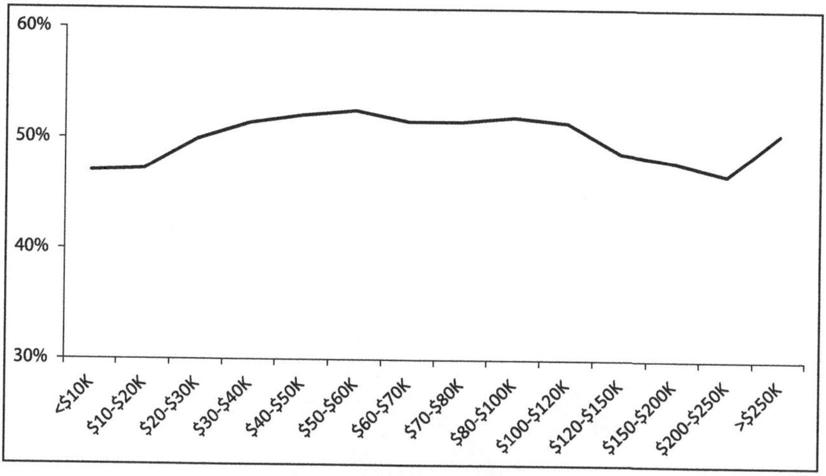

Fig. 4.3. Percent Who Wish to Repeal the Affordable Care Act, by Household Income

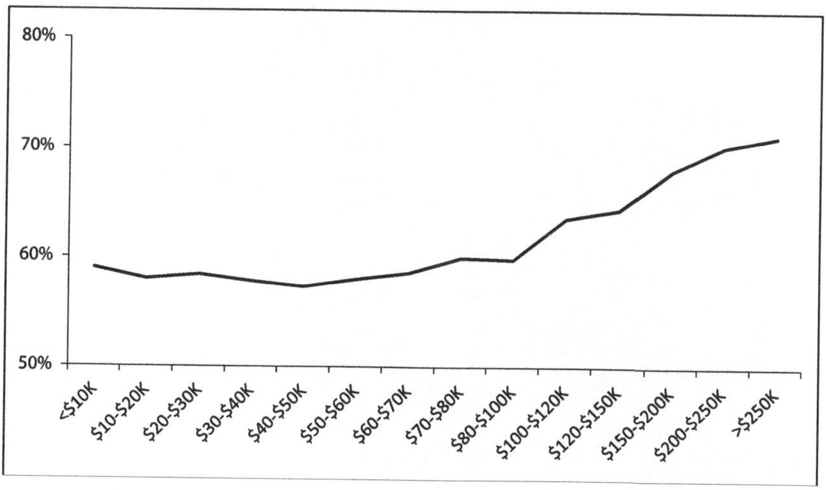

Fig. 4.4. Percent Supportive of Gay Marriage, by Household Income

different areas of the country. Figures 4.5–4.8 map citizens' mean self-placement scores, as well as mean levels of support for increasing welfare spending, repealing the ACA, and supporting gay marriage, across the country's 435 congressional districts. This figure shows that congressional districts differ substantially in their views. The most conservative and liberal districts are no surprise (9 of the 10 most liberal districts in terms of self-placement, for example, were urban areas in New York or California,

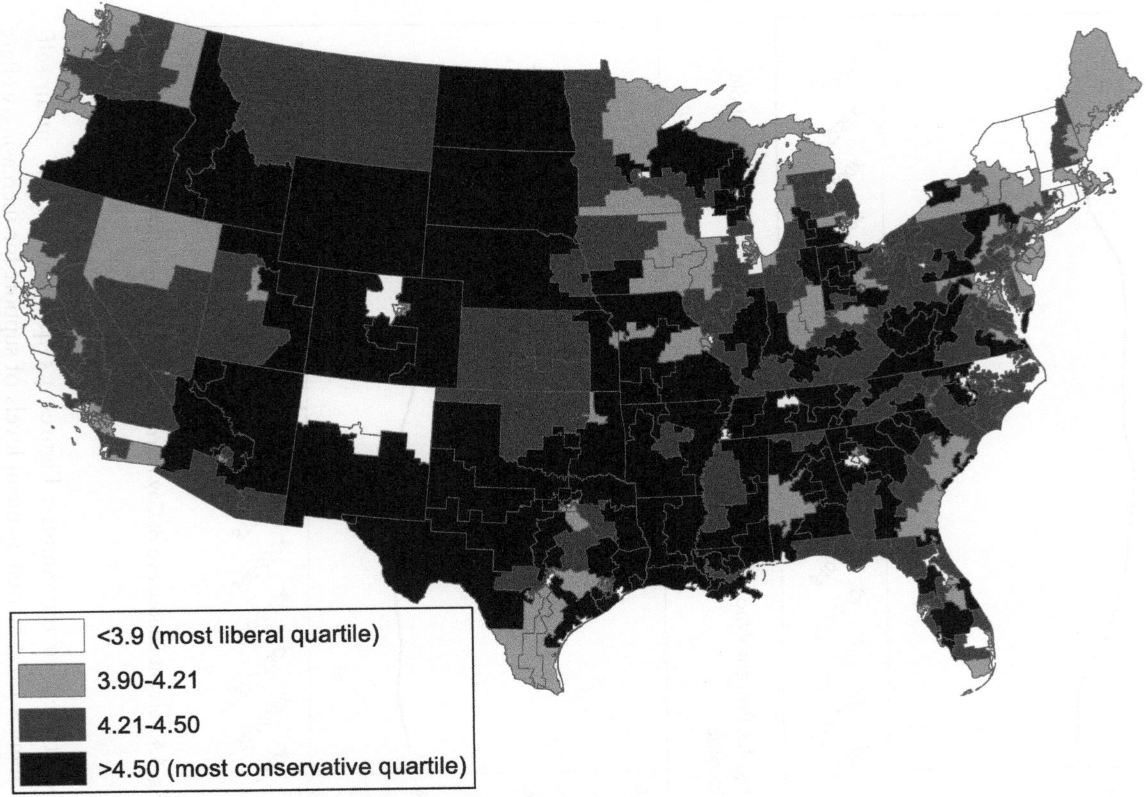

Fig. 4.5. Ideological Self-Placement, by District

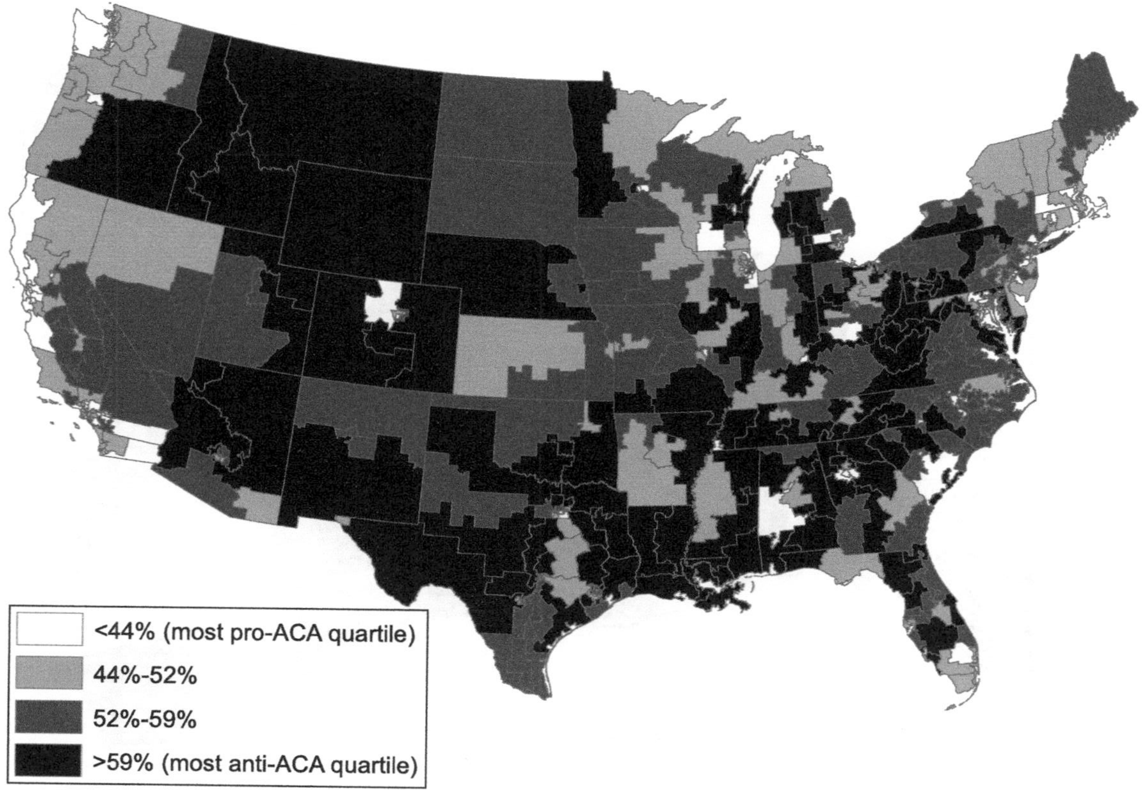

Fig. 4.6. Percent Who Want to Repeal the Affordable Care Act, by District

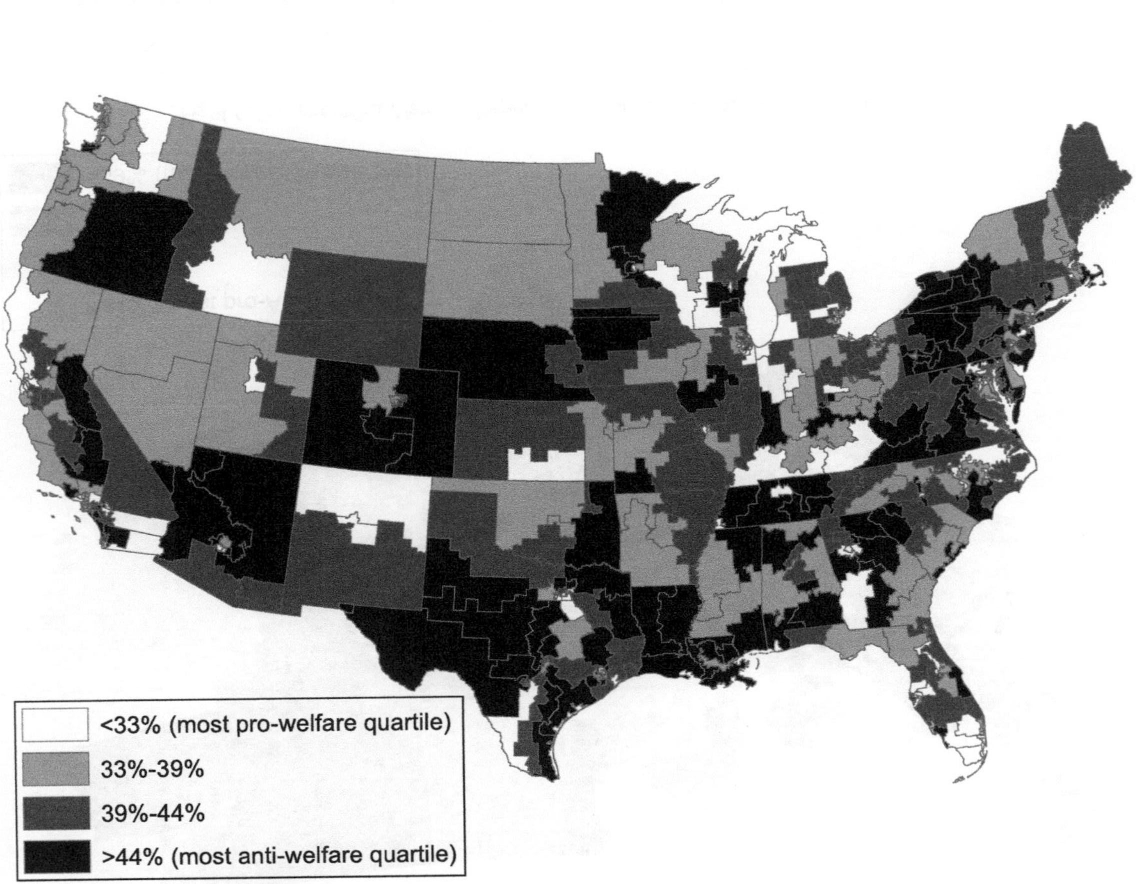

Fig. 4.7. Percent Who Want to Spend Less on Welfare, by District

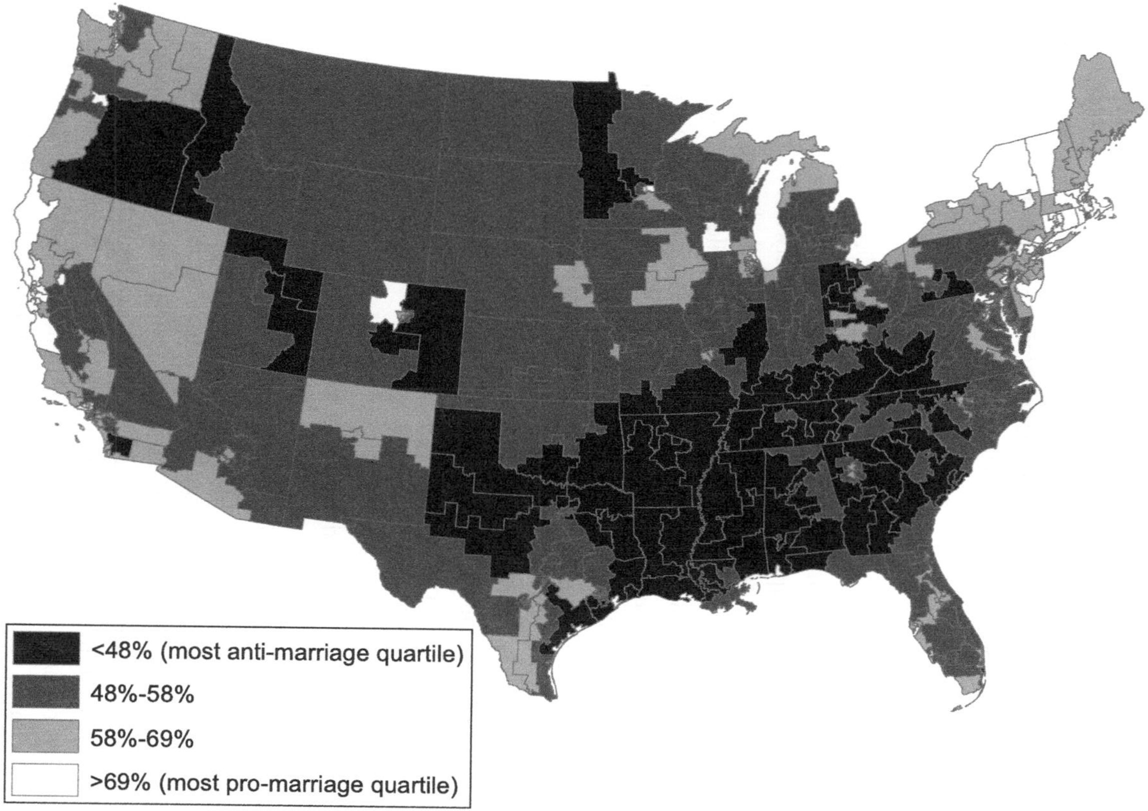

Fig. 4.8. Percent Supportive of Gay Marriage, by District

while 8 of the 10 most conservative districts were rural areas in either Texas or the Deep South). In general, the results show that variation in how different areas of the country think about politics is, in many respects, greater than variation in how rich and poor citizens think about politics. This is consistent with what is known about the state of geographic polarization in American politics, and serves to highlight the idea that different areas of the country possess markedly different political cultures that serve to both reflect and shape what citizens believe (see Gimpel and Schuknecht 2004). Knowing where someone lives is in many cases at least as good a predictor, or in some cases a better predictor, of his or her views than knowing his or her income.

More important, though, there is also evidence that the relative magnitude of rich-poor differences varies across district lines. As an example of this, figure 4.9 graphs the absolute difference between the mean policy views of top- and bottom-tercile citizens within each district with respect to self-placement. Given small by-district, by-tercile sample sizes, these opinion gaps are measured with significant noise. But we can clearly see substantial variation across districts in the size of the top-bottom tercile opinion gap: for all three measures of opinion, I can easily ($p < .001$) reject the hypothesis that opinion differences across terciles are the same across districts for this (and for the other issues illustrated in figures 4.5–4.8). Different income groups want different things from government, in other words, but the magnitudes of these differences—and the degree to which they exist at all—vary across areas of the country.

Activated Self-Interest: A General Model

We now work toward explaining the variance in rich-poor opinion divergence of the sort shown in figure 4.9. In what sorts of contexts should we expect wealthy and poor citizens to hold similar views on the proper role of government, and in what sorts of contexts should we expect such opinions to diverge? In this section, I argue that the environment in which citizens live can serve to either highlight or downplay the factors that might lead citizens to think about politics in terms of material self-interest.

As noted earlier, one's own income level could affect one's opinion on nearly all policy issues. The vast majority of policy debates (as well as the vast majority of what the federal government actually does) deal with issues of taxing, spending, redistribution, and regulation—all matters that shape "who gets what" in American society. Material self-interest might be best

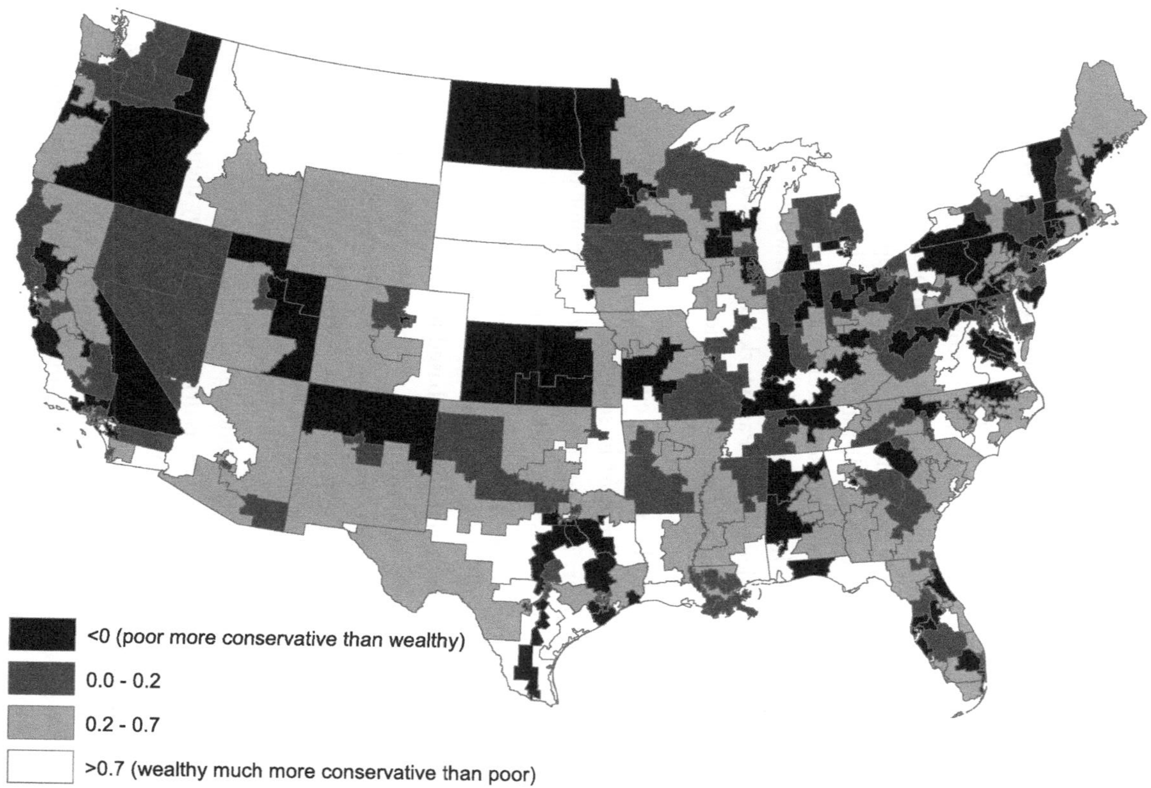

Fig. 4.9. Mean Top-Bottom Tercile Differences in Self-Placement, by District

thought of, in the language of V. O. Key (1961), as "latent opinion," one of a diverse lot of considerations on which specific policy attitudes might be built (see also Newman, Johnston, and Lown 2015).

But self-interest is only one of many possible considerations that can inform attitudes. Myriad other factors, both individual (e.g., one's religious or personal values—see Jacoby 2006) and contextual (e.g., the political and social messages to which one is exposed—Huckfeldt 1979, 1986) can also affect one's attitudes on issues. When self-interest is activated as a salient concern, in other words, citizens will be more likely to behave as many economic models predict: poorer citizens will support policies that lead to more redistribution, while wealthier citizens will support policies that lead to less redistribution. But when self-interest is not primed to be important, these other factors will dominate self-interest as a predictor of opinions.

What factors shape whether material self-interest will be activated as an important driver of policy beliefs? Past work has identified (at least) three mechanisms that are likely to enhance the salience of one's own income to policy beliefs.

First, for income to be relevant, citizens *must perceive that meaningful class differences do, in fact, exist* in society. This perception is especially important for the poor: if lower-income citizens do not perceive themselves as belonging to a class that could benefit from redistribution, there is little reason to think that they would support such redistribution. Perceiving meaningful class differences is important to priming citizens to think about politics in explicitly self-interest-based terms.

Second, and related, rich and poor must exhibit some divergence on what are perceived as the *root causes of disparities in income*. Are differences in income primarily a result of differences in worth ethic, intelligence, or creativity, or are they primarily a function of luck or the circumstances of one's birth? Is it possible for anyone, with sufficient hard work and determination, to improve their economic standing? If wealthy citizens, for example, believe that their economic success is driven primarily by their own efforts, and that anyone could achieve similar success if they were willing to work hard enough, then there is little reason to think that they will support more redistribution toward the poor (Jost and Hunyady 2005). If the wealthy, by contrast, see their success as in part a result of luck, their support for redistribution is likely to be higher.

Third, and perhaps most important, rich and poor must differ in how they *view rich and poor citizens as people*. In the absence of sophisticated policy considerations or a deep body of policy-specific knowledge, citizens' attitudes toward social programs are very often driven by simple affective orientations toward the beneficiaries of social programs and the problems that they are designed to solve (Aaroe and Petersen 2014). An emerging line of research suggests that this might be especially true for any program that redistributes wealth (see Sadin 2014; Piston 2014). Are poor citizens viewed as sympathetic or worthy of compassion? If so, then citizens will be more supportive of programs designed to benefit the poor. Are wealthy citizens viewed with anger or resentment? If so, citizens will be more supportive of programs that redistribute away from the wealthy or otherwise restrict their actions.

Table 4.3 shows responses to a variety of recent questions asked in recent surveys that address each of the three conditions noted above. The results generally comport with the notion that Americans view their society as a "meritocratic" one, where class divisions are not especially relevant, and where citizens can improve their economic lot through hard work.

TABLE 4.3. Attitudes toward Class Politics, by Income Group

	Source	All Respondents	Bottom Tercile	Middle Tercile	Top Tercile
Percent agreeing with "Most people who want to get ahead can make it if they're willing to work hard"	Pew Polarization (2014)	65%	61%	66%	69%
Percent agreeing with "Success in life is pretty much determined by forces outside our control"	Pew Values (2012)	30%	44%	26%	18%
Percent agreeing with "Hard work offers little guarantee of success"	Pew Values (2012)	30%	41%	29%	17%
Percent who view America as being divided into "haves" and "have-nots"	Pew Values (2009)	34%	44%	32%	26%
Percent who "always" or "most of the time" feel compassion toward the poor	CCES (2014)	71%	73%	71%	69%
Percent who "always" or "most of the time" feel anger toward the rich	CCES (2014)	16%	17%	17%	13%

Sources: 2012 American National Election Study; 2014 Cooperative Congressional Election Study; 2009 Pew Research Center Values Survey; 2012 Pew Research Center American Values Survey; 2014 Pew Research Center Polarization Survey.

Responses to these questions suggest that there is limited belief that society is meaningfully divided into "haves" and "have nots,"[4] or that hard work cannot lead to success. Though there are important differences across income groups—wealthy citizens are less likely to perceive class divisions, and more likely to believe that hard work can lead to success—these beliefs are broadly shared across income groups. We also see little evidence here or elsewhere that inequalities generally lead to widespread anger or resentment toward wealthier citizens (though citizens of all income levels also report feeling compassion toward the plight of the poor).

These factors are often cited as reasons why class divides are smaller in the United States than they are elsewhere: Americans, it is said, are less likely to perceive important class differences, more likely to believe that hard work leads to economic success, and less resentful toward wealthier citizens, than in other industrialized societies. These factors combine to lead citizens—particularly poor ones—to not think about politics in self-interested terms (Alesina and Glaeser 2004; van der Waal, Achterberg, and Houtman 2007). As a result, self-interest is less "activated" as a salient concern here than it might be elsewhere.

Activating Self-Interest: The Role of Political Culture

The general argument in this chapter is that the degree to which self-interest will be "activated" as an important concern in political thinking depends in part on context. What sorts of factors are likely to cause rich and poor citizens to differ in how they view disparities in wealth, and in how they view each other? First, we might examine the role that an area's dominant political culture plays in shaping such views. Comparative research has taught us a great deal about how local (and national) political cultures inform how citizens—both rich and poor—think about politics. Political cultures create the conditions under which citizens live and the belief systems into which they are socialized. Cultures serve to legitimize, or delegitimize, certain means of thinking about the political system (e.g., Noelle-Neumann 1993), and the values that a given political culture transmits have a strong conditioning effect on political opinions (Dallinger 2010).

The political culture in which one lives does not determine one's opinion about political issues, but it can play a role in how citizens define political problems, and how they view the relationship between individuals and their government. Culture, in other words, can help shape the terms under which rich and poor citizens *consider* political issues (Huckfeldt 1986), and can serve to either highlight, or downplay, the role that one's own material self-interest plays in forming political opinions.

What sorts of cultures might prime income to be a particularly important political dividing line? My most general expectation is straightforward—conservative political cultures should do more to prime the self-interest component of public opinion than liberal cultures: *opinion differences between rich and poor should be greater in politically conservative areas than in politically liberal ones.*[5] This expectation is perhaps counterintuitive, given the well-chronicled efforts of conservative lawmakers to denounce "class warfare" and attempt to reshape political discourse in a way that minimizes the importance of class conflict. But there are many reasons to think that cultures that are politically and socially conservative provide grounds for rich and poor citizens—particularly rich citizens—to think about politics in terms of narrow material self-interest. And there are also reasons to think that the opposite is true in liberal cultures.

The reasons to expect greater rich-poor opinion differences in conservative political cultures deal primarily with the notion that such cultures do substantially more to highlight individual, rather than situational, causes of income differences than do liberal ones. The values endorsed by these cultures—which tend to highlight the possibility that everyone can get ahead with sufficient effort, which view wealth as the earned rewards of working hard and playing by the rules, and poverty as at least in part a function of some individual deficiency—are transmitted in a number of formal and informal settings, including school curricula (Kaestle 1983; Alesina and Glaeser 2004), media outlets (Entman 2004; Strömbäck and Dimitrova 2006), and formal policies (like those which place significant restrictions on where poor citizens can use government support payments).[6] Given the role of culture in transmitting a set of values and ideals to all citizens, it stands to reason that the effects of this "meritocratic" worldview will be reflected in the views of both rich and poor citizens. But there are reasons to think that this effect will be particularly pronounced among the wealthy.

For the poor, the meritocratic messages received in one's political culture will clash to some extent with one's own material interests. But wealthy people, at least to some extent, have a strong motivation to see the existing political system as fair and their own wealth as justified. The natural motivation to justify one's own wealth as deserved (and, perhaps the poverty of the poor as equally deserved) will be reinforced by the messages transmitted through one's cultural context.

Liberal cultures, by contrast, tend to do more to highlight situational causes of income disparities. As a result, the perhaps natural desire to justify one's own economic standing is countered by a context that views such standing as, at least in part, a function of luck or circumstance.[7] Taken together, these points suggest that conservative cultures are likely to highlight the importance of self-interest to political views. For the wealthy, the values transmitted by such cultures are also likely to provide some rationale for self-interest to drive political views: that viewing politics in terms of narrow self-interested terms is not only in one's own economic interests but also morally just.

Activated Self-Interest: The Role of Lived Economic Experience

In addition to cultural factors, we might expect that the economic environments in which rich and poor citizens encounter each other play a significant role in understanding how differently these groups think about politics. While growing income inequality is a national trend, I have argued that it is the immediate environment in which citizens encounter this inequality that matters most to their political beliefs. How often do I see or interact with people in markedly different social positions than me? What do these interactions say about my relative economic position? About the ways in citizens in other economic positions should be viewed? It is these sorts of experiences that are likely to affect how rich and poor citizens feel and think about each other, and thus affect how differently they think about political issues. Here, I highlight two factors that might bear on the magnitude of opinion differences between rich and poor citizens: local income inequality and local population density.

Local Income Inequality

It is well established that high levels of income inequality make income differences more salient and increase one's awareness of his or her social position: put simply, high levels of inequality make wealthy people more aware that they are wealthy, and poor people more aware that they are poor (e.g., Jackman and Jackman 1985). This increased awareness of one's own class position, in turn, highlights broader perceptions of class differences that are integral to making income an especially relevant political dividing line (Conover 1984).

In addition, we might expect that local inequality differentially affects how rich and poor citizens perceive the *reasons* for disparities in wealth.

For the wealthy, high levels of inequality lead both to a desire to believe one's own wealth is justified and a desire to preserve the economic system from which one is clearly benefiting relative to others (Jost and Hunyady 2005). As a result, in highly unequal contexts, wealthy citizens are more likely to view disparities in wealth as a result of disparities in work ethic or motivation (Newman, Johnston, and Lown 2015). For the poor, highly unequal contexts produce the opposite effect: such high levels of inequality activate feelings that one's own social position is driven by factors beyond one's own control.

The result is that beliefs in the basic concept of meritocracy diverge in such contexts: wealthy people are more likely, and poor people less likely, to believe that hard work leads to success. Because divergence in perceptions of the root causes of inequality is a key condition for income-based differences in opinion to exist, I expect that *opinion differences between rich and poor should be greater in highly unequal contexts than in more equal ones:* poor citizens in such contexts should be more likely to support positions that reflect the belief in the difficulty of getting ahead on one's own, while wealthy citizens in such contexts should be more likely to reflect the belief that those who cannot get ahead are lazy or unmotivated.

Local Population Density

Of course, the degree to which inequality in a given context is experienced is driven at least in part by the ability to perceive income inequality at all. The United States, like most industrialized nations, has a considerable amount of economic segregation: rich people tend to congregate in wealthy neighborhoods, while poor people are clustered in poorer ones. This type of segregation is noted as causing people to become divorced from an understanding of, or even a perception of, people of different income groups (Danielson 1976; Lamb 2005).

This type of self-segregation is more common in rural and exurban areas, where wealthier citizens have both greater ability and motivation to isolate themselves from their poorer counterparts (Meyer 2000). While the desire, particularly among the wealthy, to avoid living and interacting with people of different income groups is not restricted to such areas (and even the most tightly packed cities have identifiable "rich" and "poor" areas), it is generally the case that people living in more densely populated areas have more day-to-day interactions, and more day-to-day contact, with people of different income groups than people living in less dense areas (Duany, Plater-Zyberk, and Speck 1991; Musterd and Ostenborf 2013).

Why might we care about the degree to which rich and poor live among one another? In a variety of contexts, psychologists have highlighted the importance of intergroup contact in helping, in the right circumstances, to reduce prejudices and improve perceptions of people from different social groups (see Pettigrew and Tropp 2006 for a review of this work). Put simply, having the experience of regular interaction with people who are different than oneself can help to improve perceptions of and reduce social distance between people of different statuses. In the context of class politics, this suggests that the opportunity for "meaningful cross-class interactions" (Oxendine 2012) is a particularly important way to bridge divides between rich and poor, and to highlight a collective sense of community and cross-class understanding. Put more directly, regularly interacting with people of different economic groups—on the street, on public transportation, in shops and restaurants—serves to humanize people of different income groups, and promote a shared sense of fate and circumstance. Not having such interactions tends to have the opposite effect, leading to a divide in how rich and poor perceive one another, and dampening perceptions that they have a stake in a common good (Soss and Jacobs 2009).[8]

This discussion suggests, then, that citizens living in densely populated areas have the sorts of regular interactions with citizens of other income groups that might serve to dampen the role that pure economic self-interest plays in shaping political attitudes.[9] Therefore, *opinion differences between rich and poor should be smaller in densely populated contexts than in less densely populated ones.*

How Rich and Poor View Each Other

This discussion offers the idea that political attitude differences between rich and poor on issues salient to the class divide should be greatest in areas where rich and poor differ in how they view each other as people. These differences in how rich and poor think are most likely to occur in contexts that are politically conservative, highly unequal, and densely populated. In this section, I explore whether context affects the degree to which these conditions are actually met.

A small subset of respondents to the 2014 CCES[10] was asked questions that are central to the arguments in this chapter, and which have been shown to be significant drivers of support for redistributive policies (see Piston 2014 and McCall 2013). Two of them dealt with positive affect toward the poor: how often citizens felt compassion for, or sympathy for, the poor. Two of them dealt with negative affect toward the rich: how often citizens felt angry, or resentful, toward the rich. These questions were coded into a four-point scale, where 0 indicates that they felt these emotions "almost never," and 4 indicates that they felt them "almost all of the time."[11] Mean scores on these measures for all citizens, and for each of the three income terciles, are presented in table 4.4.

As we also saw in table 4.3, feelings of compassion toward the poor were common, providing perhaps a bit of a corrective to the idea that the United States does not care about class differences. These attitudes were slightly less common among wealthier respondents, but even 73 percent of top tercile respondents reported feeling compassion toward the poor "most of the time" or "always" (though the expression of these attitudes are obviously prone to some social desirability biases). Negative emotion toward wealthier citizens was comparably rare: even among bottom tercile citizens, for example, only 17 percent reported that they felt angry (or resentful) toward the rich "most of the time" or "always."

More important, though, we see evidence that the degree to which rich and poor citizens differ in their responses to these questions *varies* based on context. To illustrate this, I create scales of positive affect toward the poor (by summing responses to the "sympathy" and "compassion" questions) and negative affect toward the rich (by summing responses to the "resentment" and "anger" questions). These scales (which range from 0–8) are then modeled as a function of income, measures of the three contextual variables introduced above: a district's overall liberalism (as measured by President Obama's percentage of the two-party vote in 2012),[12] level of income inequality (the Gini coefficient), and population density (a log of the number of residents per square mile), as well as interactions between

TABLE 4.4. Attitudes toward Poor and Rich Citizens

	All respondents	Top Tercile	Middle Tercile	Bottom Tercile
Sympathy toward the poor	2.88	2.83	2.86	2.95
N	869	327	319	223
Compassion toward the poor	3.05	2.99	3.06	3.09
N	869	327	319	223
Resentment toward the rich	1.21	1.08	1.27	1.24
N	851	321	311	219
Anger toward the rich	1.26	1.11	1.34	1.27
N	854	321	312	221

Source: 2014 Cooperative Congressional Election Study (Syracuse Module).

Note: Table entries are mean values on the 0–4 affective frequency scale described in this chapter. Higher values indicate that respondents reported feeling the emotion more often.

income and these contextual variables. Results are presented in tables 4.5 (attitudes toward the poor) and 4.6 (attitudes toward the rich). The first columns of each of these tables consider each contextual variable separately, while the final column models all of them together.

The results in both of these tables provide evidence that the effect of income on feelings toward both rich and poor varies across district types. In the first two sets of models (those for district liberalism and population density), the direct effects of income on positive affect toward the poor, and negative affect toward the rich, are significant and negative—consistent with table 4.4, wealthier citizens feel less positively toward the poor, and less negatively toward the rich, than do poorer ones. But at least in these first two models, these affects are moderated by district context: the relationship between one's own income and attitudes toward both rich and poor citizens are stronger in anti-Obama districts, and in less densely populated districts, than in more pro-Obama or densely populated ones. The data in table 4.5 tells us, for example, that in districts that gave 70 percent of their vote to Obama in 2012 (placing them in the 90th percentile of all districts), the expected difference in affect toward the poor among the wealthiest and poorest citizens is expected to be essentially zero. In districts that gave 30 percent of their vote to Obama (placing them around the 10th percentile of all districts), by contrast,

TABLE 4.5. Modeling Positive Affect toward the Poor

	Dependent Variable: Positive Affect toward the Poor			
Income	–0.17*	–0.16*	–0.04	0.02
	(0.07)	(0.07)	(0.26)	(0.27)
Obama percent	–1.13			–1.58+
	(0.86)			(1.07)
Income * Obama percent	0.26*			0.19
	(0.12)			(0.16)
Population Density (logged)		–0.04		0.02
		(0.07)		(0.09)
Income * Population Density		0.02*		0.01
		(0.01)		(0.01)
District Inequality			2.54	4.50
			(4.18)	(4.64)
Income * District Inequality			0.01	–0.53
			(0.57)	(0.63)
Constant	6.73*	6.36*	5.05	4.81*
	(0.48)	(0.44)	(1.92)	(1.98)
R^2	0.02	0.02	0.00	0.02
N	867	869	869	867

Note: Table entries are OLS regression coefficients (standard errors in parentheses). * $p < .05$, + $p < .10$

the difference is expected to be more than one point on the eight-point scale. A similar result for across population density: there is essentially no expected difference in how upper- and lower-income citizens view the rich and the poor in the densest districts, while the expected difference in sparsely populated districts is substantial.

District inequality does less to moderate the relationship between income and feelings toward either the poor or the rich: the substantive effects of inequality are far weaker than those for population density or liberalism, and only approach significance in the model predicting attitudes toward the poor. And combining all of the data into one model weakens the results for all the variables somewhat: the relatively small sample size, and relatively high correlation between liberalness and density, weakens the effects of both variables when placed into a model together (and both actually drop out of significance in the affect toward the rich model). In sum, though, the results provide at least suggestive evidence that in liberal and densely populated contexts, wealthy citizens feel more positively toward the poor, and less positively toward the rich, than they do in conservative contexts. The impact of one's own income on views toward rich and poor are greatest in conservative and sparsely populated contexts. This fits with much of what I have argued above: that conservative contexts transmits broadly "meritocratic" messages that are particularly appealing to the

TABLE 4.6. Modeling Negative Affect toward the Rich

	Dependent Variable: Negative Affect toward the Rich			
Income	−0.24*	−0.18*	0.54+	−0.50
	(0.08)	(0.08)	(0.30)	(0.31)
Obama percent	−1.44			−0.94
	(0.99)			(1.24)
Income * Obama percent	0.38*			0.28+
	(0.14)			(0.16)
Population Density (logged)		−0.11		−0.05
		(0.08)		(0.16)
Income * Population Density		0.03*		0.01
		(0.01)		(0.02)
District Inequality			−4.16	−1.88
			(4.85)	(5.44)
Income * District Inequality			−1.11+	0.58
			(0.66)	(0.73)
Constant	3.41*	3.29*	4.55*	4.32*
	(0.55)	(0.51)	(2.23)	(2.31)
R^2	0.01	0.01	0.01	0.01
N	849	851	851	849

Note: Table entries are OLS regression coefficients (standard errors in parentheses). * $p < .05$ + $p < .10$

wealthy, and that sparsely populated contexts provide less opportunities for the sorts of cross-class interactions that might serve to humanize people of different economic groups.

Modeling Income Differences in Opinion

We now turn to understanding opinion differences between wealthy and poor citizens, trying to understand whether the activated self-interest model can explain where such differences are likely to be largest. To do this, I explore public opinion toward three questions asked in the 2014 CCES: welfare spending, the Affordable Care Act, and ideological self-placement (measured on a seven-point scale, ranging from "extremely liberal" or "extremely" conservative"). The first two of these issues have strong and clearly identifiable redistributive effects: they are the sorts of issues on which the material self-interest of wealthy and poor citizens are strongly divergent from one another. Ideological self-placement is a simple (if imperfect) measure of a citizen's broad political leanings, and is strongly correlated with one's general attitudes toward redistributive politics (Ellis 2012a). All of these issues are coded such that higher values indicate more right-of-center views (wanting to spend less on welfare, opposing the ACA, and holding a more conservative self-placement).

As a kind of check on the results, I also analyze attitudes toward a prominent "cultural" issue: whether gays and lesbians should be allowed to legally marry. Given that I expect the contextual factors noted above to matter only to activating one's own material economic interests, we should not expect these contextual attributes to have similar effects on "cultural" issues. This issue is coded as a simply dummy variable: "1" for respondents who oppose gay marriage, and "0" for those who support it. To examine these topics, I estimate models of each of these issues as a function of income, other individual-level characteristics, the contextual characteristics discussed above, and the interactions between individual and contextual characteristics.

Individual-level covariates in these models are simply standard variables known to matter to policy views: they include measures of income (the 14-point CCES scale), education (a six-point scale measuring a citizen's highest degree earned), religious importance (measured through responses to a four-point CCES question asking respondents how important religion is to their daily lives), religious fundamentalism (a dummy variable for respondents who identify as born again Christians), race, marital status (a dummy variable for those who are married) gender, and household union membership.

The contextual covariates mirror what is illustrated above: I include the measures used above of a respondent's district's overall liberalism, level of income inequality, and population density. Finally, I interact each of these contextual characteristics with individual-measures of income, to examine how the impact of income on policy varies across different sorts of contextual conditions. As in chapter 3, I use a mixed effects modeling strategy in which individuals are clustered within districts, in order to take into account that respondents within districts are not truly independent of one another.

Results of these models are presented in table 4.7. The individual variables tend to behave as expected: men, whites, married people, and the religiously devout all hold more conservative views on welfare, the ACA, and self-placement. And all else equal, wealthy people tend to prefer less spending and place themselves farther to the right than poorer people

TABLE 4.7. Public Opinion and District Context

	Dependent Variable:			
	Self-Placement	ACA Repeal	Welfare (spend less)	Gay Marriage
Income	0.10* (0.03)	−0.07 (0.04)	0.20* (0.05)	0.16* (0.05)
South	−0.03+ (0.02)	0.01 (0.03)	−0.00 (0.03)	−0.06* (0.03)
Nonwhite	−0.44* (0.02)	−0.79* (0.02)	−0.62* (0.03)	0.11* (0.06)
Male	0.46* (0.02)	0.36* (0.02)	0.27* (0.02)	−0.70* (0.02)
Married	0.33* (0.02)	0.30* (0.02)	0.24* (0.02)	−0.51* (0.02)
Born-Again Christian	0.48* (0.02)	0.41* (0.02)	0.16* (0.03)	−1.04* (0.03)
Religious Importance	0.50* (0.01)	0.35*(0.01)	0.22* (0.01)	−0.73* (0.01)
Union Household	0.14* (0.11)	0.18*(0.02)	0.06* (0.02)	−0.05* (0.02)
Obama Percent	−0.59* (0.14)	−1.24*(0.18)	−0.51* (0.20)	0.82* (0.19)
Population Density	0.01 (0.01)	0.03+ (0.02)	0.05* (0.02)	0.01 (0.02)
District Inequality	−0.69 (0.62)	−0.52 (0.82)	−2.14* (0.96)	−2.01* (0.88)
Income * Obama Percent	−0.08* (0.02)	−0.04+ (0.02)	−0.06*(0.03)	0.02 (0.03)
Income * Population Density	−0.004* (0.002)	−0.005* (0.002)	−0.008* (0.002)	0.003 (0.002)
Income * District Inequality	−0.09 (0.08)	−0.07 (0.10)	−0.04 (0.12)	0.40* (0.12)
Constant	2.56* (0.26)	−0.92* (0.35)	−1.10* (0.42)	3.77* (0.37)
N	46,692	49,249	43,033	49,159

Note: Table entries are mixed effects regression (column 2) and mixed effects logistic regression coefficients (columns 3–5). Standard errors are in parentheses. * $p < .05$, + $p < .10$

(though the same is not true for attitudes toward the ACA). The contextual variables tend to have expected effects as well: those in pro-Obama counties hold more liberal views, for example.

Of most importance here, though, are the interactions between income and contextual effects, which indicate that the effect of income on policy views, particularly when it comes to redistributive issues, varies as a function of the political context. The interaction between income and district liberalism is significant and negative for all three issues, indicating that the relationship between income and holding right-of center views is weaker in liberal than in conservative contexts. The same is true for the interactions between income and district density: the relationship between income and policy views is weaker in densely populated contexts. The results, again, are weaker when it comes to the role of contextual inequality: the relationship between income and policy views tends to be somewhat weaker in highly unequal, as opposed to more equal, contexts. But this relationship comes close to statistical significance (or substantive importance) only when it comes to attitudes toward the ACA.

Importantly, we see little evidence that the same sorts of patterns emerge when considering gay marriage: though the individual covariates in the gay marriage model matter a great deal, the relationship between income and gay marriage attitudes is not as conditional on context as are attitudes toward any of the other three issues. This suggests, as would be expected, that the model of activated self-interest applies only to attitudes that have an economic self-interest component to them, not policy attitudes more broadly defined.

To get a sense of the relative magnitude of these effects, figures 4.10–4.12 use results from the models to display the expected ideological self-placement score, and the expected probability of preferring to "spend less" on welfare and support the ACA, for upper-income (again, operationalized here as in chapter 3 as those in the 90th percent of the income distribution) and lower-income (those in the 10th percent of the distribution) citizens as a function of a district's population density. Figures 4.13–4.15 do the same for a district's overall "liberalness," holding other variables at their mean values.

There are two takeaways from these figures. First, the figures reinforce the findings above regarding the importance of context to understanding how much the views of rich and poor differ. This is true on an issue where income is a very powerful driver of individual-level opinions (welfare), and an issue where income is a much less stronger predictor of one's views than the context in which one lives (the ACA). When it comes to welfare, for example, the opinion difference between upper- and lower-income citizens

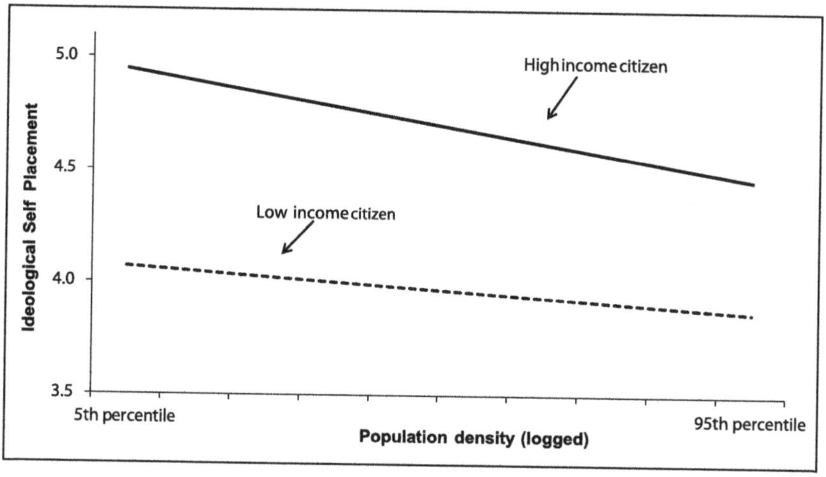

Fig. 4.10. Expected Self-Placement, by Income and District Density

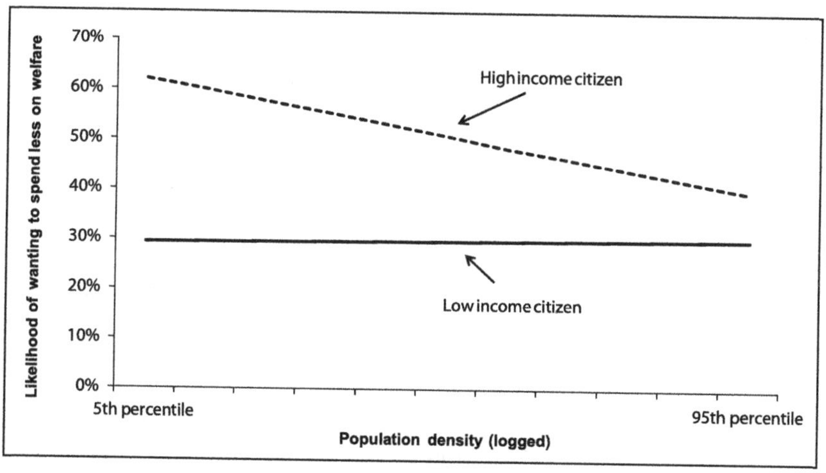

Fig. 4.11. Expected Opposition to Welfare, by Income and Population Density

in the least dense districts is expected to be roughly 35 points. But in the densest districts, it is closer to 10 points. The difference in low-density districts regarding ACA repeal is roughly 10 points. But in the densest districts, the views of upper- and lower-income citizens are a statistically indistinguishable three points different from one another.

The results for district liberalism reinforce a similar pattern. Here, we see a much bigger role for context in explaining the opinions of both rich

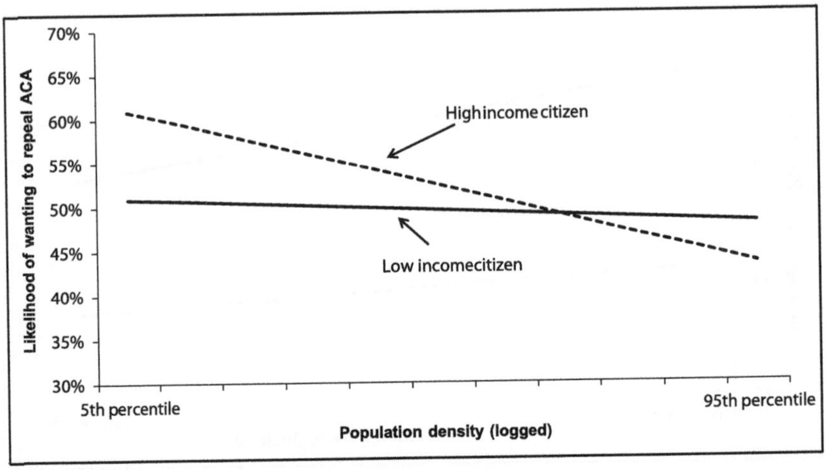

Fig. 4.12. Expected Support for ACA Repeal, by Income and Population Density

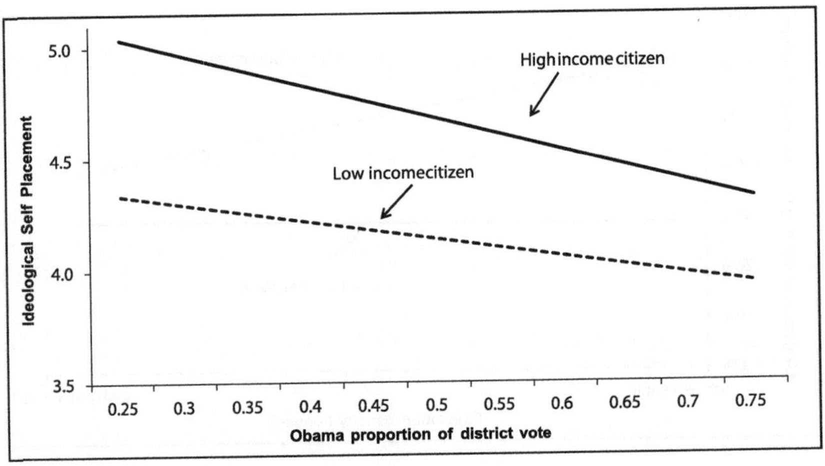

Fig. 4.13. Expected Self-Placement, by Income and Obama Vote Share

and poor: for all three issues, both upper- and lower-income citizens are substantially more liberal in pro-Obama districts than they are in anti-Obama districts. When it comes to saying that we should spend less on welfare, for example, poor citizens, even in the most anti-Obama contexts, hold views on welfare spending that are, on average, to the left of wealthy citizens in the most liberal contexts. The importance of context over income is greatest for the ACA, where divides in opinions across districts

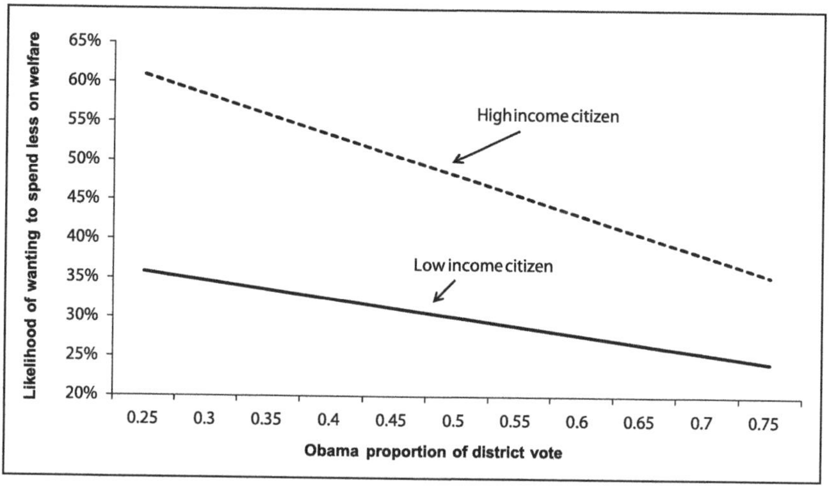

Fig. 4.14. Expected Opposition to Welfare, by Income and Obama Vote Share

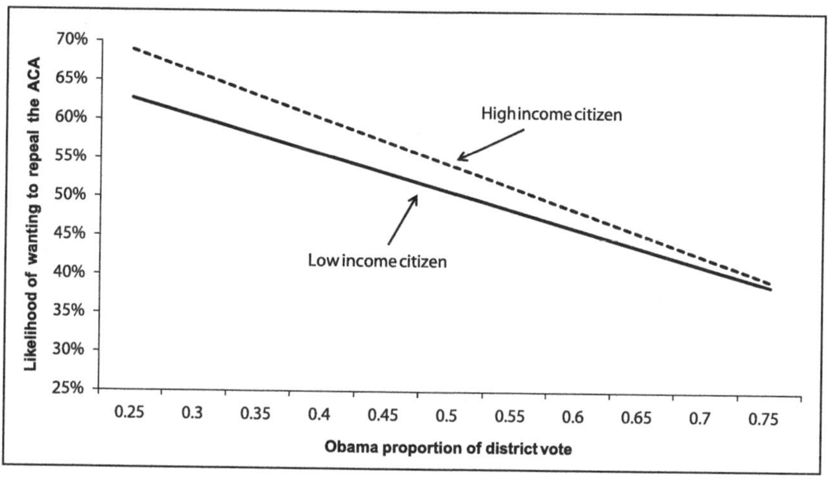

Fig. 4.15. Expected Support for ACA Repeal, by Income and Obama Vote Share

swamp any direct effects of income on attitudes. But, again, we see that the expected differences between upper- and lower-income citizens are greater in districts most hostile to the president.

Second, the graphs show that the relative size of opinion differences between rich and poor are driven, for the most part, by the opinions of wealthy citizens. This is especially true when it comes to understanding the effects of density: on all three issues, the attitudes of lower-income citizens are expected to be roughly identical regardless of district density. Instead, it is almost solely differences in the attitudes of the wealthy that are responsible for explaining the magnitude in rich-poor opinion differences across district types. This makes some sense given the discussion above—the wealthy are more likely to be receptive to the "meritocratic" justification of disparities in wealth that are transmitted in conservative or sparsely populated contexts, for example. But in any case, these results show that the idea of activated self-interest applies more strongly to wealthy citizens than to poor ones.[13]

A Note on Residential Self-Selection

Of course, many of the results above might be driven in whole or in part by residential self-selection: the tendency of citizens—particularly wealthy ones—to choose where to live based implicitly or explicitly on political attitudes. Clearly, there is reason to think that people do this: rich liberals, for example may wish to move to areas that are either densely populated, crowded with other liberals, or both. Rich conservatives may wish to do the opposite. And we have long known that citizens with the means to do so choose to live, at the margins, in areas with a mix of tax rates and public service provisions (to say nothing of political cultures) that are amendable to them (Tiebout 1956). There is certainly reason, then, to think that pure contextual effects are enhanced by the sorts of residential self-selection discussed in chapter 2: a wealthy person who wishes for government to spend more to help the poor is more likely to be attracted to living in Manhattan than suburban Houston (or suburban New Jersey, for that matter). But there is little reason to suspect that *all* of the differences found above are due to residential self-selection. Residential mobility, while more common than a century ago, is not enormously widespread: most citizens do not regularly move significant distances with any regularity.[14] In addition, political factors—or even ostensibly nonpolitical factors correlated with politics, like a desire to live in a densely populated urban area—remain important but relatively minor factors in the grand scheme of the reasons why people choose to move. More pedestrian factors like job relocation or a desire to live near family are more important than political considerations for citizens of all political stripes (see Tam Cho, Gimpel, and Hui 2013 for an extensive look at the factors behind residential migration).

We might best think of residential migration, then, as supplementing the effects that I have argued for here. Due in large part to contextual factors, wealthy people in suburban Texas have considerably different economic attitudes than wealthy people in midtown Manhattan. Wealthy people also are more likely to have choices when they move (Cadwallader 1992), and, when presented the opportunity, it is reasonable to think that wealthy people with liberal (or conservative) attitudes toward things like meritocracy, the balance between individualism and collectivism, and the like, are at the margins more likely to move to contexts that reinforce these views with similar attitudes. These choices will then be reflected in even greater differences in political opinions over time.

Conclusions

This chapter has shown us that differences in how the rich and the poor think about politics are relatively modest in scope, and often dwarfed by differences in how people in different areas of the country think about politics. We have also seen that the magnitude of these differences varies in predictable ways across contexts, with contextual factors serving to either enhance or diminish the importance of narrow economic self-interest to political views. Contextual differences in opinion are greater for the wealthy than the poor: the preferences of the poor are by no means identical everywhere, but contextual differences in views are much larger for upper-income citizens than lower-income ones. I have argued that the reasons for this are straightforward: certain contexts make it easier for wealthy citizens to view disparities in wealth as the natural outgrowth of fair processes, and make it easier for them to isolate themselves from poorer citizens in day-to-day interactions.[15]

Left out of this chapter, of course, is the important and tricky issue of whether wealthy and poor citizens *should* hold different views about politics. Though poor citizens in general favor a more progressive tax policy than the wealthy, for example, there are many poor citizens who support tax cuts for top income earners, despite the fact that the cuts will not benefit these poor citizens economically. Cutting taxes on the wealthy would represent these poor citizens' policy views well, though it may make them worse off in a material sense. Of course, there are also many wealthy citizens who favor raising taxes on themselves in order to pay for spending on the poor. Certainly, there is no shortage of commentary suggesting that poor citizens who do not demand more redistribution strongly are uninformed, misled, or somehow "duped" by political elites that do not have their best interests at heart.

It is possible to make the argument that poor citizens—regardless of culture, context, or anything else—should reject the meritocratic views of wealth that often give rise to such antiredistributive preferences. And while a focus on revealed preferences allows us an empirical understanding of what rich and poor citizens think about political issues, it says very little about whether such preferences are well informed, well considered, or wise. This issue is perhaps outside the scope of any empirical analysis (see Bartels 2007 and Lupia et al. 2007 for an excellent back and forth on this topic). Certainly, there are gaps in political knowledge and awareness between rich and poor that could, in theory, be exploited by those wishing to push poorer citizens to a particular worldview.[16] But regardless of whether these preferences are wise or not, elected officials do care about revealed preferences, and those preferences (as shown through surveys or other means) inform both what policymakers do and national political discourse more broadly defined (e.g., Stimson 2015).[17] If we care about representation, we must take seriously what citizens say.

These results make two central contributions that help further our understanding of the central issue of this book: how rich and poor are *represented* in American politics. First, the results highlight the importance of considering the "demand side" of representation, in particular trying to understand the conditions that lead the views of the rich and the poor to diverge. Much prior work suggests that when the views of wealthy and poor citizens diverge, policymakers tend to do what the wealthy want them to do. But the inequalities in substantive representation that stem from this have fairly strict "upper limits," because on many issues rich and poor citizens are asking for the same sorts of things from government.

Because of the importance of opinion divergence to representational inequality, much work has tried to interpret how often and how deeply the opinions of rich and poor citizens differ, and whether we should interpret the absolute magnitude of such differences as large (Gilens 2009a), minimal (Soroka and Wlezien 2008), or somewhere in between (Rigby and Wright 2013). But most empirical work on representational inequality takes citizen preferences as fixed and exogenous, working to see how well elected officials represent such opinions in what they choose to do or not do. These results show that additional attention needs to be paid to the processes through which rich and poor citizens form their policy views: the conditions that give rise to the types of opinion divergence—and the representational inequalities that can result.

Second, these results suggest the need to refocus attention on the role of political context in shaping both how rich and poor citizens view politics, and how elected officials respond to them. This chapter shows that the question of whether, and to what extent, wealthy and poor citizens think differently about politics is very much a contingent one: contextual factors are particularly germane to understanding how important income (as opposed to other factors such as religion, ideology, or race) is in shaping political views, and how class divisions manifest themselves differently in different political contexts.

So far, then, we have seen that context matters in shaping both how rich and poor think about politics, and how rich and poor decide to get involved in politics. Of course, public opinion, and political participation, matter to a large extent in a democracy because they should bear on what policymakers actually do. It is to this topic—the degree to which the views of rich and poor citizens are represented by their policymakers—which is the subject of the remainder of this book.

FIVE

Political Inequality in the United States

Wealthy and poor citizens in the United States are not miles apart politically. Differences between the policy views of rich and poor are usually at the margins, a matter of degree rather than magnitude. But when it comes to American policy change, as we will see, the margins are what matters. Even minor shifts in the distribution of public opinion can have substantial consequences for who is elected to office, and what they do once they get there. And while the policy views of rich and poor do have much in common, it is also true that class is alive and well as an important dividing line in American politics. The magnitude, importance, and even ideological direction of opinion differences between rich and poor vary across political contexts. But, in nearly every context, income matters: wealthy and poor citizens send different messages to policymakers regarding what they would like government to do.

This chapter turns to the issue of *representation* of these views in policy choices: the degree to which wealthy and poor citizens exert unequal influence on the actions of their members of Congress. As we have noted earlier, the topic of unequal influence has long concerned both normative theorists and policy scholars, as much of representative democracy's appeal is based on its perceived ability to segregate financial power from political power (Walzer 1993; Verba and Orren 1985).[1]

The presence of large representational inequities between rich and poor call into question the basic legitimacy of American democracy (Winters and Page 2009). But even more subtle inequities in representation can have substantial consequences for policy processes and outcomes (Griffin and Newman 2008; Stimson 2011).

The meaning of "representational inequality," like that of "representation" itself, is a complex, multidimensional concept. A deep exploration of any aspect of this concept therefore must narrow this definition down somewhat. As a perhaps simplistic shorthand, scholars have divided the concept of "representation" into four different dimensions (see Eulau and Karps 1977; Harden 2015): *policy* representation (the connection between what citizens want, and what legislators do, when it comes to issues and policies), *descriptive* representation (the degree to which officeholders look, demographically and socially, like the people they represent), *service* representation (the assistance that policymakers provide for those who require assistance from government), and *allocative* representation (the securing of funds for projects and services relevant to constituents).

When it comes to descriptive representation of the poor, we know that vanishingly small numbers of policymakers in any national representative body come from working- or lower-class backgrounds (Carnes 2013). Policymakers, overwhelmingly, "look" like the rich. Service and allocative representation are, by and large, valence issues: there are few constituents regardless of income who would prefer a representative who is unresponsive to their requests and concerns, or who is not interested in making sure that a district gets a fair share of the federal pie (Fenno 1978; Serra and Moon 1994).[2]

In this chapter, then, we narrow our focus to the issue of *policy representation*: the degree to which a citizen's preferred view of what policymakers should do with respect to salient policy matters corresponds to what policymakers actually do on these matters. When wealthy and poor citizens want different things from their policymakers, whose views do those policymakers represent? "Inequality" in representation exists, according to this definition, if the policy preferences of some citizens are more congruent than others with the choices that elected officials make—if, in this case, MCs make decisions that are more consistent with the views of the rich than the views of the poor. This definition is commonly used in studies of political representation, and provides an oft-employed standard for those examining the degree to which government treats its citizens as "political equals" (Griffin and Newman 2008; Ura and Ellis 2008; Soroka and Wlezien 2010; Gilens 2012; Ellis 2013; Flavin 2012, 2013).

The goals of this chapter are to shed light on the magnitude, consequences, and causes of economic biases in policy representation. Accordingly, following the dyadic framework laid out in chapter 2, we will examine the correspondence between what individual citizens say that they want and what their congressional representatives actually do. The dyadic relationships between individual citizens and their MCs are among the most critical links between citizens and policymaking, and such relationships have been the focus of substantial amounts of research on political representation in the United States (e.g., Miller and Stokes 1963; Achen 1978; Burden 2004; Bartels 2008).

The dyadic framework is particularly useful here in that it provides a clear standard to assess representational equality and inequality. Myriad factors—constituents' views, party leadership, interest groups, their own ideologies, an analysis of the information available to them—affect the choices that MCs make and the degree to which these choices are representative of their constituents' views. We should not expect a perfect relationship between constituents' views and what MCs do. But evidence of equality in representation would mean that a citizen's level of income should not, *on average*, affect the degree to which his or her views are reflected in their MC's choices. A system with "equal" levels of representation, put simply, would not systematically privilege the preferences of one group over another's.

In this chapter, we will focus on one specific, highly important aspect of dyadic representation: that reflected in the final votes taken by Congress members on specific pieces of legislation. To be sure, this definition leaves much out. It does not, for example, address other ways in which MCs might use their political influence to influence policy outcomes—by helping to set the political agenda, or making public pronouncements in favor of or against specific types of policy proposals.[3] But, at the same time, it provides a straightforward baseline from which to examine political equality on perhaps the most critical aspect of representation: the degree to which elected officials behave in a way consistent with their constituents' views regarding what direction policy should take. I assume that citizens prefer that their views be reflected in the actions of their elected officials, and they want government to make decisions with which they agree. As such, representation as reflected through congressional voting behavior provides a useful way to develop the idea of representational inequality in a straightforward and critically important way.

Measuring Representational Inequality

This chapter examines dyadic representation in two ways. First, I examine representation of a general, ideological sort, via an analysis of the general tenor of what MCs do across a significant period of time and across a wide variety of issues. Are MCs' actions consistent with what their constituents want, and do these actions tend to correspond more closely with the views of certain constituents over others? Second, I examine representation at the level of specific, concrete policy issues. When it comes to issues of particularly high salience and importance, do MCs tend to vote in a way that reflects the views of certain constituents over others?

Accordingly, I develop two measures of dyadic representation, both based on the votes of members of Congress and subsets of the 2012 CCES data discussed in chapter 3. The first of these measures is a broad measure of the ideological *proximity* between citizens and representatives in the 112th (2011–12) Congress.[4] This measure simply relates the ideological leanings of citizens to the ideological positions of the MCs who represent them, examining, in a rough sense, the "distance" between a citizen's ideology and that of his or her representative.

Congress members' ideologies are operationalized using first-dimension W-NOMINATE scores for the 112th Congress (McCarty, Poole, and Rosenthal 2006). Most political conflict in the United States, at least at the level of elites and policymakers, generally falls onto a single left-right dimension. Some policymakers vote in a way that places them very far to the left on this dimension, some are closer to the center, and others are very far right. NOMINATE scores provide an intuitive way of quantifying where individual MCs' ideological leanings fall on this dimension. First-dimension NOMINATE scores, which essentially scale all contested roll-call votes in a given congressional term onto a single scale, are typically interpreted as reflecting members' positions on the liberal-conservative continuum that drives most elite political conflict in the United States. They thus provide a useful summary measure of the general ideological location of members of Congress.[5]

To measure the ideological locations of citizens, I use responses to the CCES question asking respondents to place themselves on a 0 (extremely liberal) to 7 (extremely conservative) scale. I then can use these data to calculate measures of the absolute ideological distance between individual citizens and their MCs. This measure has several strengths. The first of these is breadth: NOMINATE scores reflect the sum total of MC voting behavior on contested issues, and ideological identification can serve as a simple, if imperfect, summary measure of citizens' political beliefs. The measure provides a useful way to examine patterns of representation using the widest possible conception of congressional voting. The second strength is a strong grounding in the past work: measures of ideological preferences based on aggregate roll call voting behavior (for legislators) and ideological self-placement questions (for citizens) have been used extensively in past research, both in exploring patterns of representation more generally and in biases in representation more specifically (e.g., Bartels 2008; Griffin and Newman 2005, 2007; Clinton 2006; Griffin and Flavin 2007; Erikson and Bhatti 2011). Finally, interpretation of this measure is simple: a citizen whose expressed ideological preferences fall very close to that reflected in the voting behavior of his or her MC—a citizen who places him or herself to the far right end of the self-identification scale and is represented by an MC whose NOMINATE score places them to the right of most Congress members, for example—is, all else equal, better represented than one whose ideology is quite distant from his or her MC.

Though this intuition behind this measure is straightforward, constructing it empirically is more difficult because of the long-noted difficulty of placing citizen and legislator ideologies on the same scale. The scaling problem stems from the fact that there is no obvious way to relate a citizen's ideological leanings (as stated in response to a self-placement question) to the ideological leanings of a Congress member (as measured through an aggregation of the actual choices he or she makes as a legislator).

Scholars have taken three principal approaches to dealing with this problem. The first is to simply rescale ideological identification and roll-call voting measures to the same range (Achen 1978). Others have argued that both measures should be standardized in some way (Wright 1978). Finally, others have argued that Congress members' ideologies need to be rescaled to a narrower range than that of citizens, given the relative paucity of truly "extreme" legislators (Powell 1982). There remains debate over the appropriate way to deal with this problem. Fortunately, however, the empirical consequences of the choice are relatively minor: all of the results presented in the following tables remain statistically and substantively similar regardless of the method used to map legislator and constituent preferences onto the same scale.[6]

For expository purposes, the analyses to come will use the Wright (1978) approach. To create the measure, I first standardize both citizen and legislator ideologies. I then compute a measure of ideological distance by calculating the absolute distance between a citizen's standardized ideological preferences and that of his or her congressional representative. To aid in interpretation, I then rescale to a 0–100 metric, with 0 indicating a citizen is as ideologically close to (and 100 indicating a citizen is as ideologically distant from) his or her MC as is possible to estimate with these data. *Lower values thus indicate closer ideological proximity to MCs.*

Though ideological distance measures of representation are well established in the literature, they also have some limitations. First, ideological self-identification is an imperfect, and perhaps misleading, indicator of a citizen's political outlook: many citizens simply do not understand or misunderstand the meanings of ideological labels, and have difficulty mapping their own political views onto an ideological scale (Ellis and Stimson 2012). Second, the NOMINATE measure aggregates all contested roll-call votes, even minor and highly obscure ones. It thus might be more appropriate to measure representation on a more limited, but perhaps more salient, set of votes that are both of high policy importance and likely to be of particular interest to citizens.

The second measure of representation works to address these limitations, measuring how well citizens' preferences are represented on a smaller number of specific issues. The 2012 CCES asked respondents whether they supported or opposed five key pieces of legislation voted upon by the 112th House: bills that would (a) repeal the Affordable Care Act; (b) extend NAFTA-type free trade legislation to South Korea, (c) authorize the construction of the Keystone Pipeline, (d) express support for the Simpson-Bowles budget proposal, and (e) enact Paul Ryan's "Path to Prosperity" budget proposal. Respondents were asked whether they, in principle, "favored" or "opposed" each piece of legislation.

Because respondents were asked about the same legislation on which MCs voted, we can devise a measure of representation that simply relates the proportion of the time an MC's vote on an issue corresponded to a citizen's own view on that issue. With this measure, the process of scaling citizens' and legislators' preferences together into a measure of "representation" is less arbitrary: if a citizen supported a piece of legislation, and his or her MC voted for it (or vice versa), we can say with some confidence that the citizen's preference was represented.[7]

I again use survey responses and roll-call data to compute measures of representation for each respondent. First, we code whether a citizen's preference was reflected in the vote of his or her MC on a particular issue, creating dummy variables coded "1" if a citizen supported a piece of legislation and his or her MC voted for it (or if a citizen opposed the legislation and his or her representative voted against it), and "0" if the citizen supported the legislation and his or her MC voted against it (or vice-versa). I then sum across all issues to compute a measure, which we label *key vote representation*, that divides the number of issues on which a citizen had his or her preference represented by the number of issues on which there is usable data (i.e., the issues on which a citizen expressed a preference and his or her MC cast a vote). I again scale this measure to a 0–100 metric, where the highest score indicates a citizen whose preferences were reflected in the votes of his or her MC for all issues on which there is valid data, and the lowest score indicates a citizen who preferences were opposite of that of his or her MC's votes on all issues with valid data. *Higher values mean that someone's views are consistent with their MC's votes a higher proportion of the time.*

This measure has some limitations as well. The issues chosen here, while selected for their high levels of policy importance, were not chosen at random. It is possible that a separate selection of "key votes" might yield different results.[8] And congressional votes on all of these issues, like most highly visible issues in the 112th Congress, were heavily party-line votes: only on the free-trade issue did even 15 percent of Congress members cross party lines. Thus perhaps even more than with NOMINATE scores, MC positions on these issues will be quite reflective of the extremely high levels of partisan polarization—and the dominance of party over all other factors that might influence MC behavior—that characterized the 112th Congress.[9] Given the strengths and limitations of each of these measures, employing both and finding consistent results across them can help to validate the findings for each.[10]

Representational Inequality: A Basic Look

Representation biases across income lines can only exist to the extent that there are differences in preferences across income lines. Without relevant differences in what income groups are asking from government, it is the case that all income groups' views will be represented, even if only "coincidentally" (Enns 2015): it will be functionally impossible for elected officials to ignore the views of any group, even if they wanted to. And consistent with the findings of chapter 3, the differences between rich and poor on the issues used to comprise these measures are more a matter of degree rather than magnitude. Table 4.1 presents a basic illustration of differences in political views across income terciles, showing the opinions of citizens in upper-, middle-, and lower-income terciles on the seven-point self-placement scale and the issues used to comprise the five-point "key vote" scale.

As we have seen in chapter 3, preference differences are small when it comes to ideological distance: citizens in the richest tercile place themselves as significantly ($p < .05$, two-tailed) but modestly (less than two points on the self-placement scale) more conservative than poorer ones. In addition, the relationship between ideological conservatism and income is not linear: the middle-income group is actually the most conservative of all three terciles. The differences are often larger when it comes to specific policy issues: on three of the five issues, preferences of the top and bottom terciles differ by more than 10 percentage points.

Again, district context is a strong predictor of opinion beyond income, as conservative (or liberal) districts tend to have both upper and lower citizens that are more conservative (or liberal) than average. The district-level correlation between mean top- and bottom-tercile opinion, for example, is 0.43 for self-identification, and 0.55 for a scale of roll-call vote liberalism. But even so, as we have seen in chapter 3, there is significant variation across terciles within districts.

Are wealthier citizens better represented by their Congress members? Figure 5.1 provides a very basic answer to this question, simply showing the mean ideological distance between MCs and citizens in each of the 14 income categories offered to CCES respondents. This graph makes a fairly clear point: wealthier citizens are ideologically more proximate to their MCs than poorer ones. One's level of policy representation increases in nearly every income category.[11] All told, the proximity gap between the richest and poorest citizens is more than 4 percentage points. When aggregating across income terciles, we see roughly a 1.2 percentage point ideological distance gap between the top and bottom terciles. The gap between the top and middle terciles, however, is significantly smaller according to this measure: only 0.3 percentage points. Policymakers have significant incentives to pay attention to the median voter in American politics, so there is certainly some reason to think that middle-income citizens would be better represented than the poorest ones. But though middle income

TABLE 5.1. Issue and Ideological Positions by Income Tercile

	Poorest Tercile	Middle Tercile	Richest Tercile
Mean ideological self-placement	4.16	4.30	4.21
Support repeal of Affordable Care Act (2012)	41%	45%	46%
Support extension of free trade agreements to South Korea	47%	50%	58%
Support authorization of the Keystone Pipeline	72%	75%	73%
Support Simpson-Bowles deficit reduction plan	42%	50%	57%
Support the "Path to Prosperity"	14%	19%	24%

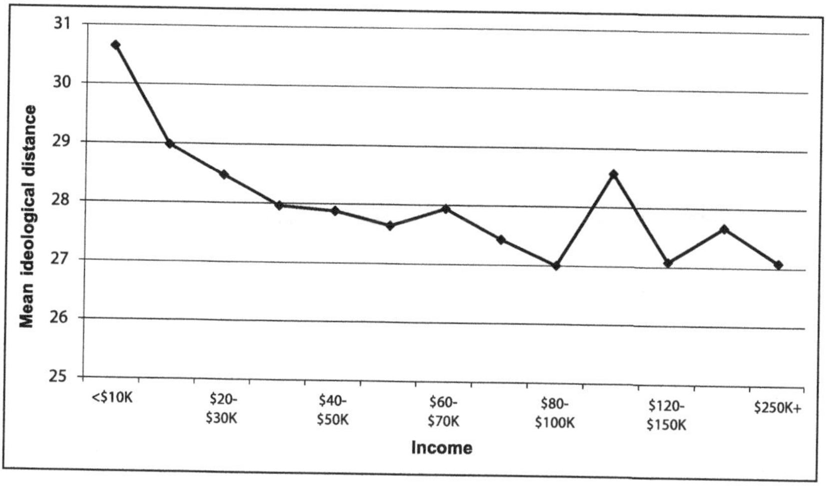

Fig. 5.1. Ideological Representation by Income Level

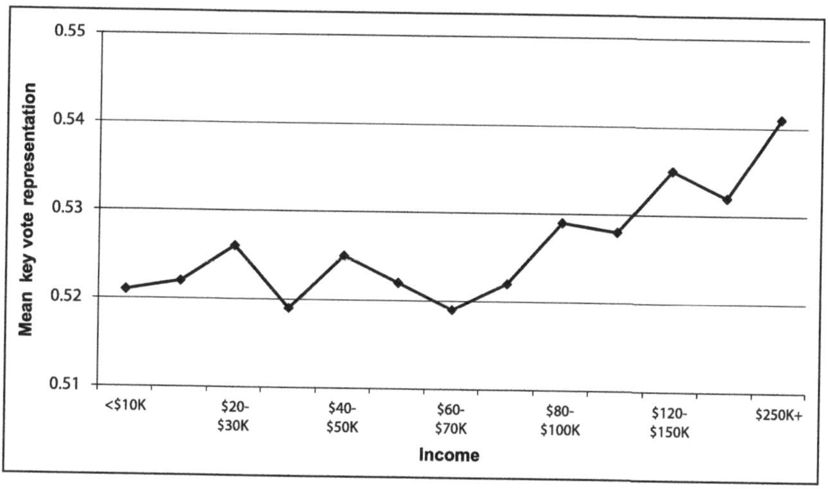

Fig. 5.2. Key Vote Representation by Income Level

citizens are far better represented than poor ones, there is a small, but real, policymaking bias in favor of the opinions of the wealthy.

The results are a bit less linear when it comes to key vote representation (figure 5.2). But even so, the data reflects the same general trends as with the proximity measure, as higher levels of income translate into a greater propensity to have one's views reflected in the choices of their MCs. The difference in representation between the richest and poorest

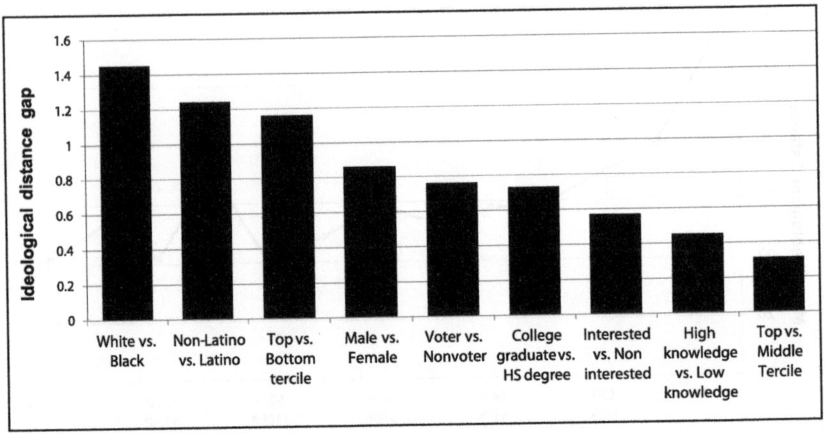

Fig. 5.3. Representational Biases across Politically Relevant Subgroups

income groups is roughly 2.5 percentage points. When looking across terciles, citizens in the wealthiest tercile, on average, have their views represented by MCs 1.1 percent more of the time than bottom-tercile citizens.[12] When it comes to this measure, middle income voters fare no better than the poor: the gap between the bottom and top terciles is only marginally larger than the gap between the middle and top terciles.

One way to put these representation biases in context is to compare them to biases across other important lines of political and demographic difference known to affect a citizen's level of political power. Figure 5.3 compares the representational inequities in key vote representation to MCs across income terciles to inequities across other sociodemographic lines. The 1.2-point differences in key vote representation between the richest and poorest terciles, for example, is comparable to or larger in size to the differences between whites and African Americans (1.5 points), between whites and Latinos (1.2 points), between those who report voting and those who do not (0.8 percentage points), between those with a college degree and those with a high school degree or less (0.7 points), and between those who are very interested in political affairs and those who are not at all interested (0.6 points).

The Policy Consequences of Unequal Representation

Both the key vote and ideological distance measure provide evidence that the views of wealthier citizens are better represented than those of the poor.

Are these differences consequential? Certainly, the answer to this question is in part subjective. Even though differences across income lines rival or exceed differences across other lines of sociodemographic difference, gaps of fewer than two points on a 100-point scale are not overwhelming. And the broad similarity in policy views between rich and poor places a natural "upper limit" (Soroka and Wlezien 2008) on how unequal policy representation can be.

Further, even if the views of rich and poor citizens do differ somewhat, the *majority* view of rich and poor citizens within districts on many salient issues is the same, so the act of representing one group's preferences will necessarily represent the other's. Large majorities of both rich and poor citizens in rural Texas support authorizing the Keystone Pipeline, for example, while large majorities of both rich and poor in Connecticut oppose the repeal of the Affordable Care Act. In these contexts and on these issues, it would be impossible for MCs to represent one group's preferences to the exclusion of others. And as we have seen in chapter 3, relative levels of public support for different policies are often similar across income terciles (see also Enns 2015; Branham, Soroka, and Wlezien 2016). Though they may differ in their absolute levels of support for these policies, for example, citizens in all groups on average support universal background checks for gun purchases more than they support keeping abortion legal in all circumstances, and on average support both of these policies more than they support increasing spending on welfare. It is not the case that wealthy people get substantial policy representation while poorer citizens get none.

But it is also clear that, given the generally incremental nature of American policy change, even the small biases in representation that we see here can have significant policy consequences. Political change in the United States happens at the margin—both public opinion and public policy rarely change dramatically in the short term. Even minor shifts in public ideology or voting patterns, for example, produce what are usually interpreted as substantial swings in public "mood" or in election results.[13] Further, most policy changes in the United States happen incrementally, as modest changes from the policy status quo. The current state of policy in the United States is determined not just by what is voted on at a given time or in a given legislative session, but is instead an accumulation of *all* past policy changes. Policies passed at a given point in time provide the basis point for the kinds of policy changes that Congress is likely to consider at future points in time. So even small differences in how rich and poor are represented can aggregate to have much more significant consequences if these gaps persist consistently over time. Stimson (2011) addresses this issue with a hypothetical example:

> A modest bias that is repeated at every policy opportunity can have quite immodest effects in the long run. Imagine that Congress changes the tax code every year—not too far from reality—and each time has just a minor tendency to bias the result in favor of the influential rich. That would produce substantial and meaningful bias in the long term.

Analyzing the specific substantive consequences of these representation biases for policy is thus a bit of a subjective enterprise, and it is impossible to say exactly what American policy would look like if rich and poor citizens were represented more equally. But even so, we can describe some more general consequences of unequal representation—looking, at least in a stylistic sense, at the real implications of unequal representation for policy outcomes. In what follows, we examine the relationship between income and representation on specific policy issues, paying particular attention to what MCs do when their wealthy and poor constituents' views on issues diverge from one another. The reason we care about unequal representation is the possibility that policy itself would be different if representation were more equal. In this section, we hone in on a few specific policy examples to examine several different ways through which unequal representation across income lines might matter for what governments actually do.

Understanding Unequal Representation: What Happens When Rich and Poor Diverge?

Under our dyadic definition of representation, MCs represent their constituents when they vote in a way that corresponds to what their constituents want. When rich and poor want basically the same thing, this means representing the views of rich and poor constituents equally well (or equally poorly). What is important from our perspective, then, is not necessarily what policymakers do when their constituents of different income groups share views on a particular issue, but instead what they do when their poor constituents' views differ across income lines in a meaningful way.

To examine this, we will look into differences in the opinions of top- and bottom-tercile citizens within particular districts.[14] The use of tercile-level opinions both here and in some analyses to come is done for practical reasons, but clearly has its limitations. Most notably, people near the bottom of the top tercile are not truly "rich" (people near the bottom of the top tercile, for example, have fared nearly as poorly in terms of wage growth over the past few decades as the poor), and inequality might mean that truly growing political influence is concentrated in a much smaller group—the top 5 percent, top 1 percent, or 0.1 percent of the population (see Page, Bartels, and Seawright 2013). Even so, representational biases between the top and bottom terciles are a significant focus of the literature on political inequality (see, e.g., Bartels 2008; Erikson and Bhatti 2011; Ellis 2012; Griffin and Newman 2013), and thus a focus on terciles allows me to draw parallels between the representational biases shown here and those commonly discussed in the literature.

To illustrate this approach, consider an example from one of the issues used to comprise our "key vote representation" scale: the issue of expanding NAFTA-style trade provisions to South Korea. The public's views on this bill were nearly equally split between support and opposition, with a majority of top-tercile citizens favoring it and a majority of bottom-tercile citizens opposing it. The bill, H.R. 3080, was introduced by Eric Cantor (R-VA), and passed 278–151. MC votes on this issue were less purely party-driven than others in the 112th Congress, with 59 Democrats joining Republican House leadership in support of the bill, and 21 Republicans voting against it. The bill also had the support of President Obama and the Democratic Senate, and became law in October 2011.

MC votes on this issue, at least in general, reflected their district's preferences: 274 MCs (63%) voted in a way that corresponded with the majority view within their district. But this general tendency to represent constituents masks the tendency to represent some constituents better than others. For purposes of illustration, we divide congressional districts into four groups based on constituents' preferences:

- Districts where a majority of both upper- and lower-income constituents (defined here by the top and bottom income terciles) *supported* the bill;
- Districts where a majority of upper-income constituents *supported* the bill, while a majority of lower-income constituents *opposed* it;
- Districts where a majority of upper-income constituents *opposed* the bill, but a majority of lower-income constituents *supported* it;
- Districts where a majority of both upper- and lower-income constituents *opposed* the bill.

Table 5.2 examines the link between constituent opinion and MC votes within these four district types. MCs represented their constituents fairly well, though clearly not perfectly, when both income groups supported the bill, voting in favor of it in 68 percent of cases. They were somewhat less representative when both groups opposed the bill, opposing it 51 percent of the time. This result clearly illustrates that other factors outside of constituent opinion affect what MCs do. But the data shows, at the least, a link between constituent opinion and MC behavior.

Of most interest, though, is what happens when the views of the two income groups diverge. The free trade bill provides a useful illustration of this, because the modal district was one in which its wealthier constituents supported the extension of free trade provisions, while its poorer ones opposed them. In such districts, MCs voted in favor of extending free trade provisions 68 percent of the time, *exactly the same rate* as when both upper- and lower-income citizens supported such provisions. In a smaller number of districts, wealthy citizens opposed free trade extensions while poorer ones supported them: in these districts, rates of MC support were roughly the same (if anything, perhaps a shade lower) than when both income groups opposed extensions.

The views of the poor, it appears, were given no weight at all in what MCs decided to do: MC votes were sensitive to what their wealthier constituents wanted, but were not responsive, even minimally, to what poor citizens wanted. On this issue, in other words, it appears that any representation that poor citizens received was incidental to whether they happened to share the views of their wealthier counterparts within a district. When the opinions of income groups diverged, MCs essentially ignored the poor entirely.

Unequal representation is not always as easy as to see as it is with the Korea issue. And other factors, well apart from even what wealthy constituents want, drive MC behavior as well. But this sort of unequal representation is not reflective only of free trade. Between 2008 and 2012, the CCES

TABLE 5.2. MC Votes and Constituent Opinion on Free Trade with Korea

	Both rich and poor constituents supported	Rich supported, poor opposed	Poor supported, rich opposed	Both rich and poor constituents opposed
Percentage of MCs who voted for Iraq withdrawal timeline	68%	68%	44%	49%
Number of districts	143	211	18	57

asked respondents for views on 18 different roll-call votes—encompassing a wide variety of issue areas—on which their MCs had the ability to cast a vote. On 16 of these issues, when the preferences of top- and bottom- tercile citizens within a district diverged, most MCs sided with the views of their wealthier constituents.

We can say with some confidence, then, that unequal representation is a regular phenomenon. What are some of the ways in which this sort of representational inequality might matter for public policy? Though this list is by no means exhaustive, in what follows we explore data from several recent Congresses (and several recent CCES surveys) to provide a typology of the ways in which unequal representation—again, conceived only through the realm of roll-call voting—can affect the nature of policy debate, and policy outcomes themselves.

Passing a Bill That Otherwise Would Have Failed: Withdrawing from Iraq

Specific bills essentially provide binary choices to legislators and policy-making bodies: either legislators support the bill or they do not, and the bill either achieves final passage or it does not. The most obvious way that unequal representation might have policy consequences, then, is if the ultimate passage or failure of certain policies depended on representing one group's preferences over another's. The 2007 resolution to mandate a strict timeline for withdrawal from Iraq provides an example of this.

The 110th Congress considered a number of bills designed to deal with the withdrawal of combat troops and defense contractors from Iraq. Arguably the most important of such bills was H.R. 2237, introduced by Representative Jim McGovern (D-MA). The bill states that troops, with the exception of those engaged in diplomacy, in fighting terrorism, or in a limited number of other activities, must begin deploying from Iraq within 90 days of the bill's passage, with final deployment to be completed within 180 days. The bill set an aggressive timeline for withdrawal, substantially more aggressive than other bills voted on or passed by the House or Senate. Though it gained some initial momentum and a number of cosponsors, support for the bill waned over time, and it ultimately was defeated in the House, 171–255.

Public support for the bill was lukewarm, but weakly in favor of its passage. In addition, there were substantial differences in support across income lines: 65 percent of bottom-tercile citizens, but only 48 percent of top-tercile citizens, supported this aggressive withdrawal timeline. Fifty-seven percent of MCs voted in a way consistent with the majority preference of their district on this issue. But again, when examining constituent representation across income lines, the results provide strong evidence that not all subconstituencies were represented equally.

As table 5.3 illustrates, MCs in general represented their districts well when upper- and lower-income citizens sent consistent cues: the MCs most likely to vote for the resolution were those who represented districts where both wealthy and poor constituents supported it, while MCs least likely to vote for it were those who represented districts where both groups opposed it.

But in the 185 districts where a majority of the poorest constituents supported the resolution while a majority of the wealthiest opposed it, only 46 percent (25%) voted for the resolution. MCs in these districts, in other words, sided with their wealthiest constituents 75 percent of the time, and their poorest constituents 25 percent of the time. If instead 50 percent of MCs in such districts had voted for the bill (thus siding with upper- and lower-income constituents an equal percentage of the time), the bill would have garnered roughly 46 additional "yea" votes, and earned narrow passage. This analysis, of course, is simplistic: among other things, it necessarily neglects all of the other factors that might affect MC behavior on this issue. But at least as an illustration, it does suggest that a more equal representation of wealthier and poorer citizens' views by MCs would have been enough to change the outcome.

Even if the bill had passed, President George W. Bush would have almost certainly vetoed it. But the bill's passage would have been a significant symbolic victory for those supportive of an aggressive timeline for withdrawal, would have put pressure on the Senate and even the president to change or accelerate postcombat operation strategies in Iraq, and at the least would have more strongly highlighted the differences between President Bush and Congress's plans for Iraq. Whatever the final nature of policy change, it is likely that the fate of this particular resolution would

TABLE 5.3. MC Votes and Constituent Opinion on Iraq Withdrawal

	Both rich and poor constituents supported	Rich supported, poor opposed	Poor supported, rich opposed	Both rich and poor constituents opposed
Percentage of MCs who voted for Iraq withdrawal timeline	60%	55%	25%	8%
Number of districts	194	11	185	26

have been different had rich and poor citizens' views on it been represented equally.

Affecting MC Choices on a "Long-Term" Issue: The Minimum Wage Debate

The Iraq case is perhaps an exception to the rule: it is not always the case that more equal representation would cause the binary outcome to change on particular bills. But even if the passage or failure of particular bills is not always determined by unequal representation, we can imagine other ways in which MC's tendencies to better represent wealthier constituents' views might matter not to the passage or failure of particular bills, but to policy more broadly defined.

The federal minimum wage is an issue that clearly bears on the material interests of the poor. The minimum wage is an enduring American policy, having been part of federal law since 1938. There is no formula or regular interval for minimum wage increases, as the wage is altered—either to keep up with inflation or to reflect changing social norms or public demands—by specific pieces of legislation. Though it has seen irregular increases, the real value of the minimum wage has declined since the 1960s, and by 2007 the real value of the wage had declined to a level not seen since the 1940s. The purpose of H.R. 2, one of the first bills taken up by the 110th Congress in 2007, was to provide the first minimum wage increase since 1997, phasing an increase in the wage from $5.15 to $7.25 per hour over two years.

The fate of H.R. 2 was never in serious doubt, and the bill passed easily, 315–116. The strong support for the bill in Congress was reflected in the public as well. Though there were some class-based differences in support for the bill—poorer citizens supported the increase more than wealthier ones—substantial majorities of rich, middle income, and poor citizens supported the increase.[15] The bill also received majority support among ideological conservatives, Republicans, and other groups not traditionally supportive of an active federal government. In fact, there was not a single congressional district in which constituency opinion was, on average, opposed to the increase. A vote against the minimum wage increase, in other words, was a vote against constituent opinion in every district.

The broad support for H.R. 2 is no exception: surveys dating back to the 1970s show supermajoritarian support for increasing the minimum wage in nearly every year that questions about it are posed. Majorities of citizens, in other words, always want the minimum wage to be higher than it currently is. It is natural, then, to ask why the real value of the minimum wage has not increased over time (or at least kept pace with inflation), given what appears to be substantial public support for larger and more regular increases to the wage. A common answer to this question is that lawmakers have other motivations—party pressures, industry lobbyists, the recommendations from economic experts—that lead them to keep the minimum wage lower than the public would, on average, like it to be. All of these motivations are undoubtedly important to some extent. But whatever the origins of opposition to minimum wage increases, it is useful to examine the contexts in which MCs are more likely (perhaps driven by these sorts of other factors) to vote against increases: when, in other words, they vote in a way at odds with their constituents by opposing minimum wage increases.

In this light, and given majority support for H.R. 2 in every district, we examine the *relative* intensity of support for the minimum wage increase across income lines—the degree to which wealthier citizens supported H.R. 2 relative to the poor. There were 68 districts where support for the increase was greater among the top than among the bottom tercile, and 352 districts where support was greater among the poor than among the wealthy. We see (table 5.4) that MCs voted for the bill at substantially higher rates when support was greater among the upper-income group than among the lower-income group. MCs were least likely to vote against constituent opinion when support for the wage increase was stronger among wealthier constituents.

If we consider the minimum wage policy as something that goes beyond this single vote, but rather as a continuum of possible wages, these differences are consequential for understanding the politics of the minimum wage. Despite the fact that majorities of all income groups express a desire to see the wage increased, poor citizens are more universally supportive of such an increase (and, in general, also place a higher priority on minimum wage increases than do wealthy citizens). But MCs are most likely to oppose wage increases when their *wealthier* constituents are not deeply supportive of such increases. There are many rationales for MCs to oppose

TABLE 5.4. MC Votes and Constituent Opinion on Minimum Wage Increase

	Wealthy supported increases more than the poor	Poor supported increases more than the wealthy
Percentage of MCs who voted for minimum wage increase	81%	70%
Number of districts	68	342

minimum wage increases. But one factor that explains whether members do employ these rationales, at the expense of constituent opinion, is tepid support for minimum wage increases among their wealthiest constituents. Put another way, strong support for minimum wage increases among the poor do not appear to be as relevant to MCs' decisions as is strong support among wealthier groups. If upper-income citizens tended to support minimum wage increases as much as the poor, it stands to reason that MCs might be more apt to follow constituent opinion when considering minimum wage issues—and that the minimum wage might be higher as a result.

Changing the Nature of Policy Debate: Cap and Trade

The 2009 American Clean Energy and Security Act, more commonly known as the "Cap and Trade" bill, was the United States' first attempt to enact a system that would place a price on carbon emissions. The Act would have placed a cap on total carbon dioxide output by U.S. industry, and would have distributed permits to businesses that allowed them to emit a certain amount of carbon. These permits would have been able to be bought and sold on the open market, giving companies an incentive to lower carbon outputs in order to be able to sell excess permits (or avoid having to buy additional permits). The end goal of the Act was to decrease total carbon emissions in the United States by roughly 20 percent by 2020. The Act was politically polarizing, with environmental activists arguing that it did not go far enough to curb carbon emissions, and business groups arguing that it would have crippling effects on both energy-intensive industries and consumers. The Act, H.R. 2454, passed the House by the very narrow margin of 219–212. But the bill's momentum waned as it left the House, and the bill died without coming to a vote in the Democratic Senate.

The climate bill is another issue on which we see clear evidence of unequal representation across income lines. The 2010 CCES asked respondents whether they supported or opposed H.R. 2454. Opinions on the issue diverged a bit along class lines, with 49 percent of top tercile, 54 percent of middle tercile, and 62 percent of bottom tercile respondents supporting it. Again, we see that MC's votes tended to represent their constituents' views well when rich and poor held similar views on the issue. But when preferences diverged, members again tended to take the side of the top tercile (see table 5.5). Sixty-nine percent of MCs voted for the bill when these constituents supported it but poor constituents opposed it, but only 36 percent voted for it when the reverse was true. If MCs had sided with rich or poor citizens an equal proportion of the time, the final vote on the bill would have been much more lopsided, passing by roughly 67 votes instead of the seven votes by which it actually passed.

Did this unequal representation make a difference to the fate of cap and trade? It is difficult to say for certain, of course, as many factors combined to the bill's eventual demise. But the Senate eventually refused to take up this bill, at least in part because of the lukewarm support, and very narrow passage, that it received in the House (Hulse and Herszenhorn 2010). Perhaps a more clear-cut passage of the bill would have made a difference in how the Senate addressed the bill, or how the media framed and discussed climate change policy in the period between consideration by the House and by the Senate. In any case, a House that represented rich and poor constituents equally would have sent a substantially different message to the Senate regarding this policy, and might have placed the bill in a different context in advance of its consideration by the Senate.

Bucking Party Pressures: Expanding Funding for Stem Cell Research

MCs' votes on all of the issues above, like most other issues that MCs consider in the contemporary House, are subject to considerable pressure from party leadership. Republicans and Democrats in Congress vote differently in part because of their own ideologies and the constituencies that they represent, but in part because of the variety of techniques that party leaders can use to encourage members to act in a way consistent with the interests of their party (Aldrich and Rohde 2000; Cox and Poole 2002). As parties have polarized in recent decades, party cohesion and party leadership have become stronger and more important, and party leadership has become better able to exert more control over how rank-and-file members act.

Still, members defect from their party, even on important pieces of legislation, for many reasons. One such reason is constituency pressure.

TABLE 5.5. MC Votes and Constituent Opinion on Cap and Trade

	Both rich and poor constituents supported	Rich supported, poor opposed	Poor supported, rich opposed	Both rich and poor constituents opposed
Percentage of MCs who voted for Clean Energy Act	75%	69%	36%	11%
Number of districts	162	13	188	35

Though party leaders have considerable power to induce MCs to vote along party lines regardless of what those MCs' constituents want, MCs are less likely to support the interests of party leadership if their constituents desire them to take a different course of action (Bullock and Brady 1983). In this light, it is useful to consider an example of how the tendency to represent wealthier constituents over poorer ones might affect how likely MCs are to vote against the desires of party leadership.

The 2007 Stem Cell Research Enhancement Act (H.R. 3) would have amended the Public Health Service Health Care Act to allow for medical research, under specific conditions, using embryonic stem cells. The bill passed by a fairly strong margin in the House (247–176) after passing in the Senate by a stronger margin (63–34), but it was vetoed by George W. Bush and never became law. The final vote was a highly partisan one, with House Democrats voting 205–18 for the bill and House Republicans voting 153–38 against it.

To be sure, party pressures mattered more to MC's eventual choices on this issue than constituency opinion: MCs of both parties were far more likely than not to vote with their party regardless of what constituents of all income groups wanted. But even after taking into account party pressures, though, we see evidence of unequal representation. Table 5.6 shows that MCs of both parties were much more likely to vote against the interests of their party if it meant following the interests of their wealthier constituents. Republicans were most apt to vote for stem cell research, and Democrats most apt to vote against it, when those votes would be consistent with the views of top-tercile constituents. But the views of poorer constituents

TABLE 5.6. MC Votes and Constituent Opinion on Stem Cell Research, by Party

	Both rich and poor constituents supported	Rich supported, poor opposed	Poor supported, rich opposed	Both rich and poor constituents opposed
Percentage of Republican MCs who voted to fund stem cell research	21%	22%	11%	14%
Number of districts	135	23	26	7
Percentage of Democratic MCs who voted to fund stem cell research	94%	95%	78%	75%
Number of districts	178	19	18	8

appeared to not matter at all to the likelihood that a member will vote against his or her party. Both Democratic and Republican MCs, in other words, were as likely to vote against party interests when only wealthy constituents thought that they should do so than when both upper- *and* lower-income constituents thought they should do so. On this issue (and on many other votes like it), MCs defected from their party primarily when wealthier constituents desired that they do so.

Guiding MCs in the Absence of Strong Party Cues: Warrantless Eavesdropping

Finally, unequal representation also matters to how MCs act when party pressures are weak or ambiguous. Though there are few major policy issues on which elite parties do not take clear and divergent stands, H.R. 6304—the 2007 "Protect America" Act—was an instance in which, at least for Democrats, party pressures on rank-and-file members were minimal. This bill amended provisions of the Foreign Intelligence Surveillance Act (FISA), which outlines procedures for the surveillance, collection, and use of information gathered from agents of foreign powers in the effort to prevent the United States from attack.

H.R. 6304 was the most substantial update to FISA since the PATRIOT Act of 2001. The bill provided an extension of FISA powers that, among other things, formally allowed the U.S. government to eavesdrop on terrorist suspects without first getting a court order if terrorist communications either originated in or were transmitted to a foreign country. It also granted immunity from litigation to telecommunications companies that assist the government in eavesdropping under a directive of the Act.

Though Republicans in the House supported the bill nearly unanimously (188–1), the bill also had some support among Democrats: 105 Democratic MCs voted for the bill, while 127 voted against it. Party leadership cues for Democrats were ambiguous. The legislation was initiated

TABLE 5.7. Democratic MC Votes and Constituent Opinion on Protect America Act

	Both rich and poor constituents supported	Rich supported, poor opposed	Poor supported, rich opposed	Both rich and poor constituents opposed
Percentage of Democratic MCs who voted for Protect America Act	55%	41%	18%	36%
Number of districts	139	41	38	14

in response to a request from President Bush, and the most outspoken opposition to the bill came from prominent liberal and Democratic leaders. But Speaker of the House Nancy Pelosi voted for the bill, and the primary sponsor of the bill was a Democrat (though its two cosponsors were Republicans). As a result, Democratic Party leaders placed little pressure on members regarding how to vote.

Free from party pressures, how did House Democrats vote on this issue? Again, more often than not, they voted in accordance with the preferences of wealthier constituents. Democratic support for the bill was highest when both top- and bottom- tercile constituents supported it (see table 5.7). But Democratic MCs were far more likely to support the bill when top-tercile constituents supported it and bottom-tercile constituents opposed it (42% of Democratic MCs in this circumstance voted for the bill) than when the reverse was true (only 18% of Democratic MCs in this circumstance voted for the bill).

These analyses have focused on differences between the top and bottom terciles. But it is also important to note what happens when opinions of middle and top tercile constituents diverge, given that we might expect middle-income citizens to be better represented than the poor. The evidence here is a mixed bag: on some issues (such as the Iraq War withdrawal or the minimum wage increase) the middle tercile's opinions seem to matter at least as much as the top tercile's; when the opinions of the two groups diverge, policymakers tend to not follow either group's preferences consistently, or exhibit a modest bias in favor of what the middle tercile wants. On others (such as warrantless wiretapping or stem cell research), policymakers tend to favor the rich at the expense of both middle- and bottom-tercile opinions. Part of the reason that middle-income voters tend to, on average, fare better than the poor is because, across districts, the views of middle-income citizens tend to be more strongly correlated with those of the wealthy than do the views of poor citizens (on the Iraq War issue, for example, district-level top- and middle-tercile opinions were correlated at 0.39, while top- and bottom-tercile opinions on this issue were correlated at 0.24). Further, top- and middle-tercile citizens are generally more likely to share the same majority preference on an issue than top- and bottom-tercile citizens.[16]

All of these analyses are necessarily counterfactual, and there are many loose ends in each. But all reinforce the same general point: when wealthy and poor constituents' views diverge, policymakers tend to represent their wealthier constituents better. These differences can have substantial consequences, not only for outcomes on particular bills, but on the ways that policy is debated and discussed, both in the short- and long-term. The statistical magnitude of representation differences between income groups is relatively small—less than 2 percentage points, on average, between the richest and poorest terciles. But these differences are consequential for understanding how MCs act and how policy gets made.

Why Are Poorer Citizens Less Well Represented?

Now that we have seen that lower income citizens are less well represented by their MCs, the important issue becomes understanding *why* they are less well represented. Low-income citizens are disadvantaged in the political process in many ways that go beyond income: they vote less, participate less, tend to know and care less about policy, and are less likely to have the political "resources" necessary to voice their views. They are also more likely to be members of demographic groups historically unequally represented in politics (e.g., Griffin and Newman 2008). These factors, to the extent that they shape whose preferences legislators hear and whose they deem important to heed, might explain why poorer citizens are less well represented.

Spurred in part by the American Political Science Association's Task Force on Inequality Report (2004), much prior discussion on this topic implicitly or explicitly points to these sorts of engagement- or resource-based factors as the driving forces behind biases in representation. Proposals to institute compulsory voting (or to at least make voting easier), to limit the amount that private citizens can donate to political campaigns, or to educate and stimulate political engagement among the poor all have their roots, at least to some extent, in a desire to remedy perceived inequalities in political influence across socioeconomic lines (e.g., Piven and Cloward 1988; Lijphart 1997).

There are, then, a number of different pathways through which socioeconomic biases in representation might work their way into the political system. From a theoretical perspective—and from the perspective of those who reform the political system to equalize political influence across income lines—it is important to understand what such pathways are, and which, if any, can explain why poorer citizens get lower levels of representation than wealthier ones.

Political Engagement and Participation

As we have seen in chapter 3, lower-income citizens are typically less politically active than their wealthier counterparts. Poor citizens tend to vote less than wealthier ones: the U.S. Census's Current Population Study shows that the turnout gap between top- and bottom-tercile citizens in the 2012 congressional election was roughly 20 percentage points. And the gap between the top- and bottom-income deciles was roughly 30 points. As we have seen, income disparities in participation are still larger with respect to more active forms of participation. And gaps are larger still—particularly between the very rich and very poor—when it comes to donating money to political causes.

There are two central reasons to expect participants to be substantially better represented than nonparticipants. First, perhaps the most direct way for a citizen to have its preferences represented is to elect representatives with like-minded views (Erikson et al. 2002). No individual can ensure that he or she is represented by a like-minded legislator, of course. But at least at the margins, those who are active in politics are more likely to be represented by MCs who share their political beliefs than those who do not. By definition, voters are more influential in shaping election outcomes than nonvoters, and political activists are disproportionately influential in electing candidates and parties that reflect their views (Layman et al. 2010).

Second, political activity and engagement can affect the actions of policymakers even apart from elections. Most classic models of representation of public opinion are driven in large part by the *threat* of electoral sanction. As Soroka and Wleizen (2005, 666–67) state: "The representation of public opinion presupposes that the public actually notices and responds to what policymakers do. Without such responsiveness, policymakers would have little incentive to represent what the public wants in policy." Legislators must balance a number of competing motivations when deciding how to act, and it makes little sense to take into account the preferences of constituents (or particular subsets of constituents) when there is minimal threat that ignoring their views will lead to electoral punishment. Those who participate in politics are perceived by lawmakers as posing more of a credible threat of electoral sanction, and are typically better represented as a result (e.g., Griffin and Newman 2005).

Education and Political Sophistication

Income and socioeconomic status are strongly correlated with the possession of political "resources," particularly education, political knowledge, and interest in politics (Delli Carpini and Keeter 1997; Verba, Schlozman, and Brady 1995). Only 13 percent of CCES respondents in the lowest income tercile (and only 6% in the poorest decile) report having a four-year college degree, compared to 48 percent of top-tercile respondents (and 68% of top-decile respondents). Lower-income respondents are also substantially less likely to say that they are interested in political affairs, and are less likely to know important facts about state and national governments.

The resources of education, knowledge, and interest are critical in shaping citizens' abilities to form stable, meaningful opinions on policy issues, and in their ability to hold policymakers accountable for their actions. Educated, attentive, and knowledgeable citizens are better equipped to form coherent, stable, and well-developed preferences on matters of public policy, and to send clear signals to policymakers regarding what they would like done. The lack of ability to form and voice coherent political preferences precludes representation, as it is unclear what "representation" of public preferences even means if those preferences are not themselves systematically meaningful (Soroka and Wlezien 2010). If educated and knowledgeable citizens send signals that are less "noisy," and more systematic, than their less educated counterparts, it is logical to expect that the former will have their preferences better represented than the latter, simply because those preferences will be clearer, more stable, and easier for policymakers to perceive.[17]

In addition, educated, attentive, and knowledgeable citizens are more likely to be attuned to the political context in general, and to their legislators' behavior in particular (Husted, Kenny, and Morton 1995; Wolpert and Gimpel 1997). Given the electoral motivations of legislators, a legislator will be more likely to disregard a portion of their constituency's preferences if that segment of the constituency is unlikely to notice that their preferences have been disregarded. Again, given the association between income and these types of political resources, socioeconomic biases could be driven in whole or in part by the disproportionately low levels of education, political knowledge, and political sophistication among lower-income citizens.

Race, Ethnicity, and Gender

For a variety of reasons, racial and ethnic minorities are typically less well represented in the voting decisions of Congress members than whites (Hero and Tolbert 1995). To a lesser extent, the same may be true of the representation of women compared to men (Griffin, Newman, and Wolbrecht 2012). Lower-income citizens are more likely to be women and members of racial and ethnic minority groups than are upper-income respondents. Since race, ethnicity, and gender are correlated with income, a substantial portion of the representation gap might be explained by these demographic factors, with socioeconomic biases inexorably intertwined with long-standing issues of racial inequality.

Modeling Economic Biases in Representation

To explore the degree to which the inequities in representation in income lines are driven by these correlates of income, we turn to multivariate analysis, modeling individuals' ideological proximity and key vote representation as a function of income and measures of the factors described above. The point of this analysis is to first estimate the effect of income on political representation without controlling for any other factors, then to examine how the independent explanatory power of income changes as we control for its politically relevant correlates.

The first row of table 5.8 presents results from a simple one-predictor model, showing the expected effects of income (as measured by the 14-point CCES income scale) on our two 100-point scale measures of representation. These results, which show significant effects of income on representation, reinforce what is seen in figures 5.2 and 5.3: wealthy citizens are, on average, both more proximate to their MCs and more likely to have their preferences reflected in MC's votes on key issues. Each one-category increase in income is expected to decrease the distance between citizens and their MC by roughly 0.16 points, and increase the proportion of the time that their preferences on the seven-issue scale are represented by 0.10 percentage points.

TABLE 5.8. Modeling Economic Biases in Representation

	Ideological Representation	Key Vote Representation
Income alone	–0.16 * (0.03)	0.10 * (0.04)
Income, controlling for race, ethnicity, and gender	–0.11 * (0.03)	0.09 * (0.04)
Income, controlling for race, ethnicity, gender, education, and voter status	–0.10 * (0.03)	0.08 * (0.04)
Income, controlling for race, ethnicity, gender, education, interest, voting, political activity and donor status	–0.10 * (0.03)	0.09 * (0.04)

Note: Table entries are maximum likelihood coefficients, with standard errors in parentheses. * $p < .05$, + $p < .10$

The remaining rows of this table illustrate what happens to the effect of income on representation when additional variables are introduced to the models.[18] The degree to which the income coefficient shrinks when these additional controls are added to the models shows the degree to which representational biases across income lines are a function of other factors correlated with income. If biases in representation across income lines were spurious, driven entirely by the fact that poorer people also are more likely to vote, donate money, or possess other characteristics that make them less likely to be represented, then we would expect the size of the income coefficient to shrink to zero after other controls are added. Conversely, if income matters above and beyond these other factors, then we would see the income effect remain even after controls for these factors are added.

The second row illustrates the effect of the income coefficient after controlling for the sociodemographic characteristics of race, ethnicity, and gender. The coefficients for these variables (not shown) generally behave as expected—blacks and Latinos are less well represented than whites, and women are modestly (but not significantly) less well represented than men—but the inclusion of these factors does little to change the size of the income effects.

Row 3 adds in controls for respondent's voter status—whether they reported voting in the most recent national election. Again, though the independent effects of interest on representation are significant in themselves, these results do not markedly change the role of income in representation.

Finally, row 4 adds in several other indicators of political engagement, including a respondent's level of formal education, level of interest in political news (measured on a 1–4 scale, ranging from "very interested" to "not at all interested,") a scale measuring the number of high-engagement political activities in which a respondent participated, and a dummy variable for respondents who donated any money to a political cause in the past year. Again, we see that these variables have only a limited effect on the independent effect of income. Income's negative effects on representation seem to be only modestly a result of poorer people being less active or less likely to contribute to politics.

The results show that income-based biases in representation cannot be explained in whole, or even in large part, by resources, political engagement, or demographic factors. The inclusion of the full list of resource and engagement variables diminishes the independent effects of income by only about 30 percent for the ideological distance measure, and 45 percent for the key vote measure.[19] The fact that poor citizens are less politically engaged does matter to how well they are represented. But lower levels of engagement only tell part of the story.

Further, the effects of income on representation are unusual in their consistency (at least when compared to resource and demographic factors) across all types of model specifications and across both measures. Variables such as education, knowledge, and participation seem, at least to some extent, to be competing to explain much of the same variance, and thus the role of each is contingent on model specification. But the role of income is unique, largely distinct from all of these factors. Together, these results show that economic biases in representation go deeper than what would be expected from resource- or sociodemographic-based explanations.

Conclusions

Taken together, the results above lead to two conclusions. First, biases in representation across income lines, though often subtle, can have substantial consequences. Second, biases in representation across income lines are nearly orthogonal to biases in representation across other lines of political difference. While the analysis does not definitively rule out all possible resource- or engagement-based factors in explaining economic biases, they do show that explanations of why biases exist need to go well beyond the fact that wealthy people know, donate, and participate more than poorer citizens.

These results raise the question of why income would have an independent effect on representation, above and beyond attentiveness, engagement, or even donating to political campaigns. Wealthier citizens, regardless of their levels of education or political interest, have better access to formal and informal political and social networks that help to set policy agendas and inform public debate on political issues (e.g., Lindblom 1977; Schlozman 1984). Wealthy people are also more likely to have their views voiced by lobbyists and special interest organizations, even if many wealthy individuals do not personally take the time to contribute to such organizations (Baumgartner et al. 2010). At a more personal level, wealthy citizens are also more likely to internalize the behavioral norms that make them apt to have their preferences taken seriously by public bureaucracies and other forms of public and private authority (e.g., Galanter 1999; Beeghley 2007). Further, most Congress members are themselves well-off, and thus might be more apt to interact with constituents who are well-off, or be disproportionately attuned to what wealthy constituents want (Carnes 2013).

All of these factors suggest, consistent with much work in political science, sociology, and other fields, that wealthier citizens are "visible" (Fallows 2000) in American political and social systems in ways that go beyond their education or political engagement. These other factors matter, but income itself—and the greater visibility of high-income citizens to policymakers—remains important after these factors are taken into account.

None of this is to say, of course, that greater equity in resources and engagement across income would not help at all in remediating biases in representation. The models also do not address some of the more complex linkages between income, representation, and political engagement: the likelihood, for example, that poor citizens participate in politics less because they feel (justifiably, given our analysis) that their preferences will be given less weight in policy. But for the purposes of reform, we can say that for those interested in remediating income-based biases in representation, a focus on increasing the political engagement of the poor, or placing restrictions on the political engagement of the wealthy (e.g., by limiting private financing of political campaigns), will be far from sufficient in eliminating income-based biases in representation without a more wide-ranging consideration of the role of wealth in shaping political and social systems.

In general, then, the results here show that an individual's income, apart from anything else about him or her, seems to confer some representational advantages in the political system. But simply saying that "wealthier people get better representation" greatly simplifies the issue. While inequalities in representation persist even after controlling for income's relevant correlates, it is also the case that poor people do receive equal representation to the wealthy, or even better representation than the wealthy, in certain contexts. Though *in general* this was not the case, the above tables reveal many specific instances in which policymakers voted with their poor constituents, and did so even in some cases where poorer constituents disagreed with wealthier ones.

If poor citizens receive better representation on certain issues and in certain contexts, the question then becomes: Why? What factors tend to enhance the political representation of the poor, and what conditions tend to make these factors prominent? I have made the argument that poorer citizens are in general less well represented because they are (in general) less visible or relevant to policymakers. Accordingly, we might expect attributes of the political context in which poor citizens live will affect how visible and relevant they are to their elected officials and, in turn, will affect the quality of the representation they receive.

SIX

Understanding Economic Biases in Representation

To this point, we have seen that whether "policy representation" is conceived in broad ideological terms, in terms of salient policy matters across a number of domains, or in terms of specific, concrete policy choices, poorer citizens are less well represented than the wealthy. These differences are often modest, but can have significant consequences. More important, these differences persist after controlling for individual-level political resource disadvantages among the poor. The fact that the poor vote less, donate less, and pay less attention to politics matters, in other words, but income itself, and the related political and social visibility that it brings, is important to representation even when taking these things into account.

The persistence of these representational biases might be thought of as endemic to the American political system: after all, a system with few restrictions on how one's private resources can be used to influence policy outcomes might generally be thought to favor the wealthy and the resource-rich. But though a tendency to cater to the views of the wealthy might be a logical outgrowth of such as system, there are circumstances in which the preferences of poor citizens are better represented than others. Indeed, we have already seen evidence of this in chapter 5: though MCs in general tended to side with the views of the wealthy over those of the poor on the specific issues highlighted, there were a number of MCs on every issue examined where MCs' votes corresponded to what their poor, and not what their wealthy, constituents wanted.

This chapter explores the issue of heterogeneity in representational inequity more broadly, using the data and measures developed in chapter 5 to illustrate, and explain, variance in representational bias across areas of the country. I draw from research into political representation in the United States and in other democracies to develop a model of contextual variation in representational inequality. This model explains how contextual factors might work to enhance (or detract from) both the *political visibility* and *political relevance* of the poor relative to the rich. Given the many competing pressures facing them, MCs have neither the time to understand what all of their constituents want nor the ability to represent all of their constituents equally. They thus must make choices when deciding who to represent. I argue that MCs, all else equal, will better represent constituents whose preferences are both easy to perceive and deemed to be particularly relevant to electoral success. The views of the poor will thus be better represented in contexts that make their views more visible and relevant to policymakers—when they reside in contexts that are more likely to give voice to their views.

District-Level Differences in Representational Inequality

We have seen that, on average, wealthier citizens are better represented by their MCs than poorer citizens. When the views of wealthy and poor constituents conflict on specific, highly salient issues, MCs more often than not choose to act in a way that corresponds with the views of the wealthy. And, in the aggregate, wealthy citizens hold political views that are ideologically closer to their MCs than those of the poor. These representational biases persist after controlling for a number of politically relevant correlates of income. But this *general* tendency for the wealthy to enjoy better representation than that of the poor masks considerable heterogeneity in how much better the wealthy are better represented—or even whether they are better represented at all.

Figure 6.1 illustrates this heterogeneity, showing the representation gaps between the top and bottom income terciles for each of the 435 congressional districts on the two measures of policy representation—ideological distance and key vote representation—described in chapter 5. The message here is clear: the modest but significant representation gaps that we observed when aggregating across all 435 congressional districts mask significant differences across districts in how large such gaps are. There is substantial variation across districts in how well upper- and lower-income groups are represented: in many districts, wealthier constituents are far

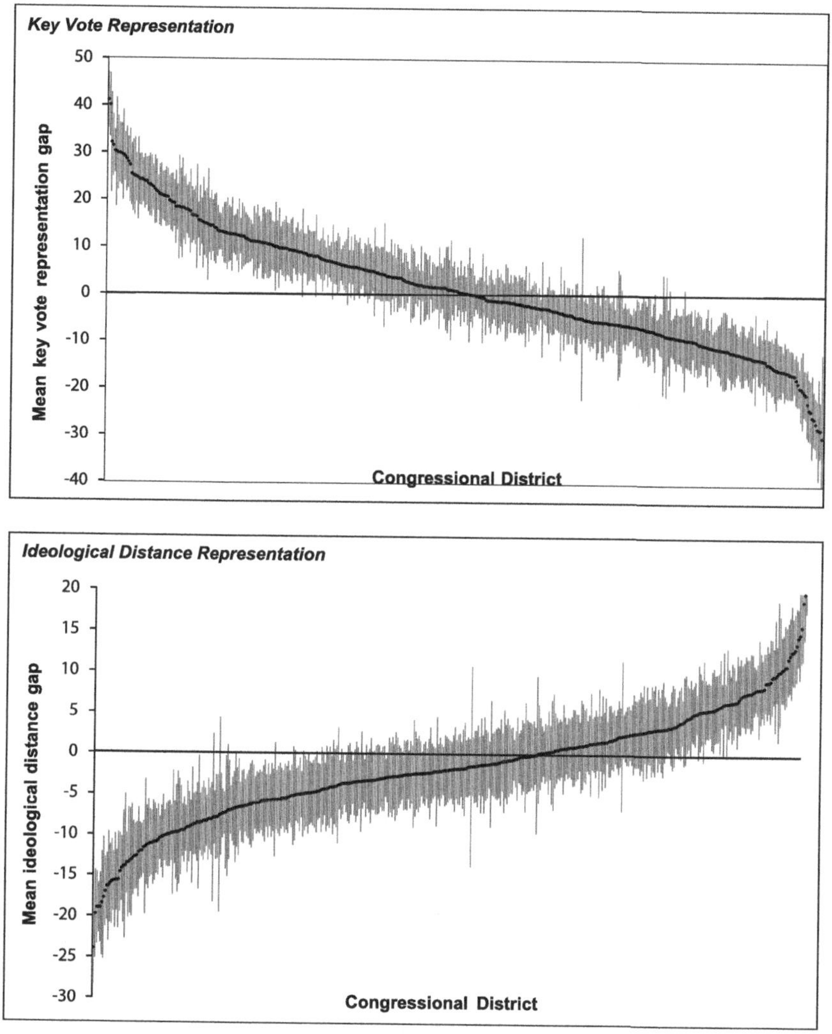

Fig. 6.1. Top-Bottom Tercile Representation Gaps, by District

better represented than the poor; in others, the differences are modest or not statistically meaningful. And in still others, poor citizens are actually more likely to get what they want from their representatives. I can easily ($p < .001$) reject the hypothesis that the representation gaps between the top and bottom terciles are equal across districts.

This chapter works to explain the sources of this heterogeneity in representation. The general argument that follows is intuitive: poor citizens will be better represented when their representatives are likely to both know and care about what they want. Though disadvantages in the individual-level political resources of the poor make it less likely that MCs will either hear from the poor or feel they need to take their views into account, I argue that contextual factors can also influence the political voice of the poor in a way that bears on how well, and how equally, their views are represented.

Subgroup Representation in American Politics

Most classic theories of MC behavior assume goal-oriented policymakers first and foremost seek to maximize their chances of reelection. Given these motivations, MCs should not systematically ignore the preferences of any segments of their constituency unless there is compelling reason to do so (Soroka and Wlezien 2010; Erikson and Bhatti 2011). Accordingly, many influential studies of the dyadic relationships between MCs and constituents (e.g., Miller and Stokes 1963; Denzau, Riker, and Shepsle 1985; Erikson 1978) explicitly consider representation as a connection between a member's actions and the preferences of a "district," broadly defined. "Representation," in this sense, is grounded in the correspondence between an MC's actions and the preferences of the median member of his or her constituency.

Other work, however, has made it clear that while this sort of representation is an integral part of what an MC does, the MC's job—and the idea of "constituency"—is far more complex than this. MCs do not and cannot see their constituency as a simple undifferentiated mass, and must make choices when trying to represent a number of diverse subconstituencies and trying to achieve a number of diverse goals.[1] These choices make it highly likely that MCs will represent certain constituents more strongly than others.

First, substantial time and resource limitations prevent MCs from being able to even perceive the preferences of all constituents within their districts: it is well known that ordinary citizens rely on heuristic cues when making political decisions on topics that they do not know that much about. But we also know that when trying to gauge what their constituents desire, MCs rely on many of the same cognitive techniques that citizens do when trying to make decisions in the context of limited time and imperfect information. Congress members simply do not have the ability to know or understand what all of their constituents want (Kingdon 1989).

Given this, MCs must make use of informational shortcuts in order to develop an understanding of what their constituents—and various subsets of constituents—want. How MCs perceive their districts is thus central to understanding how they represent their districts.

What sorts of heuristics do MCs use when trying to gauge want their constituents want? Much as citizens often make political decisions based on information that is most immediately accessible at the time a decision is required (Zaller 1992), MCs tend to rely more heavily on information about their constituency that is regularly accessible to them (Hall 1996). MCs' perceptions of their districts—and, in turn, their perceptions of how their districts should be represented—are thus based not on the universe of all possible information about their constituents, but rather on the nonrandom subset of information that they perceive and hear most prominently. This information, while it can provide a useful working guide to what citizens are thinking and saying, is often if not always an imperfect and nonrepresentative subset of all possible information that exists about an MC's constituency. The nonrepresentativeness of these cues has consequences: as Miler (2010, 6) notes, "Legislators and their staff do not see all, or even a large percentage, of the relevant constituents to whom [an] issue at hand is unimportant. This ultimately can lead to many constituents' interests going unrepresented." Constituents' views that are more accessible to their MCs, in other words, are generally better represented than views that are not as accessible.

We also know that even above and beyond these cognitive limitations, MCs must balance many competing pressures—their own ideologies, the preferences of interest groups, national party interests, the views of important political subconstituencies, and the like—when deciding how to act (e.g., Kingdon 1984; Fenno 1978; Burden 2007). When these pressures conflict, MCs must make choices in deciding whom to represent. In these contexts, policymakers seek to represent the constituencies that are deemed to be most important to the goals that they wish to achieve (Jusko 2008).

Reelection is the most proximate of these goals, as it is the goal that must be achieved "if other ends are to be attained" (Mayhew 2004, 16). If an MC cannot secure enough votes to stay in office, after all, then many of his or her second-order legislative goals become irrelevant. But other goals—the desire to wield influence in one's party or in Congress, or to achieve one's own desired policy outcomes, for example—matter as well (Fenno 1973; Aldrich and Rohde 2001).

These motivations can conflict with one another in fairly straightforward ways: an MC in a relatively centrist "swing" district may need to moderate his or her positions or otherwise pay closer attention to the preferences of his or her general election constituency in order to secure reelection. But pursuing these goals may make the member behave in a less party-centric way than his or her party leaders want. Those in safer districts, free from the most dire general election pressures, may choose to focus on behaving in a way desired by primary constituencies (in order to fend off a strong primary challenge) or party leaders (in order to curry favor with important legislative leaders).

This general discussion leads to two fairly intuitive points. First, MCs represent more strongly the views of constituents that are more *visible* and easier to perceive, and thus more salient in shaping the MC's perception of what his or her district looks like and what it wants. Second, MCs represent more strongly the views of constituents that are deemed more *relevant* to furthering the MCs goals, whether proximate (reelection) or second order.

All of these factors are relevant to understanding the representation of the poor even without taking into account context. Miler (2010) makes the intuitive argument that the use of these decision-making strategies tends to favor resource-rich constituents. MCs, of course, are more likely to hear from those who donate money, are politically active, correspond with them, vote in general and primary elections, and so on. Such citizens hold views that are more accessible when MCs are forming perceptions of what "the district" wants, and also hold views that are more relevant to what MCs want to do: after all, there are many reasons for MCs to care a great deal about what donors, influential interest groups, or politically active constituents want, and few reasons to care about those who don't vote or follow politics. Since there are strong positive relationships between income and essentially every form of political participation, it stands to reason that poorer citizens will be less well represented because they are simply not as visible, or not perceived as relevant, to their MCs.

But above and beyond these individual-level activities, there are also reasons to consider contextual variation in how visible and how relevant the poor are to elected officials. In some contexts, we might think that the views of the poor are more visible and relevant to MCs than in others, either because the proportion of poorer citizens is simply larger or because the poor are vocally represented by organizations that have their interests at heart. Similarly, we might think that the votes of the poor might be more "pivotal" (Jusko 2008) to the formation of winning electoral coalitions in some contexts than in others: in some contexts, in other words, MCs' electoral success may depend more strongly on satisfying the political interests of the poor than in other contexts.

Context and Unequal Representation

All of this suggests that contextual factors can either enhance or detract from the political visibility of the poor relative to the rich, and can make poor citizens' views more or less relevant to MCs' electoral and career success. In the following section, I isolate contextual factors that I expect to either enhance or detract from the political visibility and relevance of the poor and, in turn, affect how equally rich and poor citizens' views are represented.

Income Inequality

Comparative research on the political consequences of inequality generally supports the view that large income disparities have a negative impact on the political influence of poorer citizens. Larger concentrations of wealth provide the resources and motivation for wealthier citizens to exert greater control over the political process, and to make their views more strongly heard by policymakers relative to those of the poor (e.g., Goodin and Dryzek 1980; Solt 2008). In more unequal societies, financial resources play a larger role in shaping the decisions of policymakers and legislative bodies (Petrova 2008; Rosset, Giger, and Bernauer 2013). We have also seen evidence that, both in the United States and elsewhere, high levels of localized income inequality can dampen the political activity of the poor.

Because income inequality tends to amplify the political visibility of the wealthy while depressing it among the poor, greater economic inequality in a given democracy is generally associated with greater political inequality (Solt 2010; Rosset, Giger, and Bernauer 2013). This research is relevant here, because we have seen in chapter 2 that while inequality is increasing in the United States over time, there is also considerable cross-sectional variance in income inequality: some congressional districts have far more uneven distributions of income than others. I thus expect that poorer citizens will be less well represented relative to the rich in districts with high income inequality.

Electoral Competitiveness

Congress members in marginal districts face different incentives than those in electorally safe districts (Mayhew 2004). Though the effects of electoral safety on the behavior of MCs remains a subject of debate, one potential result of safety is that it, at least at the margins, might affect the incentives that elected officials have to be responsive to their constituents. When representatives have less fear of electoral reprisal, they are more able to act according to their own ideology (or the preferences of party leaders or other pressure groups), at the expense of their constituents' views (Fiorina 1989; Ladewig 2010). In safe districts, we might expect MCs to give more weight to the views of wealthier citizens, since such citizens have the resources that are more likely to further the MCs career goals—the desire to wield influence in his or her party or in Congress, for example—in ways that go beyond reelection (Fenno 1973; Winters and Page 2009).

In addition (and though there is controversy on this point) MCs in districts where the partisan balance is heavily tilted in his or her party's favor might also have incentives to pay closer attention to the preferences of primary electorates, given that serious electoral challenges in these districts tend to come from primaries, not general elections (Mann and Ornstein 2006). Since poor citizens are less likely to participate in primary elections than wealthier ones, this stronger focus on primary constituencies would also lead to weaker representation of the poor.

Without the need for poor citizens' votes to remain in office, in other words, legislators may disregard the preferences of the poor in the service of other constituency pressures or political goals. I thus expect that poor citizens will be less well represented relative to the rich in districts that are electorally safe.[2]

Labor Union Strength

Lobbyists and interest organizations are pivotal in shaping the voices that Congress members hear, and in helping them to understand the views and interests of their districts (Miler 2010). Though few scholars conclude that organized interests, as a matter of course, explicitly "buy" the votes of MCs, there is reason to expect that views that are voiced more strongly by interest organizations will be given more weight in the behavior of MCs than views that are not voiced by such organizations (Schlozman and Tierney 1986).

The role of interest groups in policymaking poses a problem for the representation of the poor. Though there are many interest organizations that represent trade and economic interests, and many others that represent wide cross-sections of citizens and groups, there are very few that lobby explicitly on behalf of poorer citizens (Schlozman 1984). And in terms of resources, professionalism, experience, and other metrics that determine the likely political influence of an interest group, the most well organized and connected groups nearly always represent the interests of business or wealthy constituents (e.g., Godwin 1992). To the extent that interest groups make certain types of views visible and relevant to MCs, in other words, they tend to represent the views of the wealthy.

One possible exception to this lack of poor citizens' representation in the interest group community might be organized labor. Though union members are not always (or even usually) poor, organized labor has traditionally served as a voice for the views of low-income citizens, advocating for the concerns of the poor and giving elected officials reasons to pay closer attention to the concerns of the poor (e.g., Baumgartner et al. 2010). As seen in chapter 3, labor also serves as something of a mobilizing influence for the political engagement of poorer citizens, increasing the clout of the poor further.

Labor is, of course, in a decades-long decline nationally, but it still remains a relatively strong influence on the political process in particular pockets of the country. At the low end, labor is essentially nonexistent as a political force: in a quarter of all congressional districts, labor households are less than 15 percent of all households. But at the high end, labor remains strong: roughly 10 percent of Congress members represent districts where one-third or more of all households are labor households.

It is reasonable to expect that Congress members in heavily unionized districts will be more likely to both hear the views of, and have incentives to respond to, lower-income constituents. I expect that poor citizens will be better represented relative to the rich in districts where organized labor has a strong presence.

Median Income

In addition to the income *distribution*, we might expect that the average *level* of income within a district will matter as well. Part of the reason for this expectation has to do simply with the presence of a high concentration of lower-income voters: districts with few poor voters by definition give poorer citizens less clout in the electoral process, making it less likely that they will elect a representative that shares their views. Second, even apart from elections, research from other Western democracies shows that elected officials tend to pay more attention to the needs and preferences of poor citizens when they rely strongly on them for electoral support. Low- and middle-income citizens have the greatest political power when the blocs of such voters are large enough to be pivotal to the electoral success of legislators (Jusko 2008). The preferences of poorer citizens are taken more strongly into account when the votes of the poor are perceived as necessary to forming a winning electoral coalition, and are more likely to be marginalized when their votes are perceived as less necessary.[3] This implies, then, that MCs in wealthy districts are more likely to be elected by an electoral coalition comprised largely of high-income voters, and are more likely to hear from wealthier constituents once in office. Poor citizens in high-income districts, put more directly, are less important to the electoral success of MCs, and less likely to be visible to MCs as well.

Perhaps in contrast to this, though, we have seen in chapter 3 that poorer citizens are more politically active in high-income contexts than in low-income ones: the gaps in political activity that make wealthier citizens more important to the actions of their MCs are not as prominent in these high-income contexts. Wealthier citizens still make up more of a critical mass of constituents in such districts, but the more equal levels of participation across income levels in these districts may help to mitigate these effects somewhat.

MC Party Affiliation

Finally, we might expect that MCs from the Democratic Party—which has, historically, been more closely aligned with the interests of the poor—would represent poor constituents better relative to the rich than Republican MCs. In part, this expectation comes simply from the fact that Republican MCs are almost always more conservative than Democratic ones, and so poor citizens—who, on average, are modestly more liberal on many issues than the wealthy—will tend to be less well represented by Republicans.

But party affiliation is important for other reasons as well. Party affiliation affects how MCs perceive their districts: Republicans tend to have stronger ties with corporate interests and wealthier citizens than do Democrats, and as a result the views of wealthy interests are more likely to be front and center in the minds of Republican MCs (Miler 2010). Republican MCs' perceptions of what their constituents want—and, by extension, which preferences they are more likely to represent—are generally weighted more heavily toward the views of those groups.

Modeling Contextual Influences on Representation

To test these ideas, I return to the measures of ideological distance and key vote representation introduced in chapter 5, which showed a modest but persistent representational bias in favor of wealthier citizens. The goal here is to examine whether these biases vary as a function of relevant attributes of the political context. Accordingly, the models in this chapter estimate representation on these two measures as a function of income, contextual attributes, and the interactions between income and political context.[4] Again, lower values on the ideological distance measure indicate better representation (i.e., closer ideological proximity), while higher values on the key vote measure indicate better representation (i.e., a greater congruence between public opinion and MC votes).

District-level contextual level attributes are the ones detailed above, and are measured as follows. *Income inequality* (a district-level Gini coefficient) and *median household income* are operationalized using ACS data, as in chapter 3. I operationalize *electoral safety* by taking the absolute value of each district's 2012 Cook Partisan Voting Index. This index, which is based on the district's presidential vote in the prior two election cycles, is intended to measure how electorally balanced and competitive a district is. Lower values on this measure indicate a more competitive district, while higher values indicate a district that is strongly partisan (in either direction). *Union strength* is simply the proportion of citizens in a district that reported living in a union household. *MC Party* is a dummy variable coded "1" if a district's MC is a Republican.[5]

When it comes to ideological distance representation, the interac-

TABLE 6.1. Modeling Contextual Effects on Representational Bias

	Dependent Variable: Ideological Distance Representation		Dependent Variable: Key Vote Representation	
Income	1.36*	1.39*	−0.484*	−0.48*
	(0.54)	(0.54)	(0.07)	(0.07)
Income * District Median Income	−0.33	−0.32	0.32	0.50+
	(0.22)	(0.22)	(0.28)	(0.28)
Income * District Inequality	−1.88+	−2.00+	3.73*	3.70*
	(1.07)	(1.06)	(1.40)	(1.40)
Income * District Competitiveness	−0.17*	−0.16*	0.25*	0.23*
	(0.04)	(0.04)	(0.05)	(0.05)
Income * District Unionization	0.19*	0.19*	0.05	0.04
	(0.08)	(0.08)	(0.05)	(0.05)
Income * Republican MC	−0.27*	−0.14*	1.72*	1.33*
	(0.06)	(0.06)	(0.06)	(0.08)
Income * Opinion Difference		−0.25*		0.07*
		(0.10)		(0.02)
Constant	27.28*	26.79*	90.25*	92.14*
	(4.90)	(4.02)	(5.36)	(5.42)
N	46,476	46,476	39,138	39,138

Note: Table entries are mixed effects regression coefficients (standard errors are in parentheses). * $p < .05$

tions between income and inequality, electoral safety, union strength, and Republican representation all are significant and in the expected direction: wealthy citizens are better represented relative to the poor in highly unequal contexts, electorally noncompetitive contexts, low-union contexts, and in districts represented by Republicans. For key vote representation, the interactions between income and inequality, electoral safety, and Republican representation are all significant: the interaction between income and union representation is signed in the correct direction, but is not statistically significant. In all cases, these results show that representational gaps between rich and poor are larger in contexts where the views of the poor are likely to either be less visible to their representatives or less relevant to the goals that their representatives wish to achieve.

The one hypothesis suggested above that is not supported in the data is that for district median income: in the ideological distance model, the interaction between representation and district income is not significant, and in the key vote model this interaction is incorrectly signed. This implies that the equality in participation in higher-income contexts that we saw in chapter 3 matters: perhaps the higher levels of political attentiveness among the poor in high-income contexts help to mitigate some of the advantages that wealthy citizens enjoy in these areas. The fact that high-status areas increase opportunities for political participation among the poor, without necessarily decreasing the quality of the representation that they receive, is notable.

To get a sense of the substantive impact of these findings, figures 6.2 and 6.3 display the expected effect of income on representation in a variety of situations. Figure 6.2 displays the expected relationship between income and key vote representation in four hypothetical contexts: in a high inequality district (operationalized here as a district in with a Gini coefficient in the 90th percentile of all districts) represented by a Republican, a low inequality district (a district with a Gini coefficient in the 10th percentile) represented by a Republican, a high-inequality district represented by a Democrat, and a low inequality district represented by a Democrat.[6]

This figure illustrates the heterogeneity in relative representation across district lines. Though the individual-covariates-only model from chapter 5 shows that, on average, each one-category increase in income translates to a 0.11 percent increase in key vote representation, this relationship varies across political contexts: in low-inequality districts represented by Democrats, for example, each one-category income increase is expected to *decrease* key vote representation slightly. But in high inequality districts with Republican MCs, the same one-category increase in income

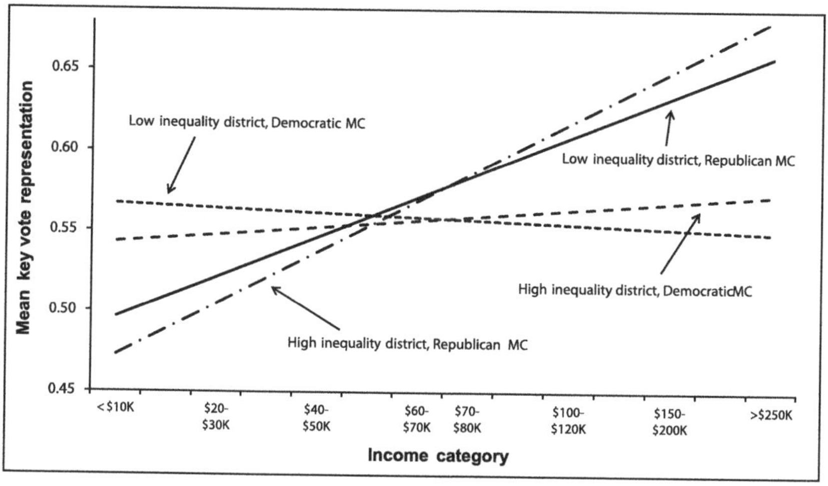

Fig. 6.2. Key Vote Representation by Income and District Inequality

is expected to increase key vote representation by more than 1 full percentage point.

These differences translate into substantively important differences in representation gaps between rich and poor across contexts. In the context most favorable to the poor—low inequality districts represented by Democratic MCs—the poorest citizens' views are modestly better represented than the wealthiest citizens' views. In high inequality Democratic districts, all income groups are expected on average to be represented equally. But in Republican-represented districts, the relationship between income and representation is strong: the difference in the relative representation of the poorest and wealthiest groups is roughly 16 points in low-inequality Republican districts and 21 points in high-income ones.

Figure 6.3 shows a similar analysis for Republican and Democratic MCs in safe districts (with an absolute PVI of 24, placing it in the 90th percentile of all districts) and very competitive districts (with an absolute PVI of 3, placing it in the 10th percentile). These results here provide even more evidence of heterogeneity in relative representation. In district contexts that are most favorable to the poor (competitive districts represented by Democratic MCs), poor citizens are better represented than wealthier ones. But this is the only context in which poor citizens receive representational advantages: in all other contexts, wealthier citizens are better than poorer ones. In the context that is least advantageous to the poor (safe districts with Republican MCs) the representation gap between

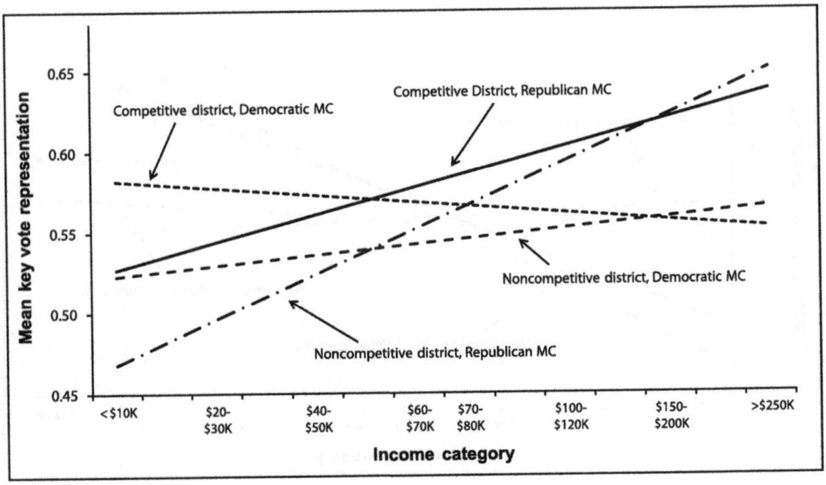

Fig. 6.3. Key Vote Representation by Income and District Competitiveness

rich and poor is again stark: nearly 20 points on the 100-point key vote representation scale.

Representation and Rich-Poor Opinion Gaps

Before moving forward, it is worth noting one other consideration that affects the relative quality of representation that rich and poor receive: the degree to which rich and poor actually want something different from government. As noted earlier, representational biases between citizens of different income levels can exist only if these groups are asking for different things: if rich and poor both want the same policy outcome, it would be impossible for policymakers to represent one group's views over the others, even if they wanted to. In chapter 4, we saw that the size of these gaps varies across contexts: there is wide variance in the degree to which the opinions of rich and poor are meaningfully discernable from one another.

To get a sense of how much opinion differences matter, I examine the size of representation gaps between wealthy and poor citizens as a function of how different wealthy and poor citizens' views are from one another. To do this, I create district-level measures of *opinion difference*, designed to proxy the degree to which rich and poor citizens within a given district disagree with one another on the conception of "opinion" that is to be represented. For the ideological distance model, this measure is the simple

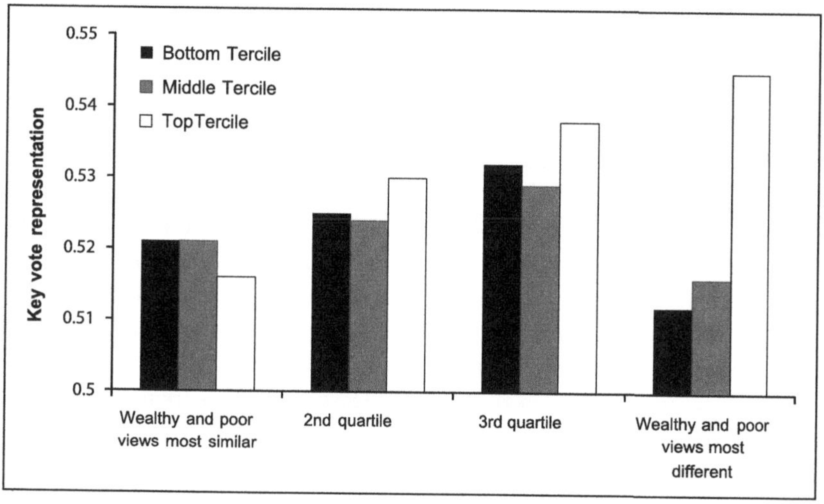

Fig. 6.4. By Tercile Key Vote Representation, by Rich-Poor Opinion Gaps

absolute difference between the mean ideological self-placement of top- and bottom- tercile citizens in a given district. For the key vote model, this variable is the sum of the absolute differences between top- and bottom-tercile opinions on each of the five key vote variables. This variable captures (albeit imperfectly) how strongly class divides in opinion are in a given district—and, by extension, how easy it would be for policymakers in that district to privilege one income group's views over another's if they chose to do so.

A sense of the substantive importance of this variable is shown in figure 6.4, which segments districts into quartiles based on their values for the opinion difference measure, and provides mean key vote representation scores for top-, middle- and bottom-tercile citizens in these four different types of districts. The results are clear: when there is very little daylight between the views of rich and poor, policymakers, unsurprisingly, represent all groups roughly equally well. But as opinion differences emerge, representation of higher-income citizens generally improves, but representation of lower-income (as well as middle-income) citizens generally gets worse.

This finding holds up to multivariate analysis: the final two columns of table 6.1 extend the previous two columns, adding an additional interaction between income and the opinion difference variable. The results show statistically significant interactions between income and these opinion difference measures for both the ideological distance and key vote models: representation gaps between rich and poor are larger when the gap in policy views between them is also large.[7] The inclusion of the income-opinion distance interaction does not do much to affect the interactions between income and the other contextual variables: the effect of opinion distance, it appears, is something that is more-or-less orthogonal to the substantive factors that affect the relative representation of the poor. But it does matter quite a bit, and speaks to a perhaps sobering interpretation of the results from chapter 3: the existence of meaningful differences in opinions across class lines may simply mean that the poor get represented less well. At the least, the presence of such differences requires policymakers to choose between representing the views of one set of constituents and representing the views of another set: in the main, at least, policymakers in such situations choose to represent their wealthier constituents.

A Closer Look at Partisanship and Ideological Extremity

Perhaps the strongest finding in the models from table 6.1 is that for partisanship: Republican MCs tend to represent their constituents less equally than do Democratic ones. As noted above, this is possibly in part due to ideological reasons, or to the fact that Republican representatives are, in general, more closely connected to higher-income constituents than are Democratic ones (Miler 2010). But if we dig a bit deeper into the reasons behind the strong impact of partisanship, another explanation emerges, one grounded more directly in the role of ideological extremity.

For a number of reasons, the views of poor citizens are less likely to be well represented by ideologically extreme policymakers. The poor are more likely to identify as "moderate" on ideological self-placement measures, and are less likely to support ideologically extreme policy positions than are wealthier citizens. They are also less likely to hold ideologically constrained views—to hold consistently liberal or conservative views on social, economic, and foreign policy issues, for example—and more likely to hold views that might reflect a mix of traditionally "liberal" and "conservative" views. These sorts of views are likely to be less well represented by an ideologically extreme, highly ideologically constrained legislative party.

Consistent with this idea, there is evidence that more extreme MCs, all else equal, tend to represent their poorer constituents less well relative to their wealthier ones. To see this, I estimate simple models of ideological and key vote representation as a function of the interaction between income and their MC's *absolute* NOMINATE score (scaled such that

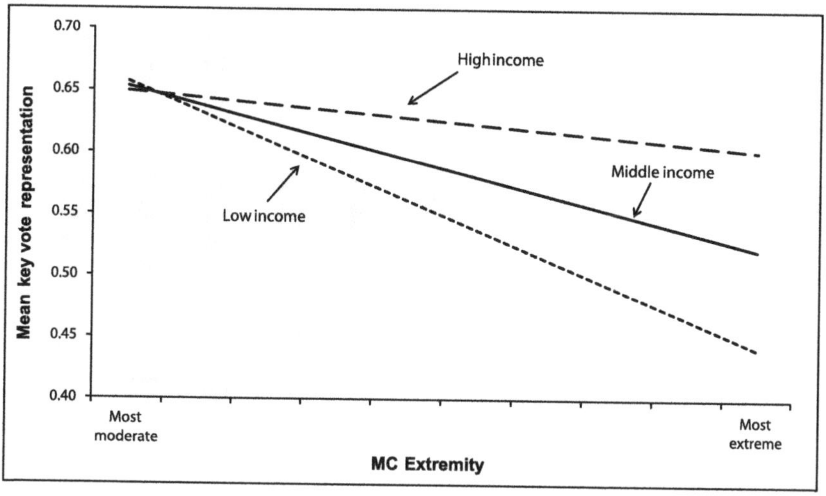

Fig. 6.5. Representational Bias by MC Extremity

higher numbers mean a more extreme MC, either liberal or conservative). Figure 6.5 presents the results of the ideological distance version of this model (the findings for the key vote model look nearly identical), showing the expected key vote representation gap between the 10th and 90th percentiles of the income distribution as a function of MC ideological extremity. The results make plain the notion that more extreme MCs represent their constituents less equally.

These findings apply regardless of MC party: more extreme Democratic MCs represent their poor constituents worse than moderate Democrats, and more extreme Republican MCs represent their poor constituents worse than moderate Republicans. But while both congressional parties have drifted toward the political extremes over the past few decades, this polarization has been asymmetric, with Republicans becoming both more ideologically homogenous and more ideologically extreme than have Democrats (Butler 2009; Hacker and Pierson 2011).

Figure 6.6 illustrates this asymmetric extremity, using absolute NOMINATE scores to classify all 435 MCs in the 113th Congress into deciles, ranging from most moderate (the leftmost portion of the figure) to most extreme (the rightmost portion of the graph). Democratic MCs are represented in gray, while Republican MCs are represented in black. The point of the figure is clear: nearly all of the most ideologically extreme MCs in Congress are Republicans. If ideological extremity has negative impacts

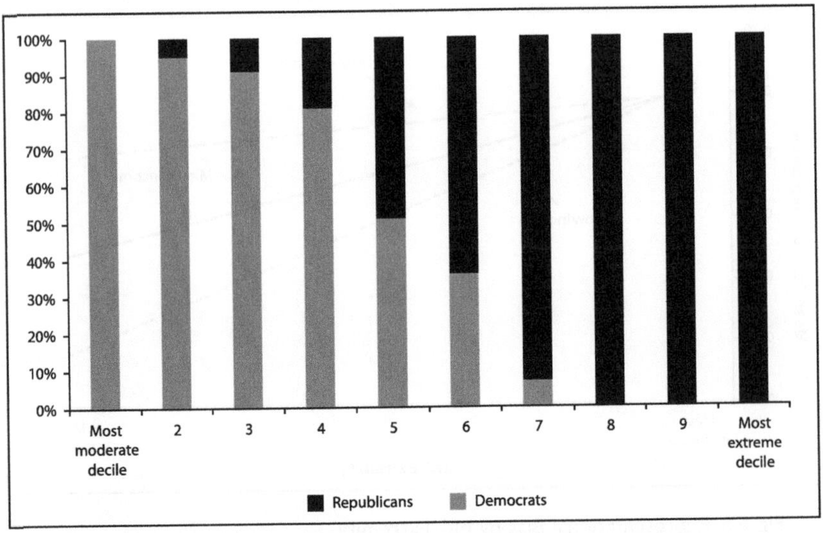

Fig. 6.6. Asymmetric Polarization in the U.S. House

on the policy representation of the poor, the impact of this extremity will be concentrated in Republican-represented districts. Adding an additional interaction between income and absolute NOMINATE score to the models in table 6.1 does, in fact, dampen the size of the interaction between income and Republican representation: in the ideological distance model, the impact of Republican representation is no longer statistically significant after controlling for MC extremity.

These findings have implications for understanding the impact of party polarization on representational inequality: we will explore this idea in depth in chapter 7. But suffice it to say for now that when trying to understand why Republicans tend to represent their constituents less equally than Democratic ones, a significant portion of the reason is the asymmetric nature of ideological polarization in Congress, and the fact that Republican MCs are, by and large, simply more ideologically extreme than Democratic ones.

Conclusions

This chapter has demonstrated the importance of political context in shaping how well, and how equally, lower-income citizens have their views represented in American politics. I have argued that broad patterns of representational inequity in general mask substantively relevant, contextually driven heterogeneity in the relative representation of the poor. I find that poorer citizens are better represented relative to the rich in low-inequality districts, in electorally competitive districts, and in districts with a Democratic MC. I also find some evidence that poor citizens are better represented relative to the rich in districts with a substantial organized labor presence. These findings all support the idea that poor citizens are better represented when they live in contexts that make their preferences more visible and more relevant to policymakers.

As in chapter 5, we should keep in mind that these results are from one Congress alone. Though the model of representation developed here is a general one and should not be bound to any particular time period, I cannot say for certain the degree to which the findings shown here are generalizable to other time periods.[8] In addition, this analysis has focused on representation as a general concept, dealing broadly with how citizens "ideological" and "issue" views are represented. This approach provides the ability to abstract away from idiosyncrasies in how MCs represent constituents on particular bills or in particular domains to gain a general understanding of the factors that affect relative representation of the poor. It is possible, however, that there is variation in representation across different types of issues, or that the issues on which wealthy or poor citizens are more advantaged might also vary across areas of the country.

This approach also only considers roll-call voting, one particular stage of the policy representation process (and, as we noted in chapter 5, one in which representational inequalities are likely to be relatively small). There are certainly other forms of representation that are also important to understanding the political influence of the poor. But the general framework—the idea that poorer citizens are better represented when their preferences are visible and relevant to policymakers—is certainly generalizable to other conceptions of representation.

Despite such limitations, these findings have important theoretical and substantive implications. Most important, we have learned that poorer citizens—because of lower levels of political engagement, attentiveness, or generally lower political and social visibility—largely hold views that are harder for policymakers to perceive, and are considered less relevant to the goals that policymakers wish to achieve. These factors combine to explain why lower-income citizens are, on balance, less well represented in the political system. But there are contextual factors that help to make the poor *more* visible and relevant to policymakers, and these factors increase the likelihood that the poor will have their voices represented.

Certain individual-level factors—the ability to donate large sums of money or communicate with policymakers in other ways, for example—increase the likelihood that individual citizens (whether rich or poor) will have their views heard and taken into account by policymakers. In much the same way, contextual factors—having organized interests ready to lobby on their behalf, or being in a location where their votes or political activity are pivotal to what MCs wish to achieve—can increase the likelihood that citizens' voices are heard and taken into account as well. In contexts where such factors overwhelmingly advantage the rich, policymakers will respond by favoring the rich. But in contexts where these factors tend to serve, at least in part, the interests of the poor, representational biases will be minimized or eliminated.

More substantively, these findings suggest that unequal representation is not necessarily a fundamental law of American political life. We need not think of representational inequality as something that is necessarily a natural outgrowth of a political system that relies heavily on private financing for campaigns, or that places relatively few restrictions on the amount that moneyed interests can spend lobbying and persuading MCs. Clearly, there is reason to suspect that such factors play a role in shaping an unequal political system (Bartels 2008). But more local contexts matter as well: even though these factors—private financing, constant contact from more resource-rich constituents—apply nearly everywhere, representational inequality is not constant everywhere. Rather, it is either exacerbated or diminished by particular institutional and contextual arrangements that affect the quality of representation that rich or poor citizens receive. The results, for example, point to specific contextual attributes that tend to enhance the political influence of the poor. To the extent that these factors might be considered in debates over districting or the like, they can provide a starting point for thinking about how political institutions can be designed in a way that equalizes political influence across income lines. I return to this point in the concluding chapter.

Still, the results in this chapter also point to two unsettling implications. The first pertains to the finding regarding the importance of rich-poor opinion gaps to representational inequality. Put simply, we see that the poor are less well represented when their views differ most sharply from the wealthy. So variance in representational inequality is driven not just by substantive factors but also by the more straightforward notion that when MCs are presented with a clear opportunity to represent the views of the wealthy over the poor, they tend, consciously or not, to take it.

Second, and perhaps more important, most of the things that we have seen in this chapter to be associated with higher levels of representational inequality *across districts* have also been increasing *over time*. At the national level, labor unions are in a sharp decline, policymakers are becoming more extreme, and income inequality is increasing. To this point, we have looked only at cross-sectional analysis, examining the landscape of opinion and representation at particular, recent points in time. But political contexts vary across time as well as across space. Have such contexts changed in a way that the political system, in general, has become less representative of the poor? It is that question to which we now turn.

SEVEN

Political Inequality over Time

We have seen that biases in representation across income lines are, in large part, context dependent, driven by the presence or absence of factors—high levels of income inequality, low levels of unionization, and the like—that serve to affect how visible and relevant poor citizens are to their MCs. The work in chapter 6, like most work on this topic, though, looks at only a single snapshot in time: it either explores representational biases at one particular point in time (e.g., Bartels 2008; Erikson and Bhatti 2011; Rigby and Wright 2013), or implicitly assumes that the representational biases between rich and poor are constant over time (Ura and Ellis 2008; Soroka and Wlezien 2010; but see Gilens 2012). But given evidence that representational bias varies across areas as a function of politically relevant contextual characteristics, there is reason to think that the factors that affect the political influence of the poor might also vary across time.

This chapter explores the time-varying nature of unequal representation, focusing on how relationships between MCs and their lower- and upper-income citizens have varied over the past several decades. Using measures of dyadic representation similar to what were developed in chapters 5 and 6, I find that the magnitude of unequal representation has increased over this time period, particularly over the past 20 years. The reasons for this increase in representational inequality are diverse and somewhat ambiguous, but point to the same sorts of contextual explanations that were discussed in chapter 6. Several aspects of the national political environment relevant to representation have changed over the past few decades, and nearly all of them have changed in a way that negatively bears on the political representation of the poor.

The results support the assertions of prominent scholars (most notably, the APSA [2004] task force on Inequality) that many recent developments in American politics—polarization, inequality, the decline of organized labor—have served to not only disadvantage the poor economically but disadvantage them politically as well. Factors that one might reasonably expect to adversely enhance the power of wealthier citizens relative to poorer ones are on the rise in the United States, in other words, so it stands to reason that inequality in political representation has grown as well. In particular, the results highlight the corrosive nature that polarization and ideological extremity has had on political representation generally, and representation of the poor specifically. The notion that party polarization decreases the congruence between citizens and their elected officials is well established in comparative research (see, e.g., Dalton and Anderson 2011): the results show that a similar dynamic is at play in the American case.

Measuring Dyadic Representation over Time

Chapters 6 and 7 used recent CCES data to introduce the idea of dyadic proximity representation: the connection between what citizens say that they want, and what elected officials do, on some broad dimension of political conflict. The goal was to relate the ideological leanings of citizens to the ideological leanings (and choices) of the MCs who represent them. This chapter seeks to operationalize this same concept, using similar measures, over a longer time period. To do so, I turn to data from the American National Election Studies (ANES). The ANES has asked citizens an ideological self-identification question (similar to that used in the CCES) since 1972: I use this seven-point self-placement to measure citizen "ideology" for purposes of this analysis, and use this measure to calculate the measure of ideological proximity representation that will be featured in this chapter.[1]

This self-placement measure suffers from the same limitations as the similar one used in chapters 5 and 6: most notably, that it provides a limited picture of where citizens stand on important political issues. In particular, as we have noted in chapter 5, political ideology among American citizens has both symbolic (the ways in which citizens think of themselves politically) and operational (the stances that citizens hold on relevant, specific, political issues) components. That these components can be conceptually distinct from one another in some cases.[2] Self-placement is the most commonly used measure of *symbolic* orientation, important to how citizens think and act. But it is only one aspect of the broader concept of ideology (Free and Cantril 1969; Jacoby 2000; Ellis and Stimson 2012). While operational and symbolic orientations are essentially indistinguishable in the minds and actions of policymakers and political elites (Ellis and Stimson 2012), they can be, and often are, distinct concepts in the minds of ordinary citizens.

To provide a check on the possible shortcomings of the self-placement measure, I also develop a simple measure of citizens' operational ideology using a specific policy-related question that also has been asked consistently since 1972: a seven-point self-placement scale asking citizens about their views on government intervention in the market economy:

> Some people feel that the government in Washington should see to it that every person has a job and a good standard of living. Others think the government should just let each person get ahead on his/her own. Where would you place yourself on this scale?

This question is obviously limited in scope, and does not get at the much broader range of policy issues that go into a full measure of operational ideology. But it does hit at a central and enduring aspect of the "proper size and scope of government" divide that comprises the central operational ideological dimension in American politics (Stimson 1999). As a practical matter, responses to this question correlate quite strongly with broader and more robust measures of operational ideology using a much wider variety of survey questions (Ellis and Stimson 2012). As in the earlier chapters, employing multiple measures of the same wide-ranging concept, and finding similar results for each, will help to validate the results to come.

Responses to these two questions are used to create two separate measures of individual-level proximity representation that simply calculate the ideological distance between a citizen's symbolic and operational placements and his or her MC's ideological leanings. As earlier, the ideologies of MCs are measured using their first-dimension DW-NOMINATE scores, both citizen and legislator measures are standardized before calculation, and proximity scores are scaled to a 0–100 scale to aid in interpretation.[3] The results are individual-level measures of proximity that relate citizens' self-placements to the NOMINATE scores of their MC in the year that their ANES survey was conducted. These measures are available for every ANES respondent who responded to the standard self-placement questions in each survey year since 1972.[4] I label the measure using ideological self-placement as *ideological proximity*, and the measure using the jobs-income scale as *operational proximity*.

At the individual level, the measures of symbolic and operational proximity correlate with one another at 0.37, suggesting that they are tapping the same general concept of representation, but are not redundant. In most of the analyses to come, I will focus on proximity representation using the ideological self-placement measure, since it has the strongest parallels to the measures created using the CCES data in earlier chapters. Results across measures, however, look very similar to one another: I will note where there are substantive differences between what is learned using the symbolic and operational proximity measures.

Income and Representation over Time

With this measure in hand, we explore the nature of inequality in representation across income lines. Because of the way in which income data is standardized in the ANES cumulative data, analysis in this chapter will focus almost exclusively on income terciles: respondents are divided into income terciles relative to others in their survey year. As discussed in more detail in chapter 5, the focus on income terciles clearly has its limitations—when commenters talk about "the rich controlling politics," it's highly unlikely that people near the bottom of the top tercile are who they have in mind. But again, tercile-level analysis is an important focus of the literature on political inequality, and allows us to understand how biases in representation as commonly defined by political scientists have changed over time.

As a first look at inequality in representation, I simply pool across all ANES years (1972–2012) to calculate the mean *ideological* and *operational* proximity for each income tercile. Table 7.1 presents these results for both measures. Aggregating across all ANES survey years, the results show something similar to what is seen using the more recent CCES data: a modest, but significant, bias in favor of wealthier citizens. The average gap between the top and bottom terciles is 1.6 points using the ideological self-placement scale, and 1.9 points using the jobs-income scale.

TABLE 7.1. Representational Biases, 1972–2012

	Ideological Representation (Self-Placement Scale)	Operational Representation (Jobs-Income Scale)
Top Tercile	21.0	24.4
Middle Tercile	21.5	24.9
Bottom Tercile	22.7	26.3

Source: American National Election Studies Cumulative File.

More important, though, is understanding how this representational bias has changed over time. Figure 7.1 disaggregates the above results, presenting the mean representation gap between the top and bottom terciles in each ANES survey year from 1972 to 2012. This chart makes a clear point: the representation gaps between rich and poor have gotten substantially bigger over time, particularly in recent years. Though wealthier citizens have nearly always enjoyed modest representational advantages over the poor, these advantages have grown both larger and more consistent in recent decades. In the period 1972–94, the average rich-poor representation gap was roughly one point, and there were three years (1972, 1980, 1984) in which poor citizens were on average closer to their MCs than were wealthy ones (though this difference is not statistically significant in any of these years).

After 1994, however, wealthy citizens are always on average more proximate to their representatives than the poor, and these differences have grown in magnitude since that point. Since 2008, the gap between rich and poor is roughly five points. The simple conclusion here is that the representational advantages that the wealthy enjoy over the poor are not time-invariant: the gap in the political influence across income lines has grown fairly substantially over time.

Understanding the Growth in Political Inequality

The remainder of this chapter works to explain why these economic biases in representation across income lines have grown over time. First, it is important to rule out three plausible explanations for growing inequality that do not fit with the data. First, growing representational inequality is not simply a function of the changing racial and ethnic composition of the citizenry. It is well known that racial and ethnic minorities tend to be disadvantaged in the political process compared to whites (e.g., Canon 1999; Hero and Tolbert 1995), and that representational inequities across racial lines appear to be an enduring aspect of American politics (Griffin and Newman 2008). Given the correlations between income and race/ethnicity, it is plausible that growing representation gaps can be attributed in whole or in part to the poorest income tercile becoming composed more fully of nonwhites.[5] But the representation gaps cannot be attributed to changing demographic patterns alone: though whites in all three terciles are on average better represented than their nonwhite counterparts of similar income, the representation gap between upper- and lower-income

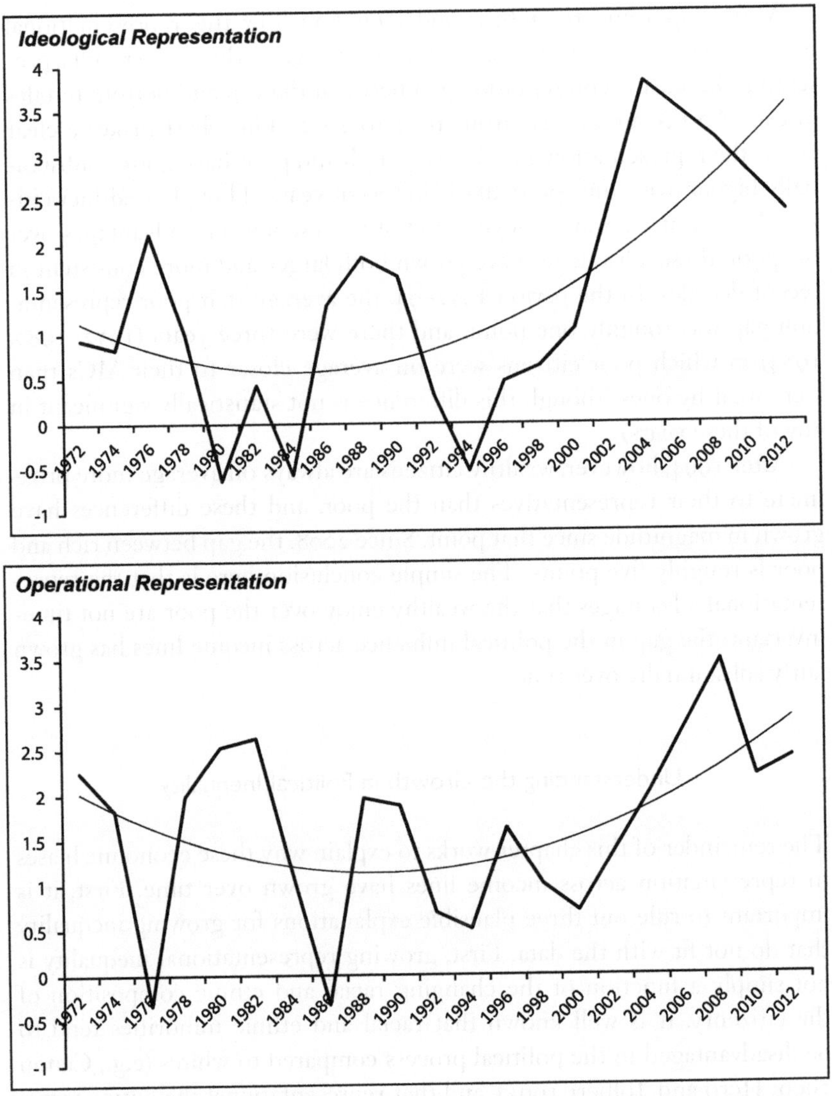

Fig. 7.1. Ideological and Operational Distance Gaps between Top and Bottom Terciles

Note: Data points represent the difference between the mean ideological distance between MCs and their top- and bottom-tercile constituents.

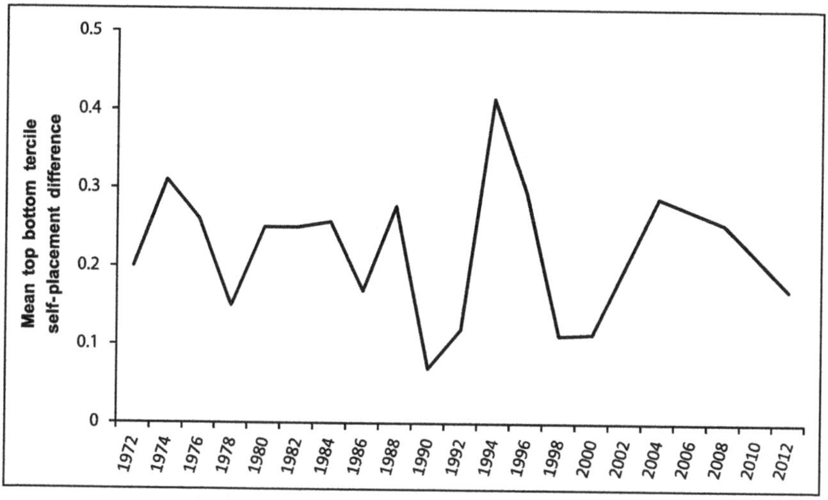

Fig. 7.2. Mean Self-Placement Preference Differences between Top and Bottom Terciles

Note: Data points represent the difference between the mean conservatism of top-tercile respondents and the mean conservatism of bottom-tercile respondents.

whites essentially mirrors that in the public as a whole: the time-series presented in figures 7.1 and similar series excluding all nonwhite respondents correlate at 0.92 (ideological proximity) and 0.94 (operational proximity).

Second, growing representational biases cannot be attributed to growing differences in what citizens of different income groups want from government. As we have argued earlier, when different groups want broadly the same thing from government, it is impossible for MCs to represent one group's views better than those of another group, even if they wanted to. But preference differences alone cannot explain the changes we see here. Figure 7.2 illustrates the mean difference between top- and bottom-tercile self-placement scores over time, showing that the mean difference between these scores has remained essentially constant. Top- and bottom-tercile citizens have always held, on average, relatively similar ideological self-placements, and this has not changed over time. A similar pattern emerges when it comes to operational views. Poor citizens have always been more in favor of government intervention (as measured by the jobs-income scale), but, again, the *magnitude* of this difference has not markedly increased over time. It is certainly the case that larger opinion divergences create the potential for larger representational biases: indeed, that is what we saw in chapter 6. But differences in the relative representation of income groups have grown even while differences in the views of these groups have not.

Third, growing representational inequalities between rich and poor are also not driven by growing *participatory* inequalities between rich and poor. We know that policymakers pay more attention to the politically active (Griffin and Newman 2009), and that differential rates in participation across income levels explain at least some (though by no means all) of the representational bias between income groups at any given point in time. But there is no evidence that wealthier people are becoming better represented because they are participating in politics at greater rates relative to the poor.

Figures 7.3 and 7.4 provide broad measures of (self-reported) political participation from the ANES: voter turnout, and a six-point scale of political activism (whether respondents have tried to influence the vote of others, attended political meetings or rallies, did volunteer work for parties or candidates, displayed political signs or stickers, donated money to parties or candidates, or written to elected officials) for all three income terciles. The results show that gaps in voter turnout across terciles have remained relatively constant over time, and gaps in political activism across terciles have become modestly smaller over time. The poor are becoming less well represented relative to the wealthy, but, at least in broad terms, this is not a result of the poor becoming disengaged from political life: if anything, the opposite appears to be true.

If growing representational inequalities cannot be explained, in full or in large part, by demographic change in the electorate, by diverging policy views of income groups, or by growing political disengagement among the poor, then we must turn to other, structural, factors to help explain growing representational bias. Chapter 6 introduced a number of factors that, at any given point in time, help to explain why poorer citizens are less well represented than upper-income ones. The purpose of the rest of this chapter is to examine the role of these factors in explaining the declining representation of the poor over time. The short version of the story is simple: the American political system has undergone a number of structural changes over the past several decades, and nearly all of these factors have changed in a way that is likely to be disadvantageous to the poor.

We have seen, for example, that ideological extremity on the part of MCs disadvantages the poor, both because extreme policymakers hold policy views that are especially out of step with their lower-income citizens, and because, on average, more extreme MCs tend to be more beholden to primary constituencies and the preferences of organized interest groups. By nearly every measure, parties have moved farther from the ideologi-

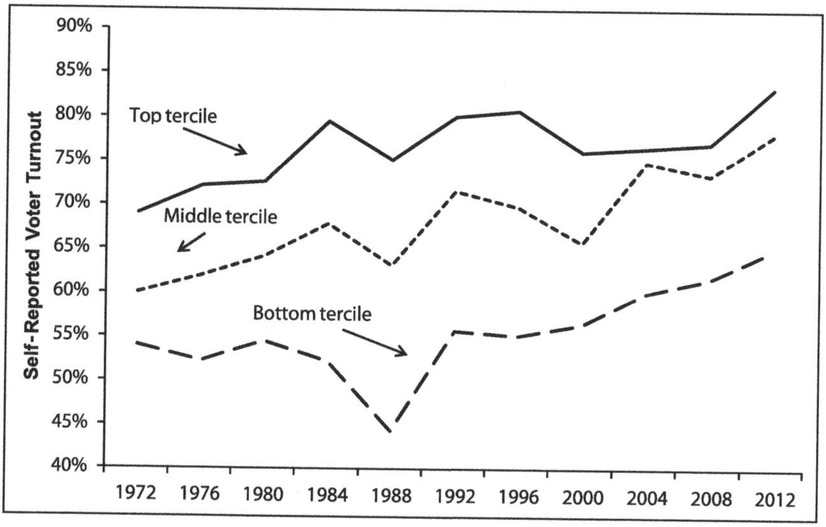

Fig. 7.3. Voter Turnout by Income Group, 1972–2012
Source: American National Election Studies Cumulative File.

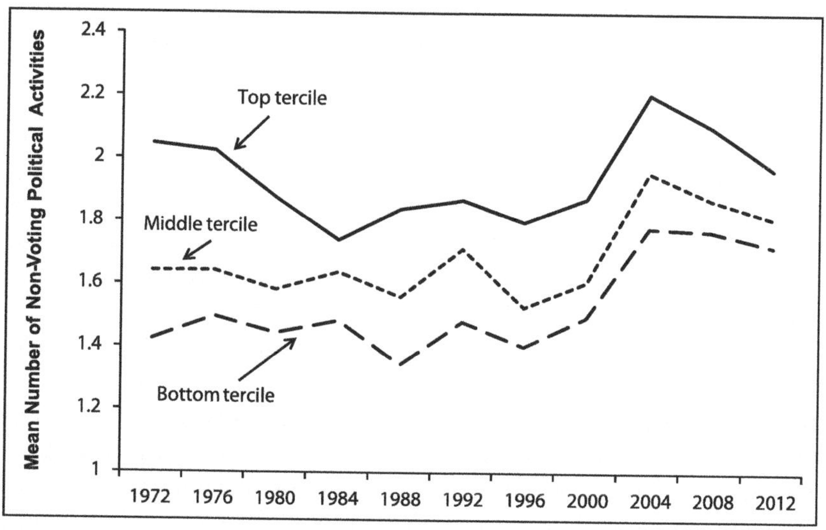

Fig. 7.4. Political Activism by Income Group, 1972–2012
Source: American National Election Studies Cumulative File.

cal center over the past few decades. The reasons behind this polarization are diverse and still subject to debate (e.g., Carson et al. 2007; Theriault 2008; Hirano et al. 2010), but the end result is clear: the level of ideological distance between Democratic and Republican elites is large and growing larger.

Polarization has increased nearly linearly since the 1970s, and the parties today are as polarized as in any era since Reconstruction. This polarization affects the representation of the poor in at least two ways. First, it almost by definition increases the mean ideological extremity of MCs—and extreme MCs represent their less affluent constituents poorly. Second, recent work also suggests that high levels of party polarization tends to inhibit the passage of legislation that might benefit the interests of the poor relative to the rich (Bonica et al. 2013; Enns et al. 2014).[6]

In addition to growing over time, we also know that this polarization is asymmetric: Republicans have moved farther from the center than have Democrats. This asymmetrical extremity is one of the reasons that Republican MCs tend to represent their upper- and lower-income constituents less equally than do Democratic MCs. This increasing Republican extremity in the House corresponds, at least in a broad sense, to a time of increasing Republican strength in the House: after controlling the House for only four years from 1933 to 1994, for example, Republicans have been the majority party more often than not since 1994.

In addition, we have seen that the poor are less well represented in districts with low levels of unionization. Unions serve as the most prominent interest lobby that works to explicitly represent the interests of lower-income citizens: low levels of union strength in a given district mean that policymakers have less incentive to represent (or even hear) the views of lower-income citizens in those districts.

Union strength has, of course, been on a decades-long decline in the United States. Again, the reasons behind the decline of organized labor, particularly private-sector organized labor, are diverse (see Wallarstein and Western 2000 for an overview), but unions are very clearly nowhere the political force, either in terms of numbers or political clout, that they were in the middle of the 20th century. Figure 7.5 illustrates this, showing the percentage of all employees, and private-sector employees, that are represented by a labor union over time. Union members have declined as a percentage of the workforce in nearly every year: in 1972, 24 percent of workers were represented by a union; in 2012, only 11 percent were.

Finally, we have seen that districts with highly uneven distributions of

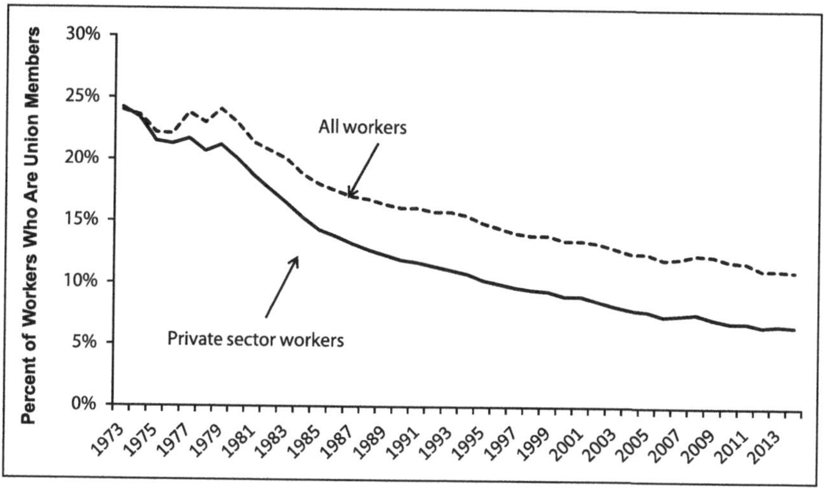

Fig. 7.5. Unionization Rates in the United States
Source: www.unionstats.com

incomes also represent lower-income citizens poorly: in both the United States and cross-nationally, greater economic inequality is generally associated with greater political inequality (e.g., Goodin and Dryzek 1980; Solt 2008). And, by nearly any measure, income inequality is increasing over time as well.

The overall trend, then, is for the factors that are associated with representational inequality across space to also be increasing over time. Figure 7.6 illustrates this, graphing the representation gaps between the top and bottom terciles from figure 1 alongside indicators of polarization (as measured by the difference in mean Democratic and Republican NOMINATE scores), Republican Party strength (as measured by the percentage of House members that are Republicans), income inequality (the U.S.'s Gini coefficient), and unionization (the percentage of private-sector workers represented by a labor union, reverse coded in the graph such that higher values correspond with lower levels of unionization). To place all of these metrics on the same scale, the graph transforms each measure into a series showing movement between its minimum and maximum values over the time period for which data is available. In all, the correlation between the growing representational inequity and each of these measures is quite high: the representation gap time series correlates with the polarization series at 0.71, the unionization series at 0.60, the Gini series at 0.64, and the Republican representation series at 0.52.

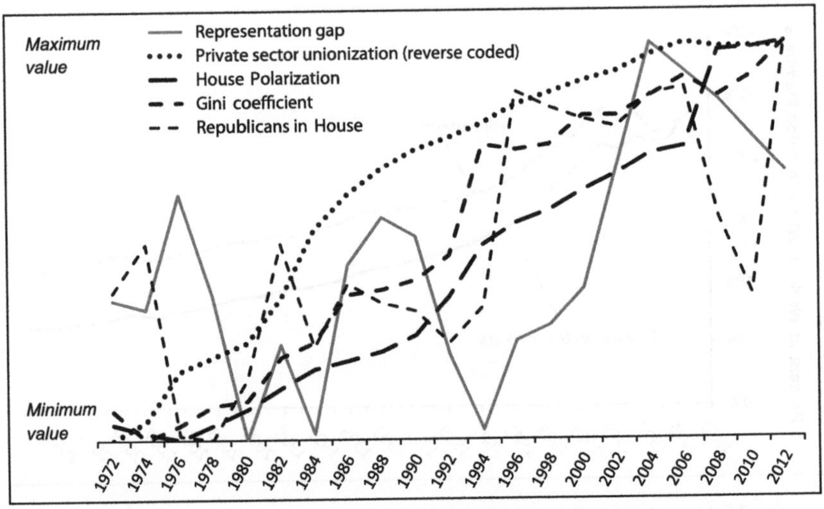

Fig. 7.6. Predictors of Economic Biases in Representation, 1972–2012

Where and Why Has Representational Bias Grown?

Teasing out the precise causes of the growth in representational inequity is empirically difficult. First, as figure 7.6 shows, many of the factors that might explain changes in representational inequity over time are changing in ways that are highly correlated with one another. In addition, the analytic leverage to address these issues at the district-level is limited: unlike in more recent years—where very large-*N* surveys such as the CCES have been regularly employed to study representation at the district level—ANES district-level samples are comparably quite small. Further complicating matters is that the ANES is designed to produce samples that are representative of the nation as a whole, not any individual district. So a large number of districts are not sampled at all in any given year. And, of course, decennial redistricting means that districts themselves are not static entities. I thus first turn to a more inductive strategy, seeking to identify patterns in the data that might suggest that certain explanations are more powerful than others.

District Partisanship and Party Control

Party control is one of the most important cross-sectional explanations of representational inequity: for a variety of reasons, Democrats tend to represent poorer constituents' views better than Republicans do. We see these representation biases in the ANES data as well. On average (pooling across the entire 1972–2012 time period), Republican MCs are nearly 5 percentage points closer to their top-tercile constituents than their bottom-tercile ones, while there is no significant difference between top- and bottom-tercile distances for Democrats.

But while Democrats tend to represent poor citizens more equally than Republicans do *in general*, there is little evidence that the trend toward weighting the views of the wealthy more strongly *relative to those of the poor* has been restricted to Republicans alone. Figure 7.7 separately graphs the top-bottom tercile ideological proximity gaps for citizens in districts represented by Republican and Democratic MCs. Though the absolute size of the gap between Republican and Democratic MCs differs significantly in nearly every year, the general trend toward greater representation of the wealthy is similar across party lines. The substantive interpretation of this trend differs across parties: for Republican districts, it means that a representational bias in favor of wealthier constituents has become even larger over time, while for Democratic districts, it means that the modest representational advantages enjoyed to poorer citizens over richer ones have disappeared or perhaps reversed. The fact that Congress has been, on average, more Republican in more recent years than it was in the past matters to understanding why unequal representation has grown—if the House is composed more heavily of representatives that, on average, represent their constituents less equally, this will have consequences for the aggregate size of representation gaps. But the greater relative emphasis given to the views of the wealthy does not appear to be a phenomenon restricted to Republicans.

In addition to individual MC party, we might also consider changes in party control of the House, or of the government in general, over time. Party control might affect relative representation for several reasons: when Republicans control the House, they may be more likely to structure the legislative agenda such that salient issues (and votes) tend to be those that divide rich and poor, for example, or they may be more likely to pursue policies that benefit the material interests of wealthier citizens at the expense of other citizens (Bartels 2008).

Here, we find at least suggestive evidence that party control may matter. For starters, the significant increase in representational inequality occurred at the same time as the initial Republican takeover in the House in 1994. Representational biases between top- and bottom-tercile citizens (as measured by ideological proximity) are greater when Republicans con-

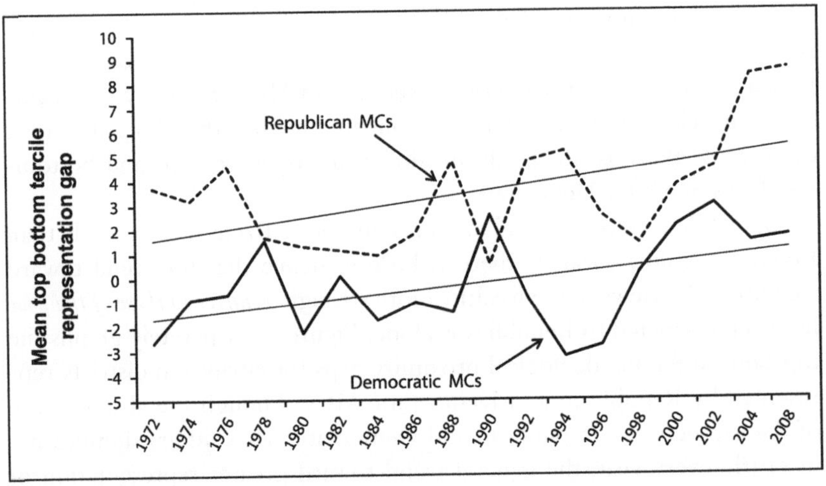

Fig. 7.7. Top-Bottom Tercile Representation Gaps by MC Party

trol the House (mean difference = 1.90, σ_{mean} = 0.65) than when Democrats control it (mean difference = 1.20, σ_{mean} = 0.32), and greatest of all when Republicans control all three branches of government (mean difference = 5.31, σ_{mean} = 0.67). But the analytic utility of these analyses is clearly limited: Republican control of the House is limited to two periods of time: the period between 1996 to 2004, and 2012 ANES surveys. Republicans had unified control of government only for the 2004 survey. So while periods of Republican control correspond with periods of greater inequality in representation, it is hard to directly point to Republican control as the cause of such inequalities. The fact that gaps between income groups did not diminish when Democrats (briefly) regained control of the House in 2008 seems to argue against a purely party-control based explanation for representational inequity, but the question remains open. With Republicans having assumed unified control of the presidency, Senate, and House of Representatives as of 2017, we might, however, reasonably expect representational inequality to continue to increase.

Polarization and Ideological Extremity

Perhaps clearer than the impact of partisanship on the relative representation of the poor is the impact of party polarization. By any measure, parties in Congress have become more ideologically distant from each other over the past few decades. One corollary of aggregate polarization, of course, is

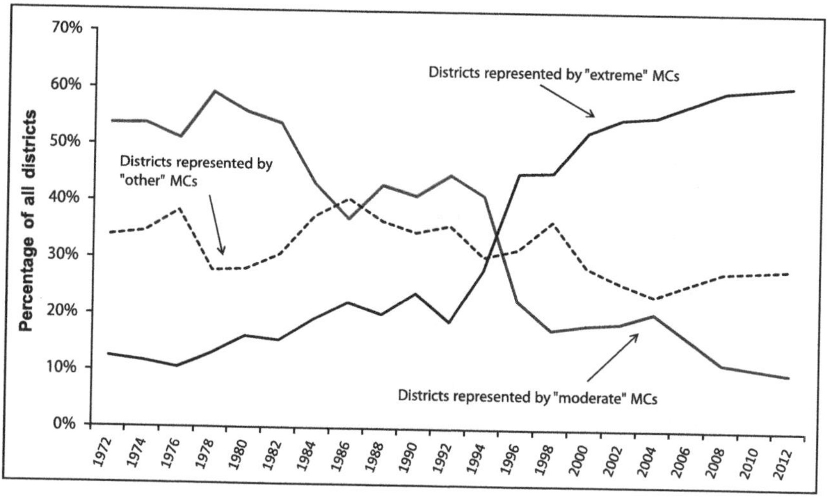

Fig. 7.8. Ideological Extremity of Individual House Members, 1972–2012

the greater ideological extremity of individual MCs. Figure 7.8 provides one way to conceptualize these changes in MC extremity, dividing districts into three categories: those represented by a "moderate" MC according to the Poole/Rosenthal (2007) definition of the term (operationalized as an MC whose absolute NOMINATE score is less than 0.25); those represented by an "extreme" MC (operationalized as an MC whose absolute NOMINATE score is greater than 0.5); and those represented by an MC who falls between these "moderate" and "extreme" categories. The trend is clear: moderates have very nearly vanished from the House, while ideologically extreme MCs have nearly become the norm.

Polarization has had a number of important effects on the linkages between citizens and elected officials. Perhaps most germane here is the argument that polarization may have weakened the representative link between citizens and policymakers (e.g., Fiorina 2012). Does ideological extremity make a difference to how wealthy and poor citizens are represented relative to one another? The ANES data strongly suggests that it does. Figure 7.9 illustrates this point, pooling the data from 1972–2012 and examining ideological distance representation, by income tercile, for each of the three types of districts shown in figure 7.8. This figure makes two clear points. First, it reinforces the findings from chapter 6 that MC extremity leads to lower levels of representation: the average distance between citizens and their MCs (of all income levels) is greater in districts with extreme members than moderate ones. Second, even apart from these

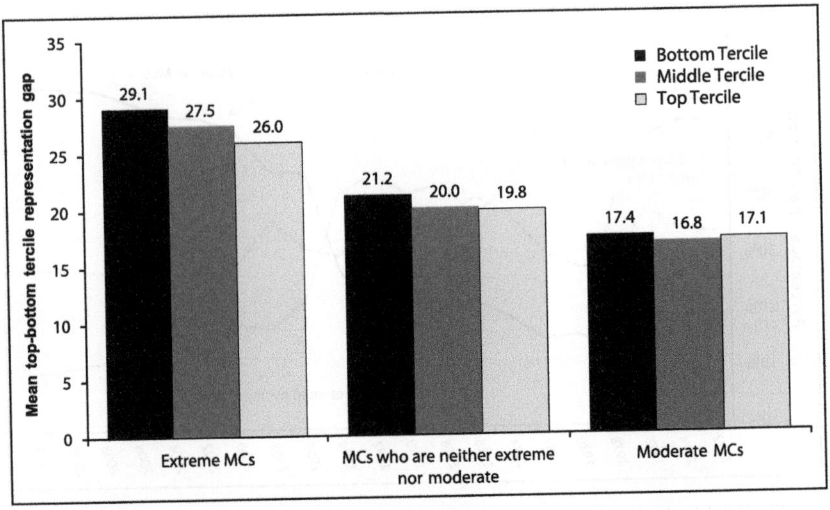

Fig. 7.9. Ideological Distance, by MC Extremity

generally low levels of representation, poor citizens are disproportionately disadvantaged by ideological extremity: there is essentially no relationship between income and ideological distance in districts with moderate MCs, while the gaps between top- and bottom tercile citizens in districts with extreme MCs is more than three points.

Differences in representational biases in "moderate" versus "extreme" districts hold across party lines as well: while Democratic MCs tend to on average represent poor constituents better than Republican MCs, moderate Democrats represent the bottom tercile better relative to the top tercile than extreme Democrats, and moderate Republicans tend to represent the bottom tercile better relative to the top tercile than extreme Republicans. The gaps also hold across time: moderate MCs represent their constituents more equally than extreme MCs in each of the four decades in which data is available. Ideological extremity on the part of individual MCs is clearly associated with representational inequality, and the mix of MCs who might be considered "extremists" has grown substantially over time.

Unionization

While unionization in the United States is in the midst of a decades-long decline, these rates of decline are not consistent across the country. Some areas of the United States have seen private-sector unionization nearly vanish over the past several decades, while the decline in other locations has been more modest (e.g., Dickens and Leonard 1985; Clark 1989; Hirsch and MacPherson 2002, 2013).

If declining unionization rates were responsible for the decrease in representational inequality over time, we would expect to see two things. First, inequality of representation across income lines would be greater in districts with low levels of unionization than in districts with high levels of unionization. Second, declines in representation over time would come primarily from contexts in which unionization rates have also seen steep declines.

Because congressional district boundaries change every 10 years, doing apples-to-apples comparisons relating changes in a district's unionization rate to changes in its representational inequity over time is impossible.[7] Data showing rates of unionization *by state*, however, are available since 1984 (Hirsch and MacPherson 2013), so we can explore the relationship between *state-level* unionization and *district-level* representation.

Doing so requires assuming that rates of unionization (and changes in the rates of unionization) that we see at the state-level are roughly mirrored at the level of each individual district within that state. This assumption is not terribly heroic in small or relatively homogenous states (Wyoming, Kentucky), but is potentially more problematic in large, geographically diverse ones (New York, California). States in which economies differ dramatically across areas of the state—a manufacturing-rich sector in one portion of the state, with a more high-tech workforce in a different part of it—are particularly problematic for this sort of classification. But at the same time, laws that make it either easier or harder to organize—"right to work" laws, most notably—are in large part state-level statutes, and thus will apply in many of the same ways to different districts within a state, regardless of the mix of economic activity within that district.

There is thus some reason to suspect that state-level unionization rates will have an association with district-level unionization rates regardless of the type of state under consideration. The use of state-level data clearly limits the inferences that can be made regarding the effects of unionization. But with these caveats in mind, this analysis can provide at least a basic look at how unionization within a given context affects the relative representation of different income groups over time.

Figures 7.10 shows levels of private-sector state level unionization at two time periods: 1984 (the first year in which state-level unionization data is available) and 2012 (the most recent year in which data is available).[8] The results illustrate the general decline in unionization over time, but also

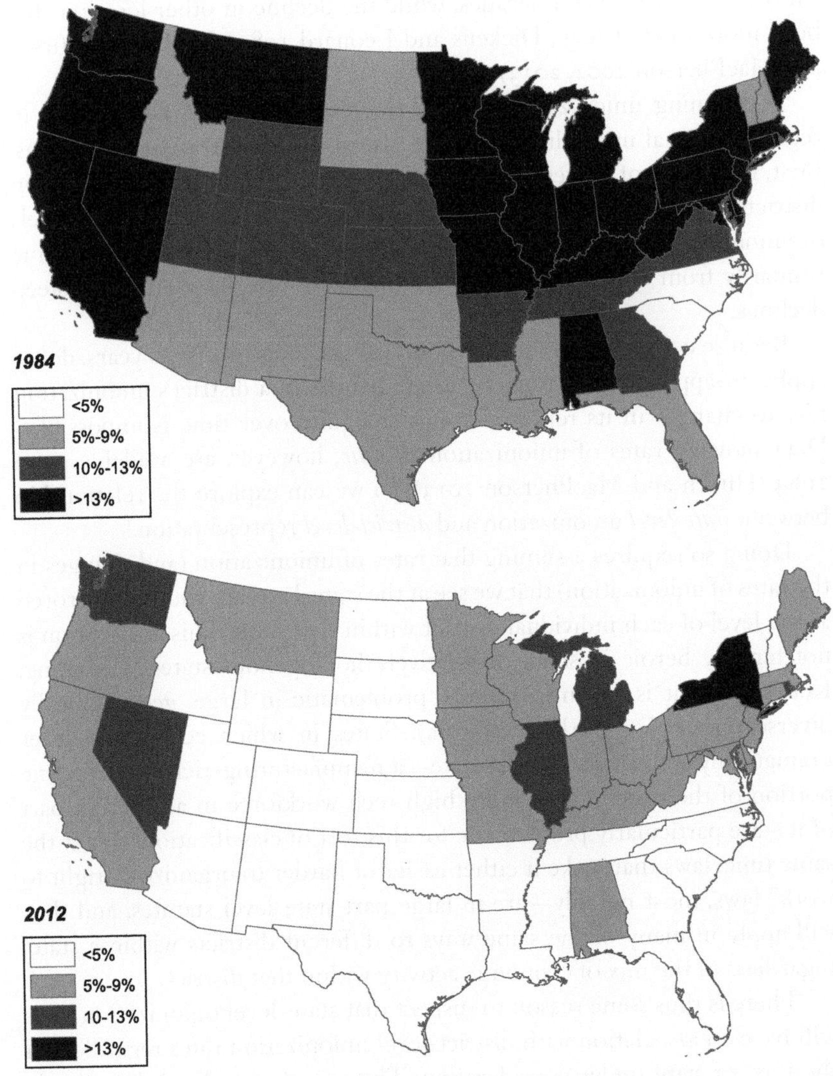

Fig. 7.10. Private-Sector Unionization Rates by State, 1984 and 2012

illustrates pockets of the country where unionization rates have changed only modestly, and other areas where they have changed fairly dramatically. Unionization rates have declined in every state from 1984 to 2012, but the magnitude of these declines varies greatly, ranging from less than 1 percent to more than 15 percent.[9]

Now we turn to the effect of unionization on representation. When it

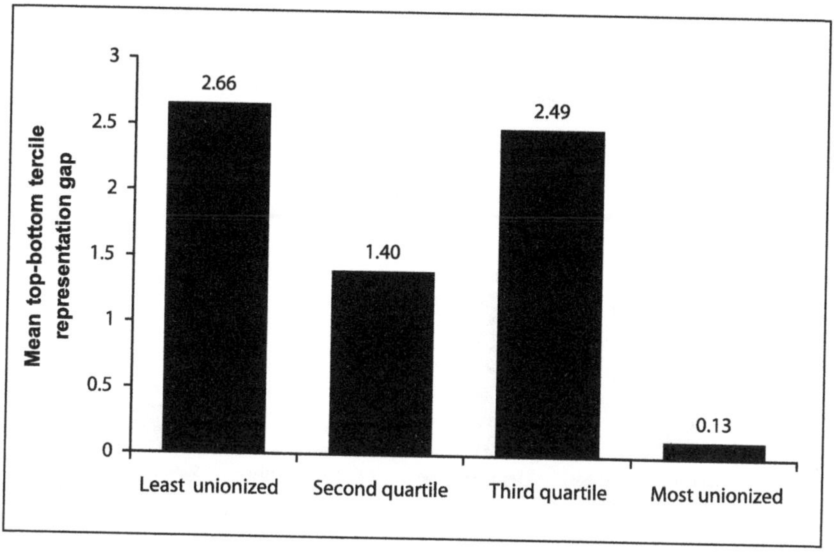

Fig. 7.11. Top-Bottom Tercile Proximity Representation Gaps, by Unionization Rate

comes to the first issue noted above—are low rates of unionization correlated with high levels of representational inequity?—the answer is, by and large, yes. Figure 7.11 pools all of the ANES data from 1984 to 2012, classifying citizens into four quartiles based on their state's rate of private-sector unionization during the year that their ANES survey was conducted. The figure displays the mean top-bottom tercile gap in representation for each of the four unionization quartiles. Representational inequities generally decrease as unionization rates increase, and in the most heavily unionized districts there is on average essentially no representation gap at all. This supports the idea that unionization matters to representational equity, but this also may simply illustrate that declines in unionization have taken place alongside declines in political equality. High-unionization districts in this pooled analysis, by and large, come from earlier time periods: nearly half of the districts in the pre-1990 era, for example, are classified as "top quartile" unionization districts, while only 3 percent of districts in post-2000 are classified this way.

A better, or at least different, way to examine the power of the unionization explanation for declining representational equity is to examine differences in how states' unionization rates have changed. Have contexts that have seen the greatest *declines* in unionization over time also seen the greatest declines in the relative representation of rich and poor? The data

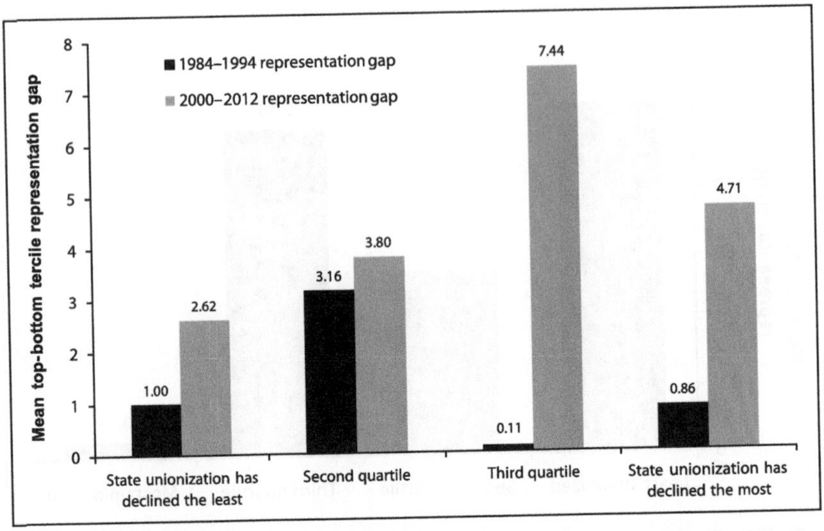

Fig. 7.12. Changes in Representation Gaps, by Changes in State-Level Unionization

again suggests that unionization can explain at least some of the growing representation gap between income groups.

Figure 7.12 divides respondents into four quartiles based on changes in their state's unionization rate from 1984 to 2012: those categorized in the bottom quartile come from states that saw the smallest decline in unionization over this time period, while those in the top quartile came from states that saw the largest decline in unionization rates. It then compares the mean gap in top-bottom tercile representation for two time periods: the first years in unionization data is available (1984–94) and the most recent years of data available (1998–2012).

Though the relationship is not quite linear across quartiles, the figure shows that contexts where unionization has declined at a faster-than-average rate have experienced faster-than-average declines in the relative representation of the poor. In states where the unionization rates has declined the slowest, representation gaps between income groups have grown, on average, 1.62 points (2.62 – 1.00) between the earliest and latest time periods. In the quartile with the fastest-declining unionization, the gap has increased more than twice as much (4.71 – 0.86 = 3.85). In the quartile with the next-fastest decline in unionization, representation gaps have grown even faster. Of course, there may still be other factors that correlate with state-level decline in unionization that is driving the differences seen in figure 7.12. But at a minimum, the evidence shows that representational inequities have grown the fastest in areas where unionized labor is showing its steepest decline.

Income Inequality

We might also consider the connections between rising income inequality and representational inequality. In the aggregate, inequality has increased fairly substantially over time in the United States, but, again, the magnitude of this rise varies quite a bit across areas of the country. We would expect, if growing income inequality is the real driver of growing political inequality, that representational bias will have grown the greatest in contexts where inequality has risen the fastest.

Again because of the limitations caused by districting and the available data, we have the ability to examine changes in inequality only at the state level—so all the caveats that apply to relating state-level changes to district-level changes also apply here. Figure 7.13 graphs state-level Gini coefficients in 1972 and 2012 (the first and last years for which ANES survey data are available). Here, the data tells a somewhat more homogenous story: every state has a markedly more unequal distribution of incomes than it did in the 1970s. But, interestingly, we see that the variation in *how* unequal incomes are across states is much greater in the later time period than the earlier one: the standard deviation of the state-level Gini measure, for example, is nearly three times as large in 2012 as it is in 1972. The country in general has grown apart when it comes to income, but that growth is much more strongly concentrated in some places than in others.

Figure 7.14 pools data from 1972–2012 to calculate the mean top-bottom tercile representation gap for four quartiles of districts based on their state's level of income inequality during their ANES survey year. Consistent with what would be expected from chapter 6, the more unequally incomes are distributed, the more unequally representation is. And as with public sector unionization, the degree to which citizens fall into a "high inequality" or "low inequality" quartile is strongly dependent on when their ANES survey was conducted: all but two states in 1972 are considered "low inequality" contexts for purposes of this analysis, while all but nine states in 2012 are considered "high inequality" contexts.

Figure 7.15 looks more explicitly at the role of changing state inequality, dividing respondents into four quartiles based on their state's degree of change in income inequality between 1972 and 2012. Districts classified in the top quartile, for example, are in states where inequality has increased at

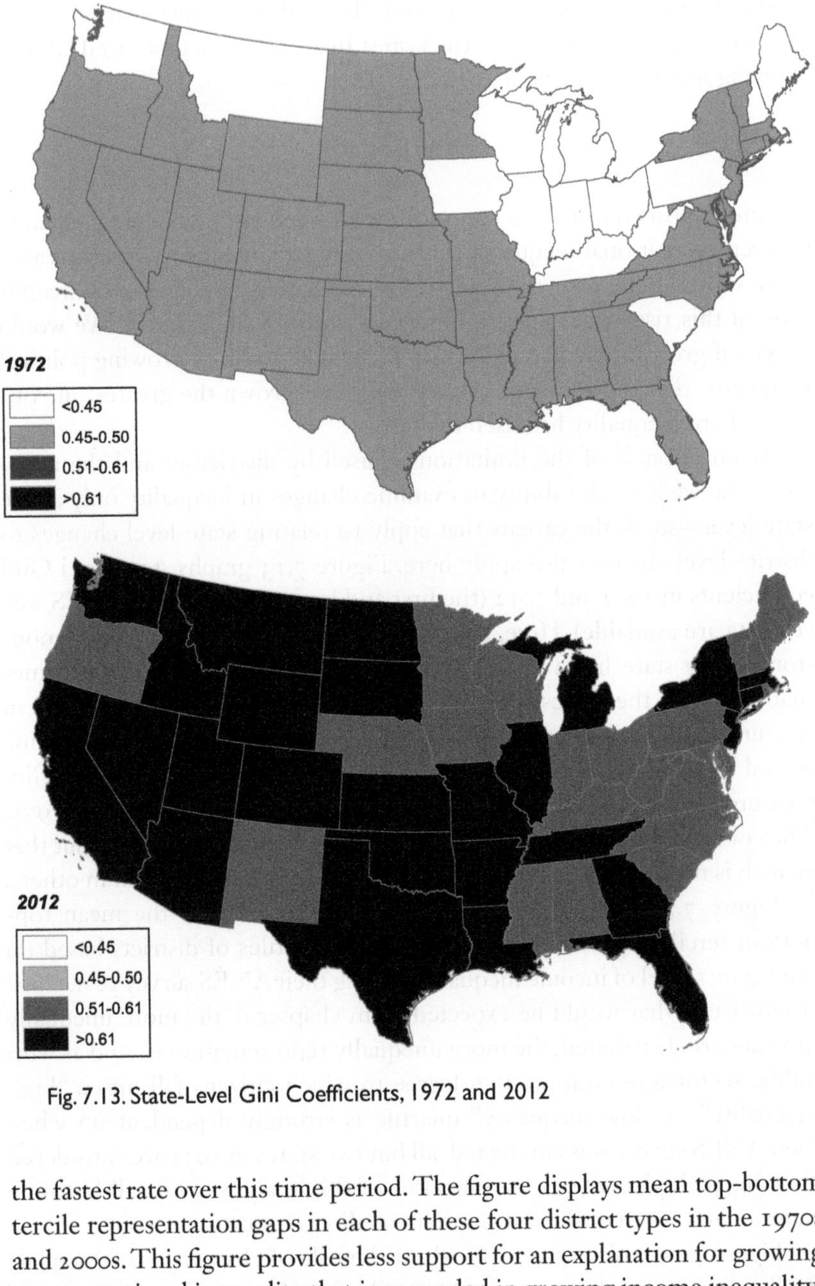

Fig. 7.13. State-Level Gini Coefficients, 1972 and 2012

the fastest rate over this time period. The figure displays mean top-bottom tercile representation gaps in each of these four district types in the 1970s and 2000s. This figure provides less support for an explanation for growing representational inequality that is grounded in growing income inequality: we might expect that representational bias would have grown the most in states where income inequality has been increasing at a similarly rapid rate.

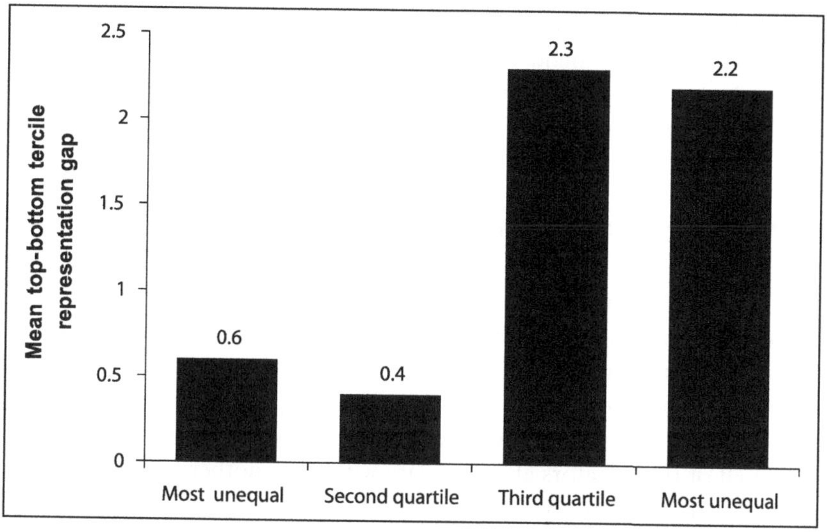

Fig. 7.14. Top-Bottom Tercile Proximity Representation Gaps, by District Inequality

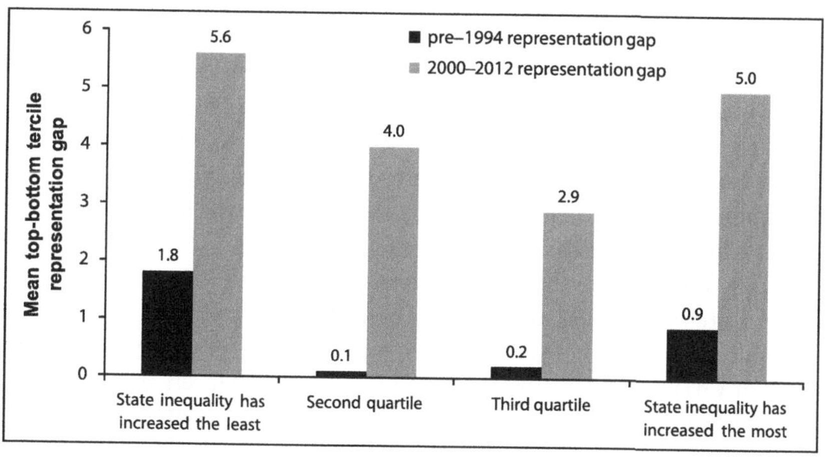

Fig. 7.15. Changes in Representational Biases, by Changes in State-Level Inequality

But there are no significant differences in "quickly growing inequality" and "slowly growing inequality" states in how representational biases have changed over time. If anything, representational bias is growing the fastest in states that have experienced relatively slow growth in income inequality.

Multivariate Analysis

The above discussion suggests several plausible reasons to explain why representational inequality has grown over time: polarization, changes in the partisan composition of the House, unionization, and (to a lesser extent) income inequality all correlate with the growing representational gaps between upper- and lower-income citizens. The problem, of course, is that all of these factors also correlate with one another (and with time), making it difficult to tease out any one as being responsible for growing representational biases.

In this section, I attempt to shed addition empirical light on the relative contribution of each of these factors to political representation, pooling data from all ANES survey years and modeling the dyadic relationship between citizen preferences and MC behavior as a function of income, the contextual characteristics outlined above, and the interaction between income and the contextual factors. These models were created by pooling the ANES data from 1972 to 2012, employing a multilevel strategy in which individuals are nested within congressional district-years, and assigning respondents the characteristics of their district (or state, in the case of unionization and inequality) at the time that their survey was conducted.

These models, like those in chapters 5 and 6, seek to explain variance in the representation (as measured here by our ideological and operational proximity measures) between a citizen and his or her MC. The key independent variables are income (measured at the tercile level) and the interactions between income and measures of the political context in which a citizen resides. I include five contextual measures in the analysis: *Republican control* (a dummy variable measuring whether Republicans are in control of the House in the year in which the survey was conducted); *Republican representation* (a dummy indicating whether a citizen's MC was a Republican); *MC extremity* (operationalized as the absolute value of a respondent's MC's NOMINATE score); *unionization* (operationalized as the rate of private-sector unionization in the respondent's state of residence in the year in which his or her survey was conducted); and *income inequality* (operationalized as the rate of private-sector unionization in the respondent's state of residence in the year in which his or her survey was conducted).

The goal here is to isolate the contextual factors that are particularly disadvantageous to the representation of the poor. The key coefficients, again, are thus those for the interaction terms: significant interactions indicate that a contextual variable affects how well top- and bottom-tercile citizens are represented relative to one another.

I estimate two sets of models: one for ideological proximity representation, and a second for operational representation. Results are presented in tables 7.2 and 7.3. The first five columns of each table present the results for each of the types of individual-contextual interactions separately, while the final column includes all five interactions.[10] The first columns provide some support for four of the five potential explanations for representational inequality: when it comes to both measures, bottom-tercile citizens are less well represented relative to the top tercile in districts represented by

TABLE 7.2. Modeling Ideological Proximity Representation, 1972–2012

	Dependent variable: Ideological Proximity					
Income (terciles)	0.25	−1.13*	0.64*	0.17+	−1.11*	−0.06*
	(0.16)	(0.34)	(0.24)	(0.10)	(0.31)	(0.20)
Income * Republican Representation	−2.71*					−1.50*
	(0.24)					(0.33)
Income * Republican Control		−0.67+				0.15
		(0.39)				(0.21)
Income * MC Extremity			−3.45*			−3.37*
			(0.55)			(0.84)
Income * Income Inequality				−0.41*		−0.26
				(0.18)		(0.33)
Income * Unionization					−0.51+	−0.33
					(0.27)	(0.30)
Republican Representation	9.08*					2.32*
	(0.72)					(0.75)
Republican Control		1.68				−0.05
		(1.74)				(1.48)
MC Extremity			31.53*			31.99*
			(1.23)			(1.88)
Income Inequality				4.81*		−0.25
				(0.39)		(0.72)
Unionization					−4.91*	−1.57*
					(0.63)	(0.60)
Constant	20.64*	24.57*	10.83*	3.82+	28.88*	12.30*
	(3.58)	(1.74)	(5.48)	(2.22)	(0.67)	(4.37)
R^2	0.02	0.01	0.11	0.03	0.02	0.11
N	25,458	25,458	25,458	25,458	18,317	18,317

Note: Table entries are OLS regression coefficients (standard errors are in parentheses). * $p < .05$, + $p < .10$

Republicans, in districts with ideologically extreme MCs, in districts with low levels of state unionization, and in districts with high levels of income inequality. There is little statistical support, however, for the "Republican control" explanation: simply living in a time where Republicans control more branches of government does not, in itself, exacerbate representational inequalities.

The final models pool all five contextual explanations together in a general model. In these final models, only Republican representation, MC extremity, and unionization remain as significant predictors in the two sets of models. Importantly, after including contextual predictors in this pooled model of representation, a simple interaction between income and time is not statistically significant in either set of models (though an income-time interaction is significant when it is included in a model without contextual predictors).[11] What this shows us is that while the poor have become less well represented than the wealthy *over* time, one need not conceive this

TABLE 7.3. Modeling Operational Proximity Representation, 1972–2012

	Dependent variable: Operational Proximity					
Income (terciles)	1.68*	−1.21*	0.55*	2.56+	−1.63*	−0.06
	(0.17)	(0.35)	(0.25)	(0.11)	(0.31)	(0.21)
Income * Republican Representation	−6.39*					−6.39*
	(0.26)					(0.36)
Income * Republican Control		−0.15				0.05
		(0.18)				(0.22)
Income * MC Extremity			−4.11*			1.28*
			(0.60)			(0.64)
Income * Income Inequality				−0.61*		−0.29
				(0.20)		(0.35)
Income * Unionization					−0.81*	−0.61+
					(0.30)	(0.33)
Republican Representation	15.53*					11.34*
	(0.57)					(0.80)
Republican Control		−0.84*				−0.08
		(0.39)				(0.48)
MC Extremity			34.11*			28.00*
			(1.29)			(2.00)
Income Inequality				4.62*		−0.34
				(0.41)		(0.35)
Unionization					−5.38*	−1.66*
					(0.65)	(0.70)
Constant	20.82*	28.63*	14.31*	1.36	33.00	15.03*
	(3.65)	(1.82)	(0.55)	(2.31)	(7.17)	(4.58)
R^2	0.02	0.01	0.10	0.02	0.02	0.13
N	28,058	28,058	28,058	28,058	19,426	19,426

Note: Table entries are OLS regression coefficients (standard errors are in parentheses). * $p < .05$, + $p < .10$

relationship as a simple function *of* time: rather, easily identifiable changes in the national environment—and, by extension, the mix of congressional districts that have low levels of unionization, a relatively extreme MC, a Republican MC, or (to a lesser extent) highly unequal distributions of income—can explain the declining political representation of the poor. Understanding growing political inequality, in other words, is a matter of understanding the changes in the political context that have served to disadvantage the poor.

Conclusions

This chapter has explored the time-varying nature of representational inequality across income lines, seeking to understand whether the representational biases identified in much recent research have persisted across recent American political history. The findings indicate that while income-based inequalities in dyadic representation are nearly always present, such biases have grown substantially in strength and consistency in recent years. The growth in the magnitude of these inequalities correlates strongly with other contextual changes in the political system that one might expect to be associated with greater disparities in political influence.

The rise in party polarization seems to be a particularly strong factor in understanding why representational inequalities have grown: ideologically extreme MCs (of both parties) represent their constituents' ideological views more equally than ideologically moderate ones, and polarization has led to a substantial rise in the number of MCs that can be considered, by historical standards, extreme. Declining unionization may also play a substantial role in why representational inequalities have grown: heavily unionized contexts are far more conducive to political inequality than less unionized ones, and the decline in the power of organized labor has led to a shrinking number of contexts in which we might expect the views of the poor to be on equal footing with those of the wealthy.

This analysis, of course, has several limitations. First, it focuses exclusively on representational disparities at the income tercile level, which very likely obscures ways in which the political influence of the extremely wealthy has grown, even compared to those who are merely "well-off." Given that the greatest increases in the concentration of wealth have happened at the very top of the income distribution (citizens in the 66th percentile of the income distribution, for example, have not fared all that much better in terms of income growth in the past few decades than citizens in the 33rd percentile), and given that very wealthy citizens might be particularly apt to use political resources to influence policy outcomes, this analysis almost certainly understates the magnitude of change in the political influence of top- and bottom-tercile citizens.

In addition, the available data and shifting nature of congressional districts over time limits the ability to make firm influences regarding the precise causes of the growth in political inequality over time. Much of the analysis here focuses on differences in congressional district "types": if changes in the political context (for example, declining unionization or polarization) are responsible for growing inequality, then it stands to reason that political inequality should be growing fastest in the contexts in which these changes are particularly pronounced. Though these aggregate analyses provide support for the idea that particular changes in the political context explain declines in representation, the available data (the ANES sample sizes are not large or representative enough to permit district-level inferences, and the survey does not sample all districts in all years) and the nature of congressional districts themselves (the boundaries of which are redrawn in multimember states each decade) do not allow for precise, consistent comparisons connecting over-time changes in a district's attributes to changes in how equally its citizens are represented.

Third, the list of explanations offered here certainly leaves out some other factors that are potentially responsible for some of the increase in political equality. Campaigns for the House of Representatives have on average gotten more expensive, for example, and the increase in the "cost" of earning a seat in the House may also serve to enhance the importance of donors and potential donors to policymakers. In addition, changes in how citizens communicate with elected officials, and how elected officials communicate with and attempt to persuade constituents, might serve to increase the influence of those who are already "resource rich" (e.g., Miler 2010).

Even with these caveats, though, this analysis has implications for our understanding of representational inequality in the United States and elsewhere. Most broadly, the results here illustrate a substantial growth in representational inequity, particularly in the past 20 years. This finding has several implications. It, of course, helps to confirm the assertion that growing income inequality has a significant political component (Bartels 2008). More important, it also provides support for the notion that growing inequality is politically self-reinforcing: rising income inequality, combined with related changes in the political system, can (by making it more likely that policymakers will disadvantage the poor) make it harder for the political system to address rising inequality through policy initiatives (see Bonica et al. 2013).

On the other hand, the analysis suggests, consistent with the cross-sectional analysis in chapter 6, that there is little inherent in the American system of government to suggest that large differences in the political voice of rich and poor is a natural facet of political life. Scholars have noted for decades that policymakers always have incentives to pay greater attention to the views of the "resource rich": those who vote, donate, or participate in other ways (Peel and Donnelly 1935; Key 1949; Piven and Cloward 1988; Lijphart 1997). And the wealthy have always had political resource advantages over the poor. But it is only in recent decades that the distance between citizens and their MCs has been strongly conditioned by income. A high level of political inequality, at least in this sense, is not necessarily the natural state of affairs in American politics. Rather, recent structural changes in American political and economic life appear to be the most important causes of this rise in political inequality. Addressing these changes in a way that might help to bring greater political equality is, of course, extraordinarily difficult. But at least such factors are identifiable.

Finally, it is worth noting that the focus here has primarily been on representational inequities—the degree to which wealthier citizens' views are better represented in government *relative to those of the poor*. But this does not mean that wealthier citizens' views have become better represented in an absolute sense: if anything, wealthier citizens' views are actually *less* well reflected by their MC's votes than they were 30 years ago. Rather, the growing divergence in the representation of rich and poor has been driven entirely by a decline in the representation of the poor, not an increase in the representation of the well-off. This suggests, building from the assertions of Fiorina (2012), that not only does party polarization appear to be a driving factor behind growing political inequality, it has served to significantly weaken the overall representational linkage between citizens and policymakers.

EIGHT

Putting Inequality in Context

In the preceding chapters, I have described and empirically examined a contextual model of class politics in the United States. At the aggregate level, large inequalities in incomes manifest themselves in a number of outcomes that we might consider normatively undesirable: among them are unequal participation in the political system and unequal representation of citizen interests in policymaking. But these outcomes do not occur uniformly or monolithically across the country; rather, they are at least in large part a function of particular contextual arrangements that serve to either depress, or exacerbate, political inequality.

This concluding chapter highlights some of the critical findings of the past few chapters, and offers some concluding thoughts on the implications of these findings for understanding representative democracy in the United States. First, I address the issue of how citizens—particularly those on the "losing end" of political inequality—view and respond to the sorts of phenomena that have been highlighted in this book. Second, I highlight the theoretical and substantive implications of the findings in the previous chapters—examining how the approach taken in this book might help us better think about the political implications of income inequality and possible solutions to the problem of unequal political influence.

Are the Poor Noticing Political Inequality?

Given the relatively low (and declining) levels of representation of the poor, it is natural to wonder whether lower-income citizens are noticing unequal representation and, if so, if they are doing anything about it. These questions in many ways dovetail with the work of scholars in a variety of fields (e.g., Bolton and Roland 1999; Hacker and Pierson 2011; Bonica et al. 2013) who ask why democratic processes—which ultimately operate on the principle of "one person, one vote"—have not slowed the widening gap between the haves and have-nots. Are poor citizens noticing and responding to the notion of unequal influence?

When it comes to noticing an unequal political playing field, the question might be framed as one of political efficacy. Table 8.1 collects questions related to the concept of efficacy from a wide variety of national surveys, and segments responses to them by income tercile.[1] The ways to conceptualize and measure political efficacy are wide-ranging and diverse, but the overall body of evidence is clear: on essentially every measure, there is a connection between income and one's confidence in the political system. Poorer citizens are more likely to see government as untrustworthy, and more likely to see corruption in the system, than are upper-income citizens.

Perhaps most tellingly, they are significantly less likely to see the system as being responsive to people like themselves. Only the last of these questions—whether one thinks his or her own MC usually does the "right thing"—gets at the specific sorts of dyadic relationships discussed in most of this book. But they are illustrative of a more general lack of faith that the political system is representative of the needs, interests, and values of the poor.

This disparity in political efficacy is important in its own right, and has a number of other implications that speak to the broader health of the democratic system. First, personal efficacy is a key part of the decision to participate in politics: citizens are less likely to get involved if they feel like their participation will not matter (Verba, Schlozman, and Brady 1995). Second, efficacy affects perceptions of the legitimacy of the political system itself (Dalton and Anderson 2011). Third, perceptions of the efficacy of the political systems are socialized into children and new participants (Easton and Dennis 1967; Campbell 2006). As a result (and particularly in an age of stagnating economic opportunity), lower-income citizens are entering the political system with a diminished belief that they can or should contribute to changing it. The consequences of all this are wide ranging, but suffice it to say for now that the fact that the political system is tilted toward the interests of upper-income citizens is not lost on those with lower incomes.[2]

TABLE 8.1. Political Efficacy by Income Level

Question	Source	Bottom Tercile	Middle Tercile	Top Tercile
Percent agreeing with "government does not care much about what people like me think"	General Social Survey (2014)	65%	57%	51%
Percent agreeing with "Most politicians are in politics only for what they can get out of it personally"	General Social Survey (2014)	63%	58%	45%
Percent who think "a lot" or "almost everyone" in government is corrupt	General Social Survey (2014)	45%	33%	32%
Percent who are satisfied with the way things are going in the country today	Pew Polarization Survey (2014)	25%	25%	33%
Percent who think that the United States' best days are behind it	Pew Polarization Survey (2014)	52%	48%	43%
Percent agreeing with "People like me don't have any say about what the government does"	Pew Political Values (2012)	58%	54%	47%
Percent agreeing with "Voting gives people like me some say about how government runs things"	Pew Political Values (2012)	64%	70%	77%
Percent who are "very" or "somewhat" optimistic about the future of the United States	Pew Political Futures (2010)	50%	57%	68%
Percent agreeing with "People like me have no say over how government runs"	Annenberg (2008)	62%	56%	46%
Percent agreeing with "sometimes politics is too complicated for people like me to understand"	Annenberg (2008)	65%	49%	33%
Percent agreeing with "My opinions on things don't count very much"	DDB Lifestyle Survey (1998)	48%	40%	29%

Source: 2008 Annenberg Election Study; 2014 General Social Survey; 2014; 2009 Pew Research Center Political Futures Study; 2012 Pew Research Center American Values Survey; 2014 Pew Research Center Polarization Survey.

Are the Poor Responding to Political Inequality?

When it comes to doing something about low levels of representation, the question becomes one of democratic accountability. Do citizens whose views are not being well represented by their elected officials hold such officials accountable, either at the ballot box or through other means? Do citizens in general, and low-income citizens in particular, respond in meaningful ways to how their policy views are represented by their MCs?

The 2014 CCES asked two questions related to the issue of democratic accountability at the level of the dyadic relationship between MCs and their constituents. First, the CCES asked respondents (on a four-point scale, ranging from "strongly approve" to "strongly disapprove") whether citizens approved of the job that their individual MC was doing in Congress.[3] Second, the survey asked respondents about their vote choice in the 2014 congressional election, getting at the question of whether they supported their incumbent MC enough to support his or her reelection bid, or planned to vote for someone else. For purposes of the analysis to come, I have coded responses to this question as simply "1" if respondents voted for their incumbent MC in the election, and "0" if they voted for someone else (nonvoters and those in districts with no incumbent running were excluded).

Although citizens decide how to evaluate their MC's job performance on a number of different dimensions, what we are interested in here is their ability to hold them responsible for policy representation specifically: whether citizens who are less well represented by the measures we have introduced earlier punish their MC, either by voting for someone else or by disapproving of their performance in office. Voting is an indicator of democratic accountability for obvious reasons. Approval can be considered a measure of accountability as well, given that a policymaker's approval rating matters for a number of reasons: it can scare off (or entice) quality challengers, and affect the sorts of things that they can accomplish in office.

To test the degree to which citizens hold elected officials accountable for policy representation, I model responses to these questions as a simple function of the ideological distance representation measure introduced in chapter 4 (as well as a control, in the vote choice model, for whether a citizen and MC shared a political party affiliation, or held opposing party affiliations). The initial results (presented in columns 1 and 4 of table 8.2) show a strong connection between ideological distance and MC approval and vote: coefficients for representation are significant and negative, meaning that citizens who were ideologically more proximate to their MCs were more approving of their job performance, and more supportive of their reelection bids, than citizens who were ideologically more distant from their MCs. This shows that, at least in this sense, democratic accountability occurs: citizens whose policy views are well represented by their MCs are more likely to reward them.

Importantly, though, we see (columns 2 and 5 of table 8.2) that these findings are moderated to a large extent by income. These columns simply interact the ideological distance variable with the CCES measure of income. These interactions are significant and negative, indicating that the impact of representation on accountability is greater for those with higher incomes—that is, that an MC's ideological proximity to upper-income citizens is more strongly rewarded than his or her proximity to citizens of lower incomes. Figures 8.1 and 8.2 give a sense of the mag-

TABLE 8.2. Income, Representation, and Accountability

	Dependent Variable: MC Approval			Dependent Variable: Voting for Incumbent MC		
	(1)	(2)	(3)	(4)	(5)	(6)
Representation	−0.50*	−0.29*	0.17*	−1.72*	−1.17*	−0.39*
	(0.01)	(0.02)	(0.02)	(0.03)	(0.07)	(0.10)
Income		0.060*	0.017 *		0.07*	0.04*
		(0.003)	(0.002)		(0.01)	(0.02)
Income * Representation		−0.31*	−0.012*		−0.08*	−0.05*
		(0.002)	(0.002)		(0.01)	(0.01)
Education			0.06*			0.10*
			(0.001)			(0.03)
Education * Representation			−0.033*			−0.10*
			(0.004)			(0.02)
Political Activism			0.19*			−0.06
			(0.001)			(0.06)
Political Activism * Representation			−0.07*			0.05
			(0.001)			(0.04)
Political Knowledge			0.50*			0.95*
			(0.01)			(0.09)
Political Knowledge * Representation			−0.34*			−0.78*
			(0.001)			(0.06)
Copartisan of MC				3.22*	3.16*	3.13*
				(0.06)	(0.06)	(0.06)
Constant	3.71*	3.29*	1.72*	1.74	1.26*	0.40*
	(0.01)	(0.02)	(0.02)	(0.02)	(0.08)	(0.13)
R^2 (pseudo-R^2)	.09	.10	.15	.36	.46	.47
N	51,499	45,823	40,028	25,750	24,278	22,917

Note: Table entries are OLS regression coefficients (columns 1–3) and logistic regression coefficients (columns 4–6). Standard errors are in parentheses. * $p < .05$

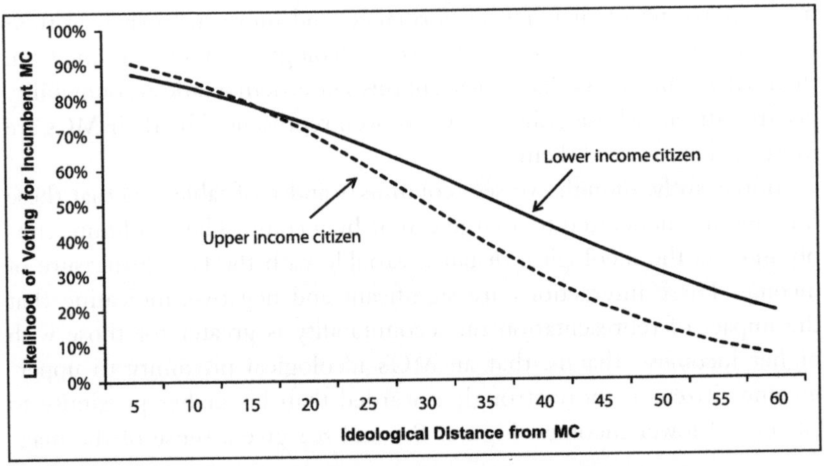

Fig. 8.1. Representation and the Likelihood of Incumbent Voting, by Income Level

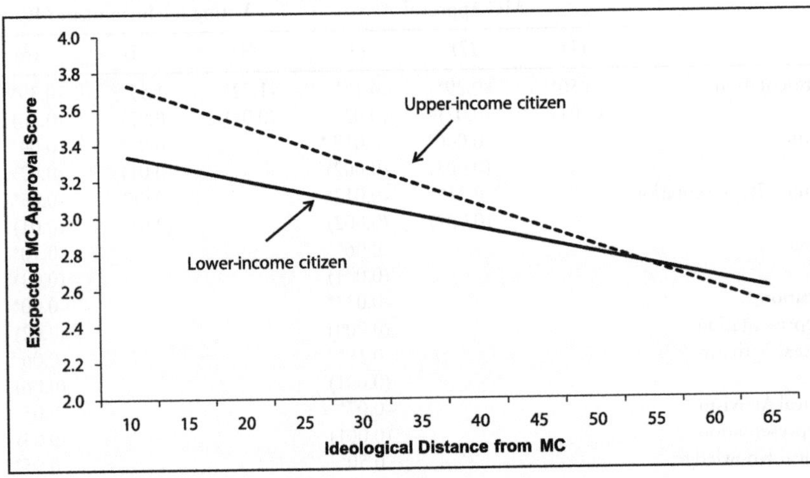

Fig. 8.2. Representation and MC Approval, by Income Level

nitude of these effects, showing the expected likelihood of voting for an incumbent MC (figure 8.1) and MC approval (figure 8.2) for hypothetical upper income (making $120,000 to $150,000 per year) and lower income (making $10,000 to $20,000 per year) citizens.[4] These citizens' expected MC approval ratings and incumbent MC vote probabilities are graphed as a function of the ideological distance between them and their MCs. The far left portion of the graphs represent citizens that we might consider very well represented (in the 90th percentile of ideological representation); the far right portion represents citizens that are very poorly represented (in the 10th percentile of ideological representation).

These figures illustrate what might be interpreted as a sizable "accountability gap" between higher- and lower-income citizens. All else equal, the "poorly represented" lower-income citizen is more likely to vote for an incumbent's reelection, and more approving of his or her job performance, than an equally poorly represented higher-income citizen. By contrast, the higher-income, well-represented citizen is more likely to both vote for and approve of an MC than a lower-income citizen who enjoys a similar level of representation. Policy representation appears to be more integral to the evaluations of upper-income citizens than lower-income ones.[5]

Importantly, these results are also robust for a variety of other factors that are correlated with both income and the ability to hold elected officials accountable. Columns 3 and 6 of table 8.2 include measures of formal education, political knowledge (using the scale developed in chapter 4), and political activism (using the scale developed in chapter 3), as well as the interactions between each of these variables and ideological distance representation. These other interactions generally behave as one would expect—the more educated, knowledgeable, and politically active exhibit a greater tendency to tie representation to approval. This makes sense: highly engaged citizens are more likely to notice and care about what their MC is doing in terms of policy. But while the inclusion of these variables explain some of the variance that had previously been attributable to income—the magnitude of the income-representation interaction decreases by around 50 percent in both models—the moderating effect of income remains strong.

It appears, then, that lower-income citizens are less likely to consider information about how well their policy views are represented when forming evaluations of their MCs, and that this tendency to be less attentive to policy representation is not simply a function of a lack of education or political attentiveness on the part of the poor. These results might be interpreted as reassuring: the fact that poorer citizens are not holding elected officials accountable for their comparably worse representation might mean that unequal representation is not necessarily a problem. If people are not likely to punish their elected officials for a particular type of behavior, it might mean that they do not really care about that sort of behavior after all. And at least at the margins, there is evidence that poor citizens care more about other things that their representatives do—bringing home distributive benefits to districts, or performing constituency service to solve individual problems—than do wealthier ones (e.g., Griffin and Flavin 2010). So perhaps a focus on policy representation is too limited to get at ways in which poorer citizens are actually receiving what they really want from elected officials.

There is some merit to this sort of view. But, on the other hand, these results might hint at even deeper problems in ensuring equality of political voice. First, while targeting benefits to specific district-level projects, or addressing the needs of particular constituents through service, certainly meet some of the needs of individuals and communities (and while these other forms of representation are undoubtedly important to forming meaningful links between citizens and their MCs), such actions in themselves are not sufficient to address the broader structural factors that underlie the rising divergence in incomes, similar divergences in economic opportunity, and the concentration of political power in the hands of more affluent citizens. Such problems are deeper and more structural (see Enns et al. 2014), and can generally only be addressed through larger-scale policy change.

Second, and perhaps more important, we should not take these findings as prima facie evidence that the poor do not care about policy representation as much as the wealthy do. Political scientists since at least Schattschneider (1960) have made a compelling case that citizens' disengagement from the mechanisms of electoral accountability is not necessarily a function of an inability or unwillingness to evaluate policymaker behavior. It is, rather, a reflection of the fact that the political agenda—the policy alternatives that both legislators and citizens get to choose between—is structured in a way that suppresses their interests and needs.

This book has said little about the topic of agenda setting in American politics. But suffice it to say for now that moneyed interests play a significant role in defining the range of acceptable policy debate and shaping the types of considerations that are a part of public debate. Money's influence over the political agenda is probably far greater than its influence over the votes or public statements that legislators make (Baumgartner et al. 2010).

Particularly paired with what we know about the lower levels of political efficacy among the poor, we might instead suggest that these results reflect a disengagement on the part of poorer citizens from a political system that does not put forth alternatives that they find compelling. Making the effort to become informed enough to hold leaders accountable for their policy positions, in other words, is less desirable when one feels that the system itself is unresponsive to your needs. This, of course, leads to a reinforcing cycle in which legislators have even less need to care about what their poorer constituents think about policy. As Erikson and Bhatti

(2012) state, "for [legislators] to ignore the poor is rational only if the poor ignore their [legislators]." If elected officials are not held accountable for not representing the poor equally—or, at a minimum, if their wealthier constituents hold them more accountable, for whatever reason—there is little compelling reason to expect them to do so.

Putting Inequality in Context

The basic point of this book is simple: context matters to how class politics manifests itself in political choices. Of course, contextual factors are not the only driver of political behavior—we have seen in nearly every analysis in this book that individual predispositions, resources, and experiences matter more than contextual ones to how citizens think. Context matters, in many if not most cases, at the margins.

But the margins matter in American politics: wild shifts in public opinion on important issues are rare, and relatively minor changes in the composition of the electorate, or the rates of participation of particular demographic groups, are enough to meaningfully change political outcomes. And even small policy shifts, particularly when they happen repeatedly, have great consequences over time for how citizens live their lives. The findings of this book illustrate that contexts matter, and do so in important, systematic, and predictable ways. When it comes to citizen behavior, local context matters because it provides the environment in which citizens encounter, and form judgments about, the social world. Though citizens are generally ignorant of detailed facts about policy and economic conditions (e.g., Gilens 2001; Soroka and Wlezien 2008), some of this information sinks through at a rudimentary level: most Americans are aware that income inequality is growing, and that job prospects for some types of lower- and middle-income workers are not what they once were.

Even so, though, these national statistics do not reflect the lived experiences of particular people in particular places—and it is these lived experiences, not aggregate conditions, that are more powerful drivers of how citizens think and act. An understanding of the political implications of inequality needs to pay close attention to how citizens experience that inequality in the course of their daily lives.

The importance of context is perhaps just as great for legislators—the environment in which a legislator's constituency is situated influences who that legislator hears from, who he or she deems important to listen to, and who is most important to the goals that he or she wishes to achieve.

These influences have important effects on what legislators do, and who they represent, in office. In some cases, these influences lead to poorer constituents enjoying representation that is as good, or even better, than their more affluent peers. Again, the main point is that while the aggregate trend toward growing inequality is clearly a central issue of modern American politics, how the political system reacts to that inequality is not monolithic, but is, at least in large part, a function of the immediate environment in which citizens and legislators experience that inequality.

Enhancing Political Equality

Of course, diagnosing the problem of political inequality is the easy part. Working to provide realistic and workable remedies for it is much harder. Part of the reason for this, of course, are that political and social institutions are deeply difficult to change—and a political system that works in many ways to disadvantage the voices of the poor is not especially likely to pass meaningful reforms that benefit the poor.

But even beyond these structural issues, the analyses in this book suggest that there are few easy or simple reforms, even in a world where some change was easy, that would work to clearly address the political disadvantages that poorer citizens face. Proposals to institute participation "floors" (such as mandatory voting) or "ceilings" (such as greatly restricted private financing of campaigns) would not fully address the problem of unequal representation. If anything, the analyses in chapter 5 speak primarily to the limited effect, at least in the short term, of some of these sorts of efforts. Disparities in political activity, as important as they are to understanding the overall health of the democratic system, collectively only explain a small part of the reasons why poorer citizens are less well represented in politics. The fact that poorer citizens are less visible and influential in all walks of social life seems to be at least as important to political inequality as the fact that poorer citizens vote or donate less.

Further, the analyses in this book suggest that some institutional or procedural reforms could work at cross-purposes to one another. A flurry of recent research (especially the excellent work of Carnes 2013) has bemoaned the near-dearth of policymakers from working-class backgrounds: such representatives, it is argued, would be much more in tune with the needs and values of lower-income citizens than policymakers from upper-class backgrounds (even if such policymakers have demonstrated a commitment to help and listen to the poor).

One might think that concentrating poorer citizens in districts that have large numbers of poor citizens would increase the likelihood that such districts would elect a representative that is sympathetic to the views of the poor, or even be from a lower-income background themselves.[6] It certainly would be easier to recruit poorer citizens to run for office in predominantly poor areas. But just as the "majority-minority" districts created by packing large percentages of racial and ethnic minorities into particular districts may have decreased the collective influence of minority interests in aggregate policymaking districts (Canon 1999), concentrating poor citizens in particular districts may have a similar effect on the collective representation of the poor. Perhaps more districts would elect representatives that care about lower-income citizens' interests, but at the expense of creating many more districts whose MCs can ignore the views of their poorer citizens entirely.

Despite these issues, the analyses here do offer insights that may be helpful in thinking about the role of contextual factors in shaping political inequality. Most important, the findings in chapters 5 and 6 sound a hopeful note: they suggest that political inequality need not be thought of as endemic to the U.S. political system, or any system that relies heavily on private funding for campaigns. Instead, this book argues that the propensity of policymakers to favor the rich over the poor is not a phenomenon that exists always and everywhere, but rather one that is best understood as context-dependent, driven in part by contextual and institutional characteristics that make it easier or harder for poor citizens to have their views represented by policymakers. Understanding the contextual factors that affect the relative representation of rich and poor citizens is important to developing a broader perspective on the relationship between income and political influence, and to thinking about the types of political institutions that might best facilitate democratic equality.

The "Double Disadvantage" of Concentrated Poverty

First and foremost, the findings reinforce the idea that poor people living in poor communities are disadvantaged in the political process. Sociologists, economists, and many others have long known that the "double disadvantage" of living in poverty in a community that is also mired in poverty has deleterious effects on educational and health status, life satisfaction, and many other outcomes. The analyses here show that these sorts of disadvantages extend to the political realm as well. Poor citizens who live in wealthier communities tend to participate more in politics and (if anything) are better represented than their counterparts in high-poverty areas. Importantly, the enhanced participation of poorer citizens in wealthy areas does not come at the expense of the participation or representation of others: when it comes to having a vibrant democracy, concentrated poverty is a deadweight loss to the system.

When combined with the findings from chapter 2 regarding the impact of population density on attitudes, what this means is that while growing economic inequality may be politically problematic, it is growing inequality combined with growing economic segregation that causes the most serious problems (see also Franko and Livingston 2015). Poor citizens in highly segregated environments do not have access to the sorts of political and social institutions that foster a healthy engagement in democratic life. And citizens of all income groups lack the regular interactions with people of different economic classes that serve to humanize and increase empathy for people who are not like oneself.

Addressing the rise of economic segregation is easier said than done. And, of course, in many communities, economic segregation is bound together with racial segregation in a way that makes dealing with it even more difficult. But these analyses show fairly clearly that addressing economic segregation is critically important to our broader political vibrancy: laws and policies that serve to segregate citizens in neighborhoods, school districts, or other geographic areas are deleterious not only because they detract from the economic opportunities and social health within given communities but because they also aggregate to create a more unequal national political system as well.

Polarization and the Declining Representation of the Poor

These results also highlight the importance of electoral safety (at the district level) and polarization (at the aggregate level) to political inequality. At the district level, we have seen that poorer citizens are more likely to be marginalized in districts where MCs can safely count on reelection. By contrast, when poor citizens are important to the formation of a winning electoral coalition—in situations, in other words, where "every vote counts"—MCs of both parties are more likely to take into account the views of lower-income citizens. Scholars in a variety of contexts have noted that the threat of electoral sanction is critical to democratic representation—as Druckman and Jacobs (2014) note, regular "scary elections" are necessary to foster accountability. This book shows that this logic especially rings true when it comes to the representation of the poor.[7]

At the aggregate level, the large number of safe, politically homogenous districts—combined with myriad other political and institutional factors—have led to a Congress that is as polarized as any in recent history. Political scientists have regularly found that, in a variety of ways, polarization and income inequality are inextricably entangled with one another: a polarized system, among other things, makes it harder for policymakers to pass inequality-reducing policies. This book illustrates a common denominator behind the connections between polarization and economic inequality: polarization makes the system less responsive to what the poor want. Much work, both academic and journalistic, has highlighted the ways in which a polarized political system poses threats to the health of American democracy. This book suggests that nowhere is this more true than when it comes to the issue of political inequality: an intractably polarized system has many negative effects, but its negative effects are greatest on the representation of the poor.

Civic Voice and Civic Mobilization

Finally, the findings of this book join the chorus of scholars calling for stronger and more robust civic participation—and, in particular, for stronger organizations to mobilize citizens who may not otherwise have the proclivity to get involved in politics. In the short term, equalized political participation is not a cure-all for the problem of political inequality: poor people are less well represented in large part because they are poor, not because they don't vote or aren't politically active. For those interested in remediating income-based biases in representation, a focus on increasing the political engagement of the poor, or placing restrictions on the political engagement of the wealthy, will be far from sufficient to eliminate income-based biases in representation without a more wide-ranging consideration of the role of wealth in shaping political and social systems. But this does not mean that participation is unimportant, particularly in shaping how policymakers consider the views of poorer citizens in the long term.

The findings in this book cannot explore, for example, the counterfactual situation where wealthy and poor did participate in politics at relatively equal rates. It is possible, for example, that an electorate in which participation was more equal across income lines might cause elected officials to pay more attention to the views of poor citizens. Such an environment would certainly make it more likely that poorer citizens have a greater say over the long-term political agenda—the sorts of issues that are regarded as legitimate topics for public debate and discourse (Schattschneider 1960).

And this book has also shown the impact that organizations mobilizing on behalf of nonwealthy citizens can play in shaping both the participation decisions and the representation of those citizens. This book has focused in particular on the role that unions play in serving as both a mobilizing force of and political voice for the poor. Low levels of unionization decrease the need for policymakers to pay attention to the views of the less fortunate: inequalities in representation are at least one consequence of this.

But unions are not the only organization that can encourage political participation among lower-income citizens: public interest and community organization groups, as well as certain types of religious institutions, have also served as an instrumental voice in providing the sorts of skills and motivations that less fortunate citizens need to participate in politics (Verba, Schlozman, and Brady 1995). These organizations have served as a political counterweight to the resource advantages that well-off citizens tend to have. This book further highlights the importance of these sorts of groups to political equality: collectively, they serve to both encourage the participation of lower-income citizens, and—perhaps more important—provide such citizens the visibility they need for lawmakers to both perceive their concerns and take such concerns seriously. In an era where labor unions appear to be in permanent decline, perhaps these organizations will be left to take up the task of mobilizing the poor and ensuring that their voices are heard by policymakers.

On Context and Political Voice

The United States is a diverse place. Different regions and areas share a common respect for and attachment to constitutional principles and fundamental democratic norms, but vary dramatically in the living environments that they offer, the political cultures that they (implicitly or explicitly) endorse, the opportunities and choices that they offer citizens, and the laws by which citizens must abide. We learn a great deal by studying the implications of these differences in how we live.

Even highly formal, aggregated models of public opinion change (e.g., Wlezien 1995; Stimson 1999; Erikson, MacKuen, and Stimson 2002) implicitly rely on citizens using local experiences to form political judgments. Citizens don't generally know the size of federal, state, or local education or infrastructure budgets, or whether such governments have increased or decreased spending in the past year. They have an easier time learning whether the local schools are hiring teachers, or whether the roads have more traffic and potholes than they used to have. In the absence of a great deal of abstract, policy-specific knowledge, citizens rely on immediate experiences to develop attitudes on what policymakers are doing, the direction the country is headed, and what should be done in the future (Soroka and Wlezien 2008). In much the same way, we can better understand the implications of growing income inequality by studying how citizens in different parts of the country—as well as the legislators who represent them—experience that inequality in their daily lives. Put simply, inequality matters. But it matters differently in certain places than in others.

We can also use the insights gained by studying contextual differences to better think about ways to deal with the problems of unequal political participation and influence. Both scholars and policymakers have long noted that state and local contexts can serve as "laboratories of democracy" (Brandeis 1932), in which we can learn much about effective (and ineffective) ways to deal with pressing social and economic problems. There is still much to learn in this realm. But contexts provide useful information both about how citizens map their own economic interests onto political choices and how legislators represent constituents of different income levels. It makes sense to use this information to think about ways to work toward the goal of greater political equality in the United States.

Notes

CHAPTER ONE

1. But we should beware the easy conclusion that *only* racial dynamics, or only dynamics unique to the American South, are at play here. Alabama's neighbor, Louisiana, for example, was recently lauded by Rutgers' Educational Law Foundation (Baker, Sciarra, and Farrie 2015) as one of the states that does the best job of targeting state funding to address the needs of high-poverty schools.

CHAPTER TWO

1. For example, the work of Duverger (1963) and others that have followed him show that myriad types of laws—whether legislators are elected proportionally or in first-past-the-post arrangements, or whether boundaries are structured to keep elections competitive or noncompetitive, for example—affect the number of political parties that are formed, their relative strength, and the ideological distance between them.

2. Of course, it is not necessarily the case that such networks need to be geographically constrained: though local opinion leaders remain important to shaping political discourse in a given context, other forms of networks (such as those driven by online communities or specific media outlets) matter a great deal as well.

3. Importantly, contextual factors can also drive the sorts of considerations (Zaller 1992) that are activated in support of particular choices. Most citizens do not have fixed, stable views on most political matters. Instead, views on any number of issues can be affected by a wide range of factors that are often loosely connected or even contradictory. Opinions on such issues are often constructed "on the fly," based in part on what is salient to citizens at the time: what considerations, in other words, are activated most strongly. Any number of these sorts of factors could bear on the attitudes citizens express toward specific political issues that they ordinar-

ily think little about. This conception of political decision making, which emphasizes how opinions are formed in real-time through sampling among competing considerations, goes a long way toward explaining framing and priming effects in both survey response and real-world political decision making. This model also can explain, in a more general sense, how citizens sort through and reconcile myriad loosely connected beliefs, values, and experiences when trying to apply them to political choices.

4. Enns et al. (2014), for example, make the argument that the U.S. political system is ill-suited to combat income inequality because it makes policy change unusually hard, and thus the system is less well equipped than those in other nations to combat broader global trends toward growing inequality. A political system that held both citizen and legislator preferences for reducing inequality constant, but that changed the rules under which the political system operated, would likely have considerably less inequality than the current one.

5. Even if someone never discusses politics with those around them, and has friends that are exclusively from outside their immediate context, in other words, they still interact in physical communities enough to form a rough sense of what the people around them are like, and how they fit into that broader community (Huckfeldt 1986; Baybeck and McClurg 2005).

6. Recent debates over the proper ways to teach the history of race in America, or the story of the country's creation, also reflect competing views on how citizens' social norms and political values should be constructed.

7. This sort of activity, then, encourages a type of feedback loop where people who live in areas where mobilization is likely participate more, which further increases the importance of targeting mobilization efforts to those areas (and vice-versa) (Rosenstone and Hansen 1993).

8. Fenton's (1969) work, for example, argued that working class voters were less reliably Democratic in rural and suburban areas than in urban ones in part because of their geographic isolation from one another: in the absence of regular and consistent social interaction, the conditions necessary for class consciousness to form in such communities did not exist.

9. And as Schattschneider (1960, 102) notes, the feelings of political efficacy that motivate participation are tied together with how the political agenda is structured in a particular context: "Abstention [from participation] reflects the suppression of the options and alternatives that reflect the needs of nonparticipants."

10. Though it is possible to replicate the vast majority of the analyses in the chapters to come with county-level measures of context instead of district-level ones. These analyses find very similar results to what is presented here.

11. And, of course, in states with more than one district, congressional district boundaries change every 10 years.

12. Because of these limitations, the use of congressional district in the analyses to come provides perhaps a particularly strong test of the impact of context on political behavior. If the effects of context as operationalized through large, somewhat diffuse congressional districts are strong and substantively important, then we might surmise the effects of smaller and perhaps more directly influential contextual units (such as county, or neighborhood) would be even stronger. Where possible in the book (particularly in chapters 3 and 4, which focus only on political

attitudes and behaviors, and not representation by members of Congress), I am able to replicate the analyses presented using county, rather than congressional district, as the contextual unit of interest. This operationalization finds results that are consistent with, and in some cases stronger than, the effects of congressional district.

13. Data for cross-national comparisons here come from the CIA World Factbook: https://www.cia.gov/library/publications/the-world-factbook/

CHAPTER THREE

1. The political agenda is also driven in large part by the interests of political participants: political activity on the part of particular social groups, for example, causes the political system to consider things that it might not have otherwise considered (e.g., Banaszak 1996; Burstein 2003).

2. In addition, political elites tend to target particular geographic areas for mobilization, so people who live in high-participation areas are more likely to be mobilized to get involved regardless of whether they, themselves, are habitual political participants or not.

3. On a more practical level, wealthier areas also generally have stronger civic and political institutions that make it easier for citizens to find out how and where to vote or participate in politics in other ways (e.g., Lenzi et al. 2012).

4. There is more economic segregation within smaller geographic units, such as counties, census tracts, or neighborhoods (see Franko and Livingston 2015).

5. Pennsylvania technically had a required photo-ID law for the 2012 election, but a key part of the law was blocked by the state courts in the months leading up to the election, on the grounds that voters were not given enough time to procure a photo identification before the election. As a result, precinct monitors were told to ask voters for photo ID, but were prohibited from actually enforcing the law.

6. Several chapters in this book make extensive use of data from the 2010, 2012, and 2014 Cooperative Congressional Election Study (CCES) surveys. This survey, conducted by the polling firm YouGov and funded by the National Science Foundation and the cooperation of several dozen research universities, is a very large *N* (>50,000) online panel survey that uses matched random sampling techniques to draw a representative sample of the U.S. population. The sampling frame of the CCES differs from conventional random-digit-dialing surveys, in that it relies on an opt-in panel. Panelists are recruited to join the YouGov panel through a variety of different means (e.g., phone sampling, direct mail, web advertising), and are randomly invited to complete particular surveys (such as this one) as part of their participation in the panel. Panelists for the survey were recruited to be representative of the American public based on gender, age, and education. Though the methodology of such surveys are somewhat novel and research into their accuracy compared to more tested methods is ongoing, the results obtained through online matched panel surveys—particularly those conducted by YouGov—provide results that are comparable (though not identical) to those obtained through more traditional methods (see Kennedy et al. 2016 for a thorough discussion of the use of nonprobability sampling in survey data). More details on the sampling technique are available at http://projects.iq.harvard.edu/cces/book/sample-design. For more information about YouGov's methods, and a comparison of its results to those

obtained through more conventional traditional RDD-based survey methods, see Twyman 2008.

7. In addition to showing that misstating participation is a matter of social desirability and not simply misremembering whether one voted or not, the fact that we see very few validated voters who reported not voting adds some validity to the Catalist validation procedure: finding large numbers of people who claimed to not vote when they are validated as having done so would be so counterintuitive that it would cast doubt on the validation procedure.

8. In addition to validated vote measures, measures of self-reported voting were also available in 2010 and 2012. Running the analyses using these self-reported measures tends to exaggerate the size of income-based gaps in voting (consistent with the notion that overreporting is more common among the wealthy than the poor), but gives substantive conclusions regarding the effect of contextual effects on income gaps that are similar to what is presented using the validated measures.

9. The CCES also asked respondents whether they were contacted by a political party or candidate in the most recent election: while being contacted by a candidate is obviously not participation per se, the importance of mobilization to participation is deeply important, so it is worth noting that there is also a significant bias in the degree to which citizens of different income levels were contacted by political candidates. In general, campaigns invest resources where they expect such investments to yield the greatest payoff: in practice, that means that upper-income citizens are more likely to be targeted for mobilization than lower-income ones.

10. The precise breakpoint of this scale varies modestly from year to year. In 2014, the categories were: <$10,000, $10,000–$19,999, $20,000–$29,999, $30,000–$39,999, $40,000–$49,999, $50,000–$59,999, $60,000–$69,999, $70,000–$79,999, $80,000–$99,999, $100,000–$119,999, $120,000–$149,999, $150,000–$199,999, $200,000–$249,999, and ≥$250,000. The range of incomes in each category varies somewhat: to see if this is driving the results, I have also redone the analyses that follow by recoding income as a pure interval scale (assigning individuals the income level that corresponds to the midpoint of their income category). Results using this alternative method do not change the conclusions presented below.

11. I have replicated all of the analyses that follow, treating income as a *relative* measure—operationalizing "income" as a citizen's income relative to the median income in his or her district of residence. This was done to take into account the possibility that income not only provides absolute advantages to citizens in terms of the resources available to them but also serves a social sorting mechanism through which citizens who are wealthier (or poorer) than most of those immediately around them are either advantaged (or disadvantaged) regardless of whether they are wealthy or poor compared to the rest of the country. The results using this alternative measure closely mirror what is presented in the tables to come.

12. I have also conducted these analyses with a separate dummy variable for each type of institutional restriction, testing the assumption that different types of identification laws have distinct, nonlinear effects and should not be collapsed into a single "restrictions on voting scale." This analysis essentially shows that a single scale is empirically appropriate here: models with separate dummy variables for each type of identification law do not fit the data better than a model where the categories are collapsed into a single scale, and the coefficients for each dummy vari-

able (and each dummy variable's interaction with income) suggest that the effects of each type of restriction on voting propensity roughly match what is seen if these restrictions worked in the way that a single-scale variable would predict.

13. The sample sizes for the 2010 model are larger than what is shown in table 3.1, because, in this year, the CCES validated voting for all survey respondents, not just those who answered the question regarding self-reported turnout.

14. The figure holds other contextual variables constant at their median values, and assumes that the citizen is a 40-year-old white, married, homeowner with a high school degree. Similar results obtain for other types of "hypothetical" citizens.

15. Consistent with this hypothesis, we see in a separate analysis that poor citizens who live in wealthy contexts are significantly more likely to be contacted by parties or candidates than poor citizens who live in poor contexts.

16. There is some reason to expect that the effects of identification requirements are nonlinear, such that they affect the poor far more than either the middle class or the rich. I have explored additional functional forms of this relationship (e.g., by interacting the voter ID measure with an income-squared term, or interacting it with a simple dummy variable for citizens who are in the bottom income tercile). There is weak evidence that this hypothesis is true—voter identification laws tend to have a modestly stronger effect on the behavior of the very poor than on the behavior of any other group—but these relationships are inconsistent, and often not statistically significant.

17. These laws were also not passed at random—among other things, they were more likely to be passed in states where other efforts to make voting more difficult were also common (Hasen 2012). This suggests that, at least in recent years, the voter identification measure is also proxying other state-level efforts to either equalize, or exacerbate, turnout inequalities. But it is important to note that the impact of the voter ID measure remains even if state dummies are included in the analysis: voter ID laws do not simply serve as a proxy for other conditions within particular types of states that might make it less likely for citizens to get involved.

18. And, importantly, the models show that the effect of contextual union density holds after controlling (in separate analyses) for individual union membership. This suggests that the presence of strong labor unions can, at least in some circumstances, affect the behavior of citizens even if they personally are not involved in a union.

CHAPTER FOUR

1. See Barker and Carman (2000) for an empirical examination of this thesis.

2. The one outlier here is on attitudes toward the Affordable Care Act, which is perhaps the most strongly redistributive social program to be signed into law in some decades. Attitudes on the ACA differ little by income and, if anything, it is supported most strongly by the very poor and the very rich. The deep ties that this issue has with recent partisan politics—the name "Obamacare" also hints at this—may lead partisan considerations to swamp all others. Indeed, partisan divisions on this issue—Democrats are more than 60 percentage points more supportive than Republicans of the ACA—are larger than on any other issue included here.

3. We might also think of support for things such as quality transportation or

education to be consistent with a broader form of "self-interest," since these sorts of programs serve to confer both immediate and ongoing benefits to all sorts of citizens (see Ellis and Stimson 2012).

4. Pew also asked a follow-up question to those who perceived a class divide, asking into which group—the "haves" or "have-nots"—they would place themselves. This question produced an expected—though far from universal—divide across income lines: 76% of top-tercile respondents, and 36% of bottom tercile respondents, placed themselves into the "have" group.

5. This expectation builds from recent empirical work (most notably Gelman 2009; see also Rueda, Stegmueller, and Idema 2014) exploring the relationship between state-level income and the vote. These studies note that income-based differences in voting behavior are greatest in "red" states when compared to "blue" ones.

6. As noted in chapter 2, there is certainly reciprocal cause and effect here: conservative (or liberal) areas create (for example) the laws and school curricula that citizens live under. But these laws and curricula then go on to affect how citizens interpret the world around them.

7. In addition, conservative contexts also promote the importance of individualism to political and social life, downplaying the notion of (and perhaps even stoking resentment to) a shared collective fate and the reliance on shared collective programs and services (Soss and Jacobs 2009). This, again, should serve to highlight the importance of self-interest to political conflict, and viewing the political system in more narrow terms of "what it can provide for me."

8. More practically speaking, people in urban areas might see themselves as more reliant on collective services—and the tax dollars that support them—instead of being resentful toward such services (see Walsh 2015).

9. Wealthy citizens in densely populated areas might also be more likely to feel some of the "negative externalities" (Rueda, Stegmueller, and Idema 2014) of income disparities that cause some well-off citizens to feel more positively toward redistribution.

10. These questions were included in the Syracuse University module of the survey. Respondents were also asked about the opposite emotions—whether they felt resentment toward the poor, or sympathetic toward the rich—but such emotions were far less common.

11. The full set of response options was "always," "most of the time," "about half of the time," "some of the time," or "almost never."

12. This measure of "liberalism" is obviously taken from just one election cycle, and may reflect factors idiosyncratic to this one cycle. To mitigate this, I have also replicated results to come with a measure derived from a district's Cook Partisan Voting Index. Though this indicator comes with its own set of problems (it is still based on election results alone, for example), it does allow for consideration of liberalism along a broader time scale. This measure produces results in the models to come that are essentially identical to the ones using Obama's 2012 share.

13. We might also consider the role of race in these analyses, as when class is more closely tied with race, income differences in views may well be stronger: wealthy people may be more opposed to redistribution, for example, in contexts where most of the poor are black (see Alesina and Glaeser 2004; Hersh and Nall

2016). To deal with this issue, I also run an additional set of models interacting income with a measure of the percentage of black residents in a given district. Although the inclusion of this variable doesn't markedly affect the results reported here, the "percent black" variable does moderate the relationship between income and welfare spending preferences (though it does not moderate the relationship between income and self-placement, gay marriage, or the ACA). This provides some support for the idea that race may add an additional complicating factor here, at least for "race coded" (Gilens 1999) issues.

14. ACS data, for example, shows that in the past year, only 6 percent of citizens moved to a different county than the year prior.

15. This analysis focused on these three high-level attributes that are emblematic of the model of activated self-interest offered here. But this model is intended to be a general one, not simply restricted to these three factors: it is certainly likely that there are other factors, not included in these analyses, that serve to heighten class divisions and produce results similar to what is reported here.

16. When it comes to the analyses in this chapter, though, it is worth noting that the views of what we might call the "knowledgeable" poor (lower-income citizens who score above average on a six-question political knowledge scale administered by the CCES) hold views that are on balance not markedly different than those of the "less knowledgeable" poor.

17. Of course, policymakers also try to shape revealed preferences as well (Druckman and Jacobs 2014).

CHAPTER FIVE

1. Dahl (1971) summarizes the point nicely: "a key characteristic of a democracy is the continuing responsiveness of the government to the preferences of its citizens, considered as political equals."

2. Though it is also not necessarily the case that all citizens care equally about the degree to which members perform constituency service and seek to secure allocative benefits (see Griffin and Flavin 2011). I return to this issue in chapter 8.

3. Given this, we might think of this analysis as providing a very conservative estimate of the degree of representative inequality. Other forms of influencing MC behavior—deciding which policy issues are most worth his or her time, shaping the content of his or her speeches or public pronouncements—require far more in the way of time and resources than does the vote (Miler 2010), so representation in policy as revealed through voting may well be the place where we see the most equality between rich and poor.

4. All of the findings here, and in chapter 6, can be well replicated using data from the prior three Congresses, and corresponding data from the 2012, 2010, and 2008 CCES surveys.

5. NOMINATE scores, like essentially all measures of MC activity in recent years, illustrate a high level of party polarization: all House Democrats possess voting records that are to the left of all House Republicans. Even so, there remains significant variance in the ideological locations of Congress members.

6. More important, it is clear that none of these measures provides a perfect representation of ideological distance. But these problems are mitigated some-

what because of our focus on relative, not absolute, representation. I can make no strong claims about the substantive meaning of any particular level of ideological distance—whether being 20 ideological "points" away from a legislator, for example, signifies that one's preferences are represented "well" or "poorly." Rather, I simply argue that a citizen whose preferences are closer to his or her MC than those of another citizen is likely to be better represented.

7. This measure also makes no assumptions that citizens' points of view follow a linear left-right ideological scale, which may be missing the fact that citizens care about a number of different issues, but do not hold ideologically constrained points of view on them (see Ahler and Broockman 2015). This measure simply counts the number of views on which a citizen's views were represented, without taking into account the ideological direction of those views.

8. In this light, it is important to note that it is possible to replicate this analysis, using older CCES data and different samples of "key votes," for the 110th and 111th Congress. Data from the 110th Congress, for example, includes votes on bills that would: (a) provide a timeline for the withdrawal from Iraq, (b) increase the minimum wage, (c) permit federal funding of stem-cell research, (d) expand warrantless eavesdropping activities under the Foreign Intelligence Surveillance Act, (e) expand access to subsidized health insurance for children, (f) ban gay marriage, and (g) provide federal assistance to homeowners at risk of foreclosure. Results from these sessions of Congress very closely mirror what is shown here. Examples of unequal representation on key votes in these Congresses will be shown later in the chapter.

9. The impact of this growing polarization on disparities in the representation of rich and poor will be explored in chapter 6.

10. These two measures might also be considered to be capturing representation on two separate dimensions of public preference: a symbolic dimension of identification (as measured by self-placement), and an operational dimension of aggregated preferences on specific policy issues (as measured by the roll-call vote scale) (see Ellis 2012a).

11. At least when it comes to ideological distance, there is perhaps some evidence that the relationship between income and representation is exponential, with much lower levels of representation occurring at the very lowest income levels. But the nonlinear aspect of this relationship is not strong: a model of the relationship between income and representation that includes any of a number of plausible quadratic terms (e.g., income-squared) does not fit the data better than a simple linear model.

12. A limitation of both of these scales is that they measure the degree to which a citizen's preferences are congruent with MC behavior, not whether such citizens are actually influencing MC behavior. The greater congruence between wealthier citizens' preferences and MC behavior could result from greater influence of the wealthy over MC action. It might also result in part from two other factors: that wealthier citizens' preferences are more likely to be influenced by the behavior of their MCs, or that wealthier citizens, because of their higher levels of political understanding and participation in public debate, are more likely to react to real-world conditions in a way that mirrors their MCs. There is reason to think that meaningful differences in congruence also imply meaningful differences in influ-

ence (see Gilens 2005 and Griffin and Newman 2008 for broader discussions of this point). But given the data and approach, we cannot rule out either possibility explicitly, and it is possibly the case that both are true to some extent.

13. The difference in the popular vote received by John Kerry in 2004—a narrow loser—and Barack Obama in 2008—a landslide winner—was roughly 5 percentage points. The difference between defeat and landslide victory, in other words, was the results of roughly one voter in 20 changing their minds. The 1.4 percentage point difference we see in ideological representation, then, is properly placed in context not in terms of the entire 100-point ideology scale, but in a much narrower band that defines the actual range of American ideological preferences.

14. Tercile categories here were generated using district-level measures of income (so that, for example, citizens classified in the "top tercile" are citizens whose income falls into the top third of incomes for that particular district, not for the nation as a whole). Using national-level tercile estimates produces similar results.

15. An ABC News/*Washington Post* poll taken at the time that the minimum wage increase was being debated in Congress found that a slim majority of Americans (52%) felt that the minimum wage should actually be higher than $7.25 per hour.

16. All of this can create a situation akin to what Enns (2016) calls "coincidental representation": even though wealthy and middle-income citizens differ in the magnitude of their support or opposition to some bills, they may share both a majority preference for an MC to vote either for or against a bill and a rough ranking of which bills should garner the most support. In cases like these, we would expect the preferences of both groups to be represented roughly equally well, even if MCs were only following the views of the rich.

17. In addition, the inability to form or express attitudes *at all* might be another way in which the quality of the representation of the poor suffers. Citizens who do not express views on important policy matters, by definition, cannot have their views represented by policymakers, and poor citizens are significantly more likely in these and other surveys to answer "don't know," "no response," or "not interested" in respond to queries about politics (in the 2014 CCES, for example, 10 percent of bottom-tercile respondents, but only 3 percent of top-tercile respondents, refused to place themselves on the seven-point self-placement scale). In the analyses in this and subsequent chapters, I do not include citizens who do not hold preferences in the analysis. But it is at least important to note that not only do the wealthy tend to have their preferences better represented by policymakers, they are also more likely to hold preferences that can, in theory, be represented.

18. For presentation purposes, this table reports only the results for the income variable in each model.

19. Copartisanship is the only variable that "moves the needle" in diminishing the independent role of income on representation. It is thus clearly the case that low-income citizens have a much better chance of having their views represented well if they share their MC's party affiliation. But it is still important to note that copartisanship alone does not diminish the impact of income itself: on both measures (and for both Republican and Democratic MCs), high-income copartisans are better represented by their MCs than their low-income counterparts.

CHAPTER SIX

1. Fenno's (1978) classic study of Congress member behavior, for example, is especially illustrative in this regard. Among other things, Fenno highlights the important differences between MC's geographical, election, and primary constituencies. Representing the views of one of these constituencies will mean, in many cases, neglecting those of one or more of the others.

2. With some exceptions, MCs that are in districts with heavy partisan tilts in one direction or another also tend to be ideologically extreme, with safe Democratic MCs generally more liberal than the average Democrat, and safe Republican MCs more conservative than the average Republican. I return to the role of ideological extremity in shaping representational inequality later in this chapter.

3. These findings are consistent with evidence in the American states that legislatures craft policies more supportive of poorer citizens' interests when the poor are more politically active (Hill and Leighley 1992; Hill, Leighley, and Hinton-Andersson 1995).

4. To streamline the presentation of these models, the results shown in this chapter exclude the other individual-level controls (e.g., race, gender, political activism, and the like) used in chapter 5. The inclusion of such variables, however, does little to affect the results presented here.

5. In the rare case when districts were represented by members of two different parties in a single term (because a sitting representative died or resigned), these data include only the voting records of the member that served the longest during that term.

6. A district near the 10th percentile of income inequality has a district Gini coefficient of approximately 0.42—corresponding to districts such as central Pennsylvania's PA-1 (represented in the 113th Congress by Republican Tom Marino) and Orange County's CA-46 (represented by Democrat Loretta Sanchez). A 90th percentile district has a Gini coefficient of roughly 0.49—corresponding to districts such as suburban Phoenix's AZ-6 (represented by Republican David Schweikert) or Brooklyn's NY-9 (represented by Democrat Yvette Clarke).

7. I also tested for the presence of three-way interactions here: whether the relationship between representational bias and opinion gaps is stronger in certain contexts than others. There is some suggestive evidence that this relationship is stronger in Republican-represented districts—that Republican representatives represent their constituents more unequally in the context of large opinion divides than Democratic representatives do—but this result is somewhat sensitive to model specification.

8. Though they do hold in the other two recent Congresses for which CCES data are available.

CHAPTER SEVEN

1. The wording of this question: "Here is a seven-point scale on which the political views that people might hold are arranged from extremely liberal to extremely conservative. Where would you place yourself on this scale?"

2. See Ellis and Stimson (2012) for a fuller discussion of the conceptual and empirical distinctions between operational and symbolic measures of preferences.

3. The American National Election Studies (ANES) works to provide a nationally representative sample of citizens. Unlike the CCES, however, its sampling frame does not aim for representative samples of individual congressional districts—and in any given year, many congressional districts have no respondents at all. The analyses here are necessarily based on individual-level data—relating individual citizens to their MCs—and it is not possible to make more aggregated statements about changes in particular districts.

4. Subsamples of ANES respondents in some years were asked versions of both the ideological self-placement and jobs-income scales using experimental question wording different from the traditional wording. These respondents are excluded from the analysis. In recent years, the ANES has experimented with some methods of collecting responses (phone and Web-based interviewing) that differ from its standard face-to-face format. These respondents are included, though excluding them does not change the substantive conclusions reported here.

5. All income terciles have become less white over time, but the increase in the nonwhite population is most pronounced in the lowest income group. In the pre-1980 surveys, for example, 19% of the poorest tercile, and 5% of the wealthiest tercile, identified as a race other than white. In the post-2000 surveys, 53% of the poorest tercile, and 26% of the wealthiest, identified as nonwhite.

6. There are many reasons for this finding, but perhaps the most important one is that polarization—and the resultant policy gridlock that it brings—inhibits the political system's ability to respond to external changes in the economic or demographic environment. If economic factors (such as globalization or skill-based technological change) are disadvantageous to the poor, a political system with a heavy "status quo bias" will tend to see rising levels of inequality because its policies cannot change as quickly in response to external forces.

7. Data on unionization rates by district are not consistently available until post-2000, so comparisons of this sort are not possible given available data in any case.

8. Data on state-level unionization is based on data from Current Population Surveys, and is compiled and made publicly available through Barry Hirsch and David MacPherson's Union Membership and Coverage Database: www.unionstats.com

9. The states that have experienced the greatest declines in unionization are typically rust-belt states (Indiana, Michigan, Ohio, Pennsylvania, Wisconsin) that have seen struggles in industries that typically employ many unionized workers. The states that have seen the smallest declines are more heterogeneous, including states that had low levels of unionization to begin with (South Carolina, Louisiana) and states that have worked more strongly than others to protect organized labor (Vermont, Hawaii).

10. Because of data limitations, the models including unionization include only respondents from 1984 to 2012. Reestimating the full model in the final column without the unionization variable, and including the full range of the dataset, produces results for the other variables that are similar to what is presented in the

table. In addition, restricting all other models to the 1984-and-later period does not affect the substantive importance (or statistical significance) of any variable.

11. And, importantly, there is no evidence of a meaningful triple interaction between income, time, and party: Republicans and Democrats have not changed relative to one another over time in how equally they represent constituents across income levels. This relationship between income and unionization rates does not also appear to be time varying: it appears, in other words, that it is the decline in unionization rates themselves, not anything about the political power of unions to represent the views of the poor, that is behind the exacerbation of representational inequality.

CHAPTER EIGHT

1. Though this table reports findings at the tercile level only, the effect of income on efficacy is very nearly linear in most cases: the higher a citizen's household income, the higher his or her level of political efficacy.

2. When time series of these questions were available, I also attempted to discern trends in the political efficacy of various income groups over time. There is some evidence (consistent with what we would expect from chapter 7) that differences in the efficacy levels of rich and poor are increasing over time, but this finding was not consistent across all question types. There is a general trend, however, for the political efficacy of all citizens to be declining over time.

3. In the aggregate, 58% of those with an opinion approved of their MC's job performance. This fits with what is largely known about Americans' evaluations of Congress: that citizens dislike the institution itself, but are on balance satisfied with the performance of their own MC.

4. In these figures, a citizen is assumed to be a political independent.

5. The MC approval question also provided the option for respondents to say that they had "never heard of" their representative. These responses (about 17% of the total sample) are removed from the analysis, but it is worth noting that the propensity to give this response decreases with income: 24% of citizens in the bottom tercile, but only 10% in the top tercile, admitted that they had never heard of their representative. Given that knowing the identity of a representative is very likely a necessary precondition for holding him or her responsible for his or her actions, the gaps between how accountable wealthy and poor citizens hold MCs for their job performance is probably greater than what is reported here.

6. And perhaps such efforts could be undertaken through creative gerrymandering (which citizens seem to not care much about, provided that it serves other goals, such as better representation—see Christenson and Makse 2015), rather than by the geographic concentration of poor citizens that we know to be harmful in a variety of contexts.

7. This point clearly leads to discussions of districting procedures. Creative redistricting is clearly not the only—nor maybe even a—cause of increasing polarization (Theriault 2008), so districting is clearly not a cure-all for the issue of political equality (and certainly not for polarization more broadly defined). Even so, many scholars have explored the effects of congressional redistricting on how citizens and elected officials act. While there has been much research on the effects of

districting on representation generally (e.g., Gelman and King 1994; Buchler 2005) and on the representation of racial minorities specifically (e.g., Canon 1999; Lublin 1999), the results here suggest that the districting process might also have significant implications for economic inequality in representation, if districts are drawn in a way that either increases or decreases the prevalence of the factors identified here (electoral competitiveness, income inequality, and the like) as mattering to relative representation of the poor. These factors can provide a starting point for thinking about how political institutions can be designed in a way that might best serve the goal of representational equity across income lines.

References

Aarøe, Lene, and Michael Bang Petersen. 2014. "Crowding Out Culture: Scandinavians and Americans Agree on Social Welfare in the Face of Deservingness Cues." *Journal of Politics* 76:684–97.

Aaronson, Daniel, and Bhashkar Mazumder. 2008. "Intergenerational Economic Mobility in the United States, 1940 to 2000." *Journal of Human Resources* 43:139–72.

Abrams, Samuel J., and Morris P. Fiorina. 2012. "'The Big Sort' That Wasn't: A Skeptical Reexamination." *PS: Political Science & Politics* 45:203–10.

Achen, Christopher. 1978. "Measuring Representation." *American Journal of Political Science* 22:502–21.

Ahler, Douglas J., and David E. Broockman. 2015. "Does Polarization Imply Poor Representation? A New Perspective on the 'Disconnect' between Politicians and Voters." Working paper, University of California, Berkeley.

Aldrich, John H., and David W. Rohde. 2000. "The Consequences of Party Polarization in the House." In *Polarized Politics: Congress and the President in a Partisan Era*, ed. Jon Bond and Richard Fleisher. Washington, DC: Congressional Quarterly Press.

Aldrich, John, and David Rohde. 2001. "The Logic of Conditional Party Government: Revisiting the Electoral Connection." In *Congress Reconsidered*, 7th ed., ed. Lawrence C. Dodd and Bruce I. Oppenheimer. Washington, DC: Congressional Quarterly Press.

Alesina, Alberto, and Edward Glaeser. 2004. *Fighting Poverty in the US and Europe: A World of Difference*. Oxford: Oxford University Press.

Alesina, Alberto, and Eliana La Ferrara. 2002. "Who Trusts Others?" *Journal of Public Economics* 85:207–34.

Alex-Assensoh, Yvette M. 1998. *Neighborhoods, Family, and Political Behavior in Urban America*. New York: Garland.

Althaus, Scott. 2003. *Collective Preferences and Democratic Politics: Opinion Surveys and the Will of the People*. Cambridge: Cambridge University Press.

Alvarez, R. Michael, and Paul Gronke. 1996. "Constituents and Legislators: Learning about the Persian Gulf War Resolution." *Legislative Studies Quarterly* 21:105–27.

American Political Science Association. 2004. *American Democracy in an Age of Rising Inequality*. http://www.apsanet.org/imgtest/taskforcereport.pdf

Anderson, Dewey, and Percy Davidson. 1943. *The Democratic Class Struggle*. Palo Alto: Stanford University Press.

Andrain, Charles. 2014. *Economic Inequality: A Comparative Policy Approach*. New York: Rowman-Littlefield.

Annie Casey Foundation. 2014. *Early Reading Proficiency in the United States*. http://www.aecf.org/resources/early-reading-proficiency-in-the-united-states/

Ansolabehere, Stephen, and Eitan Hersh. 2012. "Validation: What Big Data Reveal about Survey Misreporting and the Real Electorate." *Political Analysis* 20:437–59.

Ansolabehere, Stephen, Marc Meredith, and Erik Snowberg. 2014. "Macro-Economic Voting: Local Information and Micro-Perceptions of the Macro-Economy." *Economics & Politics* 26:380–410.

Axelrod, Robert M. 1997. *The Complexity of Cooperation: Agent-Based Models of Competition and Collaboration*. Princeton: Princeton University Press.

Bageant, Joseph. 2008. *Deer Hunting with Jesus: Dispatches from America's Class War*. New York: Broadway Books.

Baker, Bruce, David Sciarra, and Danielle Farrie. 2015. *Is School Funding Fair? A National Report Card*. Rutgers Education Law Center. http://www.schoolfundingfairness.org/

Banaszak, Lee Ann. 1996. *Why Movements Succeed or Fail*. Princeton: Princeton University Press.

Barker, David C., and Christopher Jan Carman. 2000. "The Spirit of Capitalism? Religious Doctrine, Values, and Economic Attitude Constructs." *Political Behavior* 22:1–27.

Bartels, Larry M. 1991. "Constituency Opinion and Congressional Policy Making: The Reagan Defense Buildup." *American Political Science Review* 85:457–74.

Bartels, Larry M. 2007. "Homer Gets a Warm Hug: A Note on Ignorance and Extenuation." *Perspectives on Politics* 5:785–90.

Bartels, Larry. 2008. *Unequal Democracy: The Political Economy of the New Gilded Age*. Princeton: Princeton University Press.

Baumgartner, Frank R., Jeffrey M. Berry, Marie Hojnacki, David C. Kimball, and Beth L. Leech. 2010. *Lobbying and Policy Change*. Chicago: University of Chicago Press.

Baumgartner, Frank R., Suzanna L. De Boef, and Amber E. Boydstun. 2008. *The Decline of the Death Penalty and the Discovery of Innocence*. Cambridge: Cambridge University Press.

Baybeck, Brady, and Scott D. McClurg. 2005. "What Do They Know and How Do They Know It? An Examination of Citizen Awareness of Context." *American Politics Research* 33:492–520.

Beeghley, Leonard. 2007. *The Structure of Social Stratification in the United States*. New York: Allyn and Bacon.

Belli, Robert F., Michael W. Traugott, and Matthew N. Beckmann. 2001. "What Leads to Voting Overreports? Contrasts of Overreporters to Validated Voters and Admitted Nonvoters in the American National Election Studies." *Journal of Official Statistics* 17:479–98.

Benabou, Roland, and Jean Tirole. 2011. "Identity, Dignity and Taboos: Beliefs as Assets." *Quarterly Journal of Economics* 126:805–55.

Beramendi, Pablo, and Christopher Anderson. 2008. *Democracy, Inequality, and Representation: A Comparative Perspective*. New York: Russell Sage Foundation.

Berelson, Bernard R., Paul F. Lazarsfeld, and William N. McPhee. 1954. *Voting: A Study of Opinion Formation in a Presidential Election*. Chicago: University of Chicago Press.

Berger, Jonah, Marc Meredith, and S. Christian Wheeler. 2008. "Contextual Priming: Where People Vote Affects How They Vote." *Proceedings of the National Academy of Sciences* 105:8846–49.

Berinsky, Adam J., Nancy Burns, and Michael W. Traugott. 2001. "Who Votes by Mail? A Dynamic Model of the Individual-Level Consequences of Voting-by-Mail Systems." *Public Opinion Quarterly* 65:178–97.

Berube, Alan. 2014. "All Cities Are Not Created Unequal." Working paper, Brookings Institution.

Beyer, Landon E., and Daniel P. Liston. 1996. *Curriculum in Conflict: Social Visions, Educational Agendas, and Progressive School Reform*. New York: Teachers College Press.

Bishop, Bill. 2009. *The Big Sort: Why the Clustering of Like-Minded America Is Tearing Us Apart*. New York: Houghton Mifflin Harcourt.

Blais, André. 2006. "What Affects Voter Turnout?" *Annual Review of Political Science* 9:111–25.

Bolton, Patrick, and Gerard Roland. 1997. "The Breakup of Nations: A Political Economy Analysis." *Quarterly Journal of Economics* 112:1057–90.

Bonica, Adam, Nolan McCarty, Keith T. Poole, and Howard Rosenthal. 2013. "Why Hasn't Democracy Slowed Rising Inequality?" *Journal of Economic Perspectives* 27 (3): 103–23.

Bonica, Adam, Nolan McCarty, Keith Poole, and Howard Rosenthal. 2015. "Congressional Polarization and Its Connection to Income Inequality: An Update." In *American Gridlock: The Sources, Character and Impact of Political Polarization*, ed. James Thurber and Antoine Yoshinaka. Cambridge: Cambridge University Press.

Books, John W., and Charles L. Prysby. 1991. *Political Behavior and the Local Context*. New York: Praeger.

Brady, Henry E. 2004. "An Analytical Perspective on Participatory Inequality and Income Inequality." In *Social Inequality*, ed. Kathryn Neckerman, 667–702. New York: Russell Sage Foundation.

Brady, Henry E., Kay Lehman Schlozman, and Sidney Verba. 1999. "Prospecting for Participants: Rational Expectations and the Recruitment of Political Activists." *American Political Science Review* 93:153–68.

Brady, Henry E., Sidney Verba, and Kay Lehman Schlozman. 1993. "Beyond SES: A Resource Model of Political Participation." *American Political Science Review* 89:271–94.

Brandeis, Louis. 1932. "Dissenting Opinion." *New State Ice Co. v. Liebmann*, 285 U.S. 262, 311.

Branham, J. Alexander, Stuart Soroka, and Christopher Wlezien. 2017 (forthcoming). "When Do the Rich Win?" *Political Science Quarterly.*

Brockington, David. 2009. "It's about the Benefits: Choice Environments, Ideological Proximity, and Individual Participation in 28 Democracies." *Party Politics* 15:435–54.

Brooks-Gunn, Jeanne. 1997. *Neighborhood Poverty: Context and Consequences for Children.* New York: Russell Sage Foundation.

Buchler, Justin. 2005. "Competition, Representation and Redistricting: The Case against Competitive Congressional Districts." *Journal of Theoretical Politics* 17:431–63.

Bullock, Charles S., and David W. Brady. 1983. "Party, Constituency, and Roll-Call Voting in the U. S. Senate." *Legislative Studies Quarterly* 8:29–43.

Burden, Barry. 2004. "A Technique for Estimating Candidate and Voter Locations." *Electoral Studies* 23:632–39.

Burden, Barry C. 2007. *Personal Roots of Representation.* Princeton: Princeton University Press.

Burns, Nancy. 1992. *The Formation of American Local Governments.* New York: Oxford University Press.

Burstein, Paul. 2003. "The Impact of Public Opinion on Public Policy: A Review and an Agenda." *Political Research Quarterly* 56:29–40.

Butler, Daniel M. 2009. "The Effects of the Size of Voting Blocs on Incumbents' Roll-Call Voting and the Asymmetric Polarization of Congress." *Legislative Studies Quarterly* 34:297–318.

Cadwallader, Martin T. 1992. *Migration and Residential Mobility: Macro and Micro Approaches.* Madison: University of Wisconsin Press.

Campbell, Angus, Philip E. Converse, Warren E. Miller, and Donald Stokes. 1960. *The American Voter.* New York: Wiley.

Campbell, David E. 2006. *Why We Vote: How Schools and Communities Shape Our Civic Life.* Princeton: Princeton University Press.

Canon, David T. 1999. *Race, Redistricting, and Representation.* Chicago: University of Chicago Press.

Carnes, Nicholas. 2013. *White-Collar Government: The Hidden Role of Class in Economic Policymaking.* Chicago: University of Chicago Press.

Carsey, Thomas, and Jeffrey Harden. 2010. "New Measures of Partisanship, Ideology, and Policy Mood in the American States." *State Politics and Policy Quarterly* 10:136–46.

Carson, Jamie, Michael Crespin, Charles Finocchiaro, and David Rohde. 2007. "Redistricting and Party Polarization in the US House of Representatives." *American Politics Research* 35:878–904.

Cho, Wendy K. Tam, and James G. Gimpel. 2009. "Presidential Voting and the Local Variability of Economic Hardship." *Forum* 7:1–23.

Cho, Wendy K. Tam, and Thomas J. Rudolph. 2008. "Emanating Political Participation: Untangling the Spatial Structure behind Participation." *British Journal of Political Science* 38:273–89.

Christakis, Nicholas A., and James H. Fowler. 2009. *Connected: The Surprising Power of Our Social Networks and How They Shape Our Lives.* New York: Little, Brown.

Christenson, Dino, and Todd Makse. 2015. "Mass Preferences on Shared Representation and the Composition of Legislative Districts." *American Politics Research* 43:451–78.

Citrin, Jack, and Donald Philip Green. 1990. "The Self-Interest Motive in American Public Opinion." *Research in Micropolitics* 3:1–28.

Citrin, Jack, Eric Schickler, and John Sides. 2003. "What if Everyone Voted? Simulating the Impact of Increased Turnout in Senate Elections." *American Journal of Political Science* 47:75–90.

Claassen, Ryan L., and Andrew Povtak. 2010. "The Christian Right Thesis: Explaining Longitudinal Change in Participation among Evangelical Christians." *Journal of Politics* 72:2–15.

Clark, Gordon L. 1989. *Unions and Communities under Siege: American Communities and the Crisis of Organized Labor*. Cambridge: Cambridge University Press.

Clinton, Joshua D. 2006. "Representation in Congress: Constituents and Roll Calls in the 106th House." *Journal of Politics* 68:397–409.

Cohen, Barney, Samuel H. Preston, and Eileen M. Crimmins, eds. 2011. *Explaining Divergent Levels of Longevity in High-Income Countries*. Washington, DC: National Academies Press.

Conover, Pamela Johnston. 1984. "The Influence of Group Identifications on Political Perception and Evaluation." *Journal of Politics* 46:760–85.

Cox, Gary W., and Keith T. Poole. 2002. "On Measuring Partisanship in Roll-Call Voting: The U.S. House of Representatives, 1877–1999." *American Journal of Political Science* 46:477–89.

Crenson, Matthew A. 1983. *Neighborhood Politics*. Cambridge: Harvard University Press.

Dahl, Robert A. 1971. *Polyarchy: Participation and Opposition*. New Haven: Yale University Press.

Dallinger, Ursula. 2010. "Public Support for Redistribution: What Explains Cross-National Differences?" *Journal of European Social Policy* 20:333–49.

Dalton, Russell J. 2008. "Citizenship Norms and the Expansion of Political Participation." *Political Studies* 56:76–98.

Dalton, Russell J., and Christopher J. Anderson, eds. 2011. *Citizens, Context, and Choice: How Context Shapes Citizens' Electoral Choices*. Oxford: Oxford University Press.

Danielson, Michael N. 1976. "The Politics of Exclusionary Zoning in Suburbia." *Political Science Quarterly* 91:1–18.

Davis, Mike. 2000. *Prisoners of the American Dream: Politics and Economy in the History of the US Working Class*. 2nd ed. New York: Verso.

Delli Carpini, Michael X., and Scott Keeter. 1997. *What Americans Know about Politics and Why It Matters*. New Haven: Yale University Press.

Denzau, Arthur, William Riker, and Kenneth Shepsle. 1985. "Farquharson and Fenno: Sophisticated Voting and Home Style." *American Political Science Review* 79:1117–34.

Dickens, William T., and Jonathan S. Leonard. 1985. "Accounting for the Decline in Union Membership: 1950–1980." *Industrial and Labor Relations Review* 38: 323–34.

Downs, Anthony. 1957. "An Economic Theory of Political Action in a Democracy." *Journal of Political Economy* 65:135–50.

Druckman, James N., and Lawrence R. Jacobs. 2014. *Who Governs? Presidents, Public Opinion, and Manipulation*. Chicago: University of Chicago Press.

Duany, Andres, Elizabeth Plater-Zyberk, and Jeff Speck. 1991. *Suburban Nation: The Rise of Sprawl and the Decline of the American Dream*. New York: Macmillan.

Duverger, M. 1963. *Political Parties: Their Organization and Activity in the Modern State*. New York: Wiley.

Dyck, Joshua J., and James G. Gimpel. 2005. "Distance, Turnout, and the Convenience of Voting." *Social Science Quarterly* 86:531–48.

Easton, David, and Jack Dennis. 1967. "The Child's Acquisition of Regime Norms: Political Efficacy." *American Political Science Review* 61:25–38.

Eaton, Susan. 2014. "How a 'New Secessionist' Movement Is Threatening to Worsen School Segregation and Widen Inequalities." *Nation*, May 15. http://www.thenation.com/article/how-new-secessionist-movement-threatening-worsen-school-segregation-and-widen-inequal/

Ellis, Christopher. 2012a. "Public Ideology and Political Dynamics in the United States." *American Politics Research* 40:327–54.

Ellis, Christopher. 2012b. "Understanding Economic Biases in Representation." *Political Research Quarterly* 65:938–51.

Ellis, Christopher. 2013. "Social Context and Economic Biases in Representation." *Journal of Politics* 75:773–86.

Ellis, Christopher R., and James Stimson. 2012. *Ideology in America*. Cambridge: Cambridge University Press.

Enns, Peter K. 2015. "Relative Policy Support and Coincidental Representation." *Perspectives on Politics* 13:1053–64.

Enns, Peter K., and Paul M. Kellstedt. 2008. "Policy Mood and Political Sophistication: Why Everybody Moves Mood." *British Journal of Political Science* 38: 433–54.

Enns, Peter K., Nathan J. Kelly, Jana Morgan, Thomas Volscho, and Christopher Witko. 2014. "Conditional Status Quo Bias and Top Income Shares: How US Political Institutions Have Benefited the Rich." *Journal of Politics* 76:289–303.

Enns, Peter, and Christopher Wlezien. 2011. *Who Gets Represented?* New York: Russell Sage Press.

Entman, Robert M. 2004. *Projections of Power*. Chicago: University of Chicago Press.

Erikson, Robert S. 1978. "Constituency Opinion and Congressional Behavior: A Reexamination of the Miller-Stokes Representation Data." *American Journal of Political Science* 22:511–35.

Erikson, Robert S., and Yosef Bhatti. 2011. "How Poorly Are the Poor Represented in the U.S. Senate?" In *Who Gets Represented?*, ed. Peter Enns and Christopher Wlezien. New York: Russell Sage Press.

Erikson, Robert S., Michael B. MacKuen, and James A. Stimson. 2002. *The Macro Polity*. Cambridge: Cambridge University Press.

Eulau, Heinz, and Paul D. Karps. 1977. "The Puzzle of Representation: Specifying Components of Responsiveness." *Legislative Studies Quarterly* 2:233–54.

Evans, Geoffrey. 2000. "The Continued Significance of Class Voting." *Annual Review of Political Science* 3:401–17.

Fallows, James. 2000. "The Invisible Poor." *New York Times Magazine*, March 19, 68–78.

Fenno, Richard F. 1973. *Congressmen in Committees*. Boston: Little, Brown.

Fenno, Richard F. 1978. *Home Style: House Members in Their Districts*. Boston: Little, Brown.

Fenno, Richard F. 2006. *Congressional Travels: Places, Connections, and Authenticity*. New York: Routledge.

Fenton, John H. 1969. *Midwest Politics*. New York: Holt, Rinehart and Winston.

Fiorina, Morris. 1989. *Congress: Keystone of the Washington Establishment*. 2nd ed. New Haven: Yale University Press.

Fiorina, Morris P. 2012. *Disconnect: The Breakdown of Representation in American Politics*. Norman: University of Oklahoma Press.

Fischer, Ronald, Taciano L. Milfont, and Valdiney V. Gouveia. 2011. "Does Social Context Affect Value Structures? Testing the Within-Country Stability of Value Structures with a Functional Theory of Values." *Journal of Cross-Cultural Psychology* 42:253–70.

Flavin, Patrick. 2012. "Income Inequality and Policy Representation in the American States." *American Politics Research* 40:29–59.

Flavin, Patrick. 2013. "Does Higher Voter Turnout among the Poor Lead to More Equal Policy Representation?" *Social Science Journal* 49:405–12.

Flavin, Patrick. 2015a. "Lobbying Regulations and Political Equality in the American States." *American Politics Research* 43:304–26.

Flavin, Patrick. 2015b. "Campaign Finance Laws, Policy Outcomes, and Political Equality in the American States." *Political Research Quarterly* 68:77–88.

Form, William H., and Joan Huber. 1971. "Income, Race, and the Ideology of Political Efficacy." *Journal of Politics* 33:659–88.

Frank, Thomas. 2005. *What's the Matter with Kansas? How Conservatives Won the Heart of America*. New York: Holt.

Franko, William W. 2015. "More Equal Than We Thought? Using Vote Validation to Better Understand Participation Inequality in the States." *State Politics & Policy Quarterly* 15:91–114.

Franko, William W., and Avery Livingston. 2015. "Income Inequality, Economic Segregation, and Support for Redistribution." Paper presented at the 2015 meeting of the American Political Science Association, San Francisco.

Free, Lloyd A., and Hadley Cantril. 1969. *The Political Beliefs of Americans: A Study of Public Opinion*. New Brunswick, NJ: Rutgers University Press.

Galanter, Marc. 1999. "Farther Along." *Law and Society Review* 33:1113–23.

Galbraith, James K., and J. Travis Hale. 2008. "State Income Inequality and Presidential Election Turnout and Outcomes." *Social Science Quarterly* 89:887–901.

Gay, Claudine. 2001. "The Effect of Black Congressional Representation on Political Participation." *American Political Science Review* 95:589–602.

Gelman, Andrew. 2009. *Red State, Blue State, Poor State: Why Americans Vote the Way They Do*. Princeton: Princeton University Press.

Gelman, Andrew, and Gary King. 1994. "Enhancing Democracy through Legislative Redistricting." *American Political Science Review* 88:541–59.

Gilens, Martin. 1999. *Why Americans Hate Welfare*. Chicago: University of Chicago Press.

Gilens, Martin. 2001. "Political Ignorance and Collective Policy Preferences." *American Political Science Review* 95:379–96.

Gilens, Martin. 2005. "Inequality and Democratic Responsiveness." *Public Opinion Quarterly* 69:778–96.

Gilens, Martin. 2009. "Preference Gaps and Inequality in Representation." *PS: Political Science & Politics* 42:335–41.

Gilens, Martin. 2011. "Policy Consequences of Representational Inequality." In *Who Gets Represented?*, ed. Peter Enns and Christopher Wlezien. New York: Russell Sage.

Gilens, Martin. 2012. *Affluence and Influence: Economic Inequality and Political Power in America*. New York: Russell Sage Press.

Giles, Michael, and Marilyn K. Dantico. 1982. "Political Participation and Neighborhood Social Context Revisited." *American Journal of Political Science* 26:144–50.

Gimpel, James G., and Iris S. Hui. 2015. "Seeking Politically Compatible Neighbors? The Role of Neighborhood Partisan Composition in Residential Sorting." *Political Geography* 48:130–42.

Gimpel, James G., and Jason E. Schuknecht. 2004. *Patchwork Nation: Sectionalism and Political Change in American Politics*. Ann Arbor: University of Michigan Press.

Godwin, R. Kenneth 1992. "Money, Technology, and Political Interests." In *The Politics of Interests*, ed. Mark Petracca. Boulder: Westview Press.

Goodin, Robert, and John Dryzek. 1980. "Rational Participation: The Politics of Relative Power." *British Journal of Political Science* 10:273–92.

Gorman, Thomas J. 2000. "Cross-Class Perceptions of Social Class." *Sociological Spectrum* 20:93–120.

Griffin, John D., and Patrick Flavin. 2007. "Racial Differences in Information, Expectations, and Accountability." *Journal of Politics* 69:220–36.

Griffin, John D., and Patrick Flavin. 2011. "How Citizens and Their Legislators Prioritize Spheres of Representation." *Political Research Quarterly* 64:520–33.

Griffin, John D., and Brian Newman. 2005. "Are Voters Better Represented?" *Journal of Politics* 67:1206–27.

Griffin, John D., and Brian Newman. 2007. "The Unequal Representation of Latinos and Whites." *Journal of Politics* 69:1032–46.

Griffin, John D., and Brian Newman. 2008. *Minority Report: Evaluating Political Equality in America*. Chicago: University of Chicago Press.

Griffin, John D., and Brian Newman. 2012. "The Presidency and Political Equality." Paper prepared for the Annual Meeting of the American Political Science Association, New Orleans, August 28–September 1.

Griffin, John D., and Brian Newman. 2013. "Voting Power, Policy Representation, and Disparities in Voting's Rewards." *Journal of Politics* 75:52–64.

Griffin, John D., Brian Newman, and Christina Wolbrecht. 2012. "A Gender Gap in Policy Representation in the US Congress?" *Legislative Studies Quarterly* 37:35–66.

Grill, Christopher J. 2007. *The Public Side of Representation*. New York: SUNY Press.

Grumbach, Jacob M. 2015. "Does the American Dream Matter for Members of Congress? Social-Class Backgrounds and Roll-Call Votes." *Political Research Quarterly* 68:306–23.

Hacker, Jacob. 2006. *The Great Risk Shift: The New Insecurity and the Decline of the American Dream.* Oxford: Oxford University Press.

Hacker, Jacob S., and Paul Pierson. 2011. *Winner-Take-All Politics: How Washington Made the Rich Richer—and Turned Its Back on the Middle Class*. New York: Simon and Schuster.

Hacker, Jacob, et al. 2005. "Inequality and Public Policy." In *Inequality and American Democracy: What We Know and What We Need to Learn*, ed. Larry Jacobs and Theda Skocpol. New York: Russell Sage.

Hall, Richard L. 1996. *Participation in Congress*. New Haven: Yale University Press.

Hansford, Thomas G., and Brad T. Gomez. 2010. "Estimating the Electoral Effects of Voter Turnout." *American Political Science Review* 104:268–88.

Hansford, Thomas G., and Brad T. Gomez. 2015. "Reevaluating the Sociotropic Economic Voting Hypothesis." *Electoral Studies* 39:15–25.

Harden, Jeffrey. 2015. *Multidimensional Democracy: A Supply and Demand Theory of Representation in American Legislatures*. Cambridge: Cambridge University Press.

Hasen, Richard L. 2012. *The Voting Wars: From Florida 2000 to the Next Election Meltdown*. New Haven: Yale University Press.

Haspel, Moshe, and H. Gibbs Knotts. 2005. "Location, Location, Location: Precinct Placement and the Costs of Voting." *Journal of Politics* 67:560–73.

Hero, Rodney E., and Caroline J. Tolbert. 1995. "Latinos and Substantive Representation in the U.S. House." *American Journal of Political Science* 39:640–52.

Hersh, Eitan D., and Clayton Nall. 2016. "The Primacy of Race in the Geography of Income-Based Voting: New Evidence from Public Voting Records." *American Journal of Political Science* 60:289–303.

Hershey, Marjorie. 2009. "What We Know about Voter-ID Laws, Registration, and Turnout." *PS: Political Science & Politics* 42:87–91.

Highton, Benjamin, and Raymond E. Wolfinger. 2001. "The Political Implications of Higher Turnout." *British Journal of Political Science* 31:179–223.

Hill, Kim Quaile, and Patricia A. Hurley. 1999. "Dyadic Representation Reappraised." *American Journal of Political Science* 43:109–37.

Hill, Kim Quaile and Jan E. Leighley. 1992. "The Policy Consequences of Class Bias in State Electorates." *American Journal of Political Science* 36:351–65.

Hill, Kim Quaile, Jan E. Leighley, and Angela Hinton-Andersson. 1995. "Lower-Class Mobilization and Policy Linkage in the U.S. States." *American Journal of Political Science* 39:75–86.

Hirano, Shigeo, James M. Snyder Jr., Stephen Ansolabehere, and John Mark Hansen. 2010. "Primary Elections and Partisan Polarization in the US Congress." *Quarterly Journal of Political Science* 5:169–91.

Hirsch, Barry T., and David A. Macpherson. 2002. "Union Membership and Coverage Database from the Current Population Survey." *Industrial and Labor Relations Review* 56:349–54.

Hirsch, Barry, and David Macpherson. 2013. "Union Membership and Coverage Database." Available online at www.unionstats.com

Hitlin, Steven. 2003. "Values as the Core of Personal Identity: Drawing Links between Two Theories of Self." *Social Psychology Quarterly* 66:118–37.

Hochschild, Jennifer. 1981. *What's Fair? American Beliefs about Distributive Justice*. Cambridge: Harvard University Press.

Hopkins, Daniel J. 2009. "Partisan Reinforcement and the Poor: The Impact of Context on Explanations for Poverty." *Social Science Quarterly* 90:744–64.

Huckfeldt, Robert. 1979. "Political Participation and the Neighborhood Social Context." *American Journal of Political Science* 23:579–92.
Huckfeldt, Robert. 1986. *Politics in Context: Assimilation and Conflict in Urban Neighborhoods.* New York: Agathon Press.
Huckfeldt, R. Robert, Paul E. Johnson, and John D. Sprague. 2004. *Political Disagreement.* Cambridge: Cambridge University Press.
Huckfeldt, Robert, and John Sprague. 1992. "Political Parties and Electoral Mobilization: Political Structure, Social Structure, and the Party Canvass." *American Political Science Review* 86:70–86.
Hulse, Carl, and David M. Herszenhorn. 2010. "Democrats Call Off Climate Bill Effort." *New York Times*, June 23.
Husted, Thomas A., Lawrence W. Kenny, and Rebecca B. Morton. 1995. "Constituent Errors in Assessing Their Senators." *Public Choice* 83:251–71.
Jackman, Mary R., and Robert W. Jackman. 1985. *Class Awareness in the United States.* Berkeley: University of California Press.
Jackman, Robert W. 1987. "Political Institutions and Voter Turnout in the Industrial Democracies." *American Political Science Review* 81:405–23.
Jackson, Robert A., Robert D. Brown, and Gerald C. Wright. 1998. "Registration, Turnout, and the Electoral Representativeness of US State Electorates." *American Politics Research* 26:259–87.
Jacobs, Lawrence R., and Theda Skocpol. 2005. *Inequality and American Democracy: What We Know and What We Need to Learn.* New York: Russell Sage.
Jacoby, William G. 2000. "Issue Framing and Public Opinion on Government Spending." *American Journal of Political Science* 44:750–67.
Jacoby, William G. 2006. "Value Choices and American Public Opinion." *American Journal of Political Science* 50:706–23.
Janda, Kenneth. 1993. "Comparative Political Parties: Research and Theory." In *Political Science: The State of the Discipline II*, ed. Ada W. Finifter. Washington, DC: American Political Science Association.
Jones, Bradford S., and Barbara Norrander. 1996. "The Reliability of Aggregated Public Opinion Measures." *American Journal of Political Science* 40:295–309.
Jost, John T., and Orsolya Hunyady. 2005. "Antecedents and Consequences of System-Justifying Ideologies." *Current Directions in Psychological Science* 14:260–65.
Jost, John T., Mahzarin R. Banaji, and Brian A. Nosek. 2004. "A Decade of System Justification Theory: Accumulated Evidence of Conscious and Unconscious Bolstering of the Status Quo." *Political Psychology* 25:881–919.
Jusko, Karen Long. 2008. "The Political Representation of the Poor." PhD diss., University of Michigan.
Kaestle, Carl. 1983. *Pillars of the Republic: Common Schools and American Society, 1780–1860.* New York: Macmillan.
Kawachi, Ichiro, Bruce P. Kennedy, Kimberly Lochner, and Deborah Prothrow-Stith. 1997. "Social Capital, Income Inequality, and Mortality." *American Journal of Public Health* 87:1491–98.
Kelleher, Christine, and David Lowery. 2004. "Political Participation and Metropolitan Institutional Contexts." *Urban Affairs Review* 39:720–57.
Kelleher, Christine A., and David Lowery. 2009. "Central City Size, Metropolitan Institutions and Political Participation." *British Journal of Political Science* 39:59–92.

Kelly, Nathan. 2009. *The Politics of Income Inequality in the United States*. Cambridge: Cambridge University Press.

Kennedy, Courtney, Andrew Mercer, Scott Keeter, Nick Hatley, Kyley McGeeney, and Alejandra Gimenez. 2016. "Evaluating Online Nonprobability Surveys." Pew Research Center. http://www.pewresearch.org/2016/05/02/evaluating-online-nonprobability-surveys/

Kerrissey, Jasmine, and Evan Schofer. 2013. "Union Membership and Political Participation in the United States." *Social Forces* 91:895–928.

Key, V. O. 1949. *Southern Politics in State and Nation*. New York: Knopf.

Key, V. O. 1961. *Public Opinion and American Democracy*. New York: Knopf.

Kingdon, John W. 1984. *Agendas, Alternatives, and Public Policies*. Boston: Little, Brown.

Kingdon, John W. 1989. *Congressmen's Voting Decisions*. New York: Harper and Row.

Krehbiel, Keith. 2010. Chicago: *Pivotal Politics: A Theory of US Lawmaking*. Chicago: University of Chicago Press.

Ladewig, Jeffrey W. 2010. "Ideological Polarization and the Vanishing of Marginals: Retrospective Roll-Call Voting in the U.S. Congress." *Journal of Politics* 72:499–512.

Lamb, Charles M. 2005. *Housing Segregation in Suburban America since 1960*. Cambridge: Cambridge University Press.

Lancee, Bram, and Herman G. Van de Werfhorst. 2012. "Income Inequality and Participation: A Comparison of 24 European Countries." *Social Science Research* 41:1166–78.

Lawrence, Eric D., and John Sides. 2014. "The Consequences of Political Innumeracy." *Research & Politics* 1:1–8.

Layman, Geoff, Thomas Carsey, John C. Green, Richard Herrera, and Rosalyn Cooperman. 2010. "Activists and Conflict Extension in American Party Politics." *American Political Science Review* 104:324–46.

Leighley, Jan. 1990. "Social Interaction and Contextual Influences on Political Participation." *American Politics Research* 18:479–95.

Leighley, Jan E., and Jonathan Nagler. 2007. "Unions, Voter Turnout, and Class Bias in the US Electorate, 1964–2004." *Journal of Politics* 69:430–41.

Lenzi, Michela, et al. 2012. "How Neighborhood Structural and Institutional Features Can Shape Neighborhood Social Connectedness: A Multilevel Study of Adolescent Perceptions." *American Journal of Community Psychology* 51:451–67.

Leventhal, Tama, and Jeanne Brooks-Gunn. 2000. "The Neighborhoods They Live In: The Effects of Neighborhood Residence on Child and Adolescent Outcomes." *Psychological Bulletin* 126:309–37.

Lijphart, Arend. 1997. "Unequal Participation: Democracy's Unresolved Dilemma." *American Political Science Review* 91:1–14.

Lindblom, Charles. 1977. *Politics and Markets: The World's Political-Economic Systems*. New York: Basic Books.

Lipset, Seymour Martin. 1997. *American Exceptionalism: A Double-Edged Sword*. New York: W. W. Norton.

Lipset, Seymour Martin, and Gary Marks. 2000. *It Didn't Happen Here: Why Socialism Failed in the United States*. New York: W. W. Norton.

Lublin, David. 1999. *The Paradox of Representation*. Princeton: Princeton University Press.

Lupia, Arthur, Adam Seth Lavine, Jesse O. Menning, and Gisela Sin. 2007. "Were Bush Tax Cut Supporters 'Simply Ignorant?' A Second Look at Conservatives and Liberals in 'Homer Gets a Tax Cut.'" *Perspectives on Politics* 5:773–84.

Lyman, Brian. 2014. "Alabama Takes Look at New Funding Plan for Students." *Montgomery Advertiser*, October 13. http://www.montgomeryadvertiser.com/story/news/local/alabama/2014/10/12/alabama-takes-look-new-funding-plan-students/17144707/

Mann, Thomas E., and Norman Ornstein. 2006. *The Broken Branch: How Congress Is Failing America and How to Get It Back on Track*. Oxford: Oxford University Press.

Massey, Douglas S. 1996. "The Age of Extremes: Concentrated Affluence and Poverty in the Twenty-First Century." *Demography* 33:395–412.

Mayhew, David R. 2004. *Congress: The Electoral Connection*. 2nd ed. New Haven: Yale University Press.

McCall, Leslie. 2013. *The Undeserving Rich: American Beliefs about Inequality, Opportunity, and Redistribution*. Cambridge: Cambridge University Press

McCarty, Nolan, Keith T. Poole, and Howard Rosenthal. 2006. *Polarized America: Ideology and the Dance of Unequal Riches*. Cambridge, MA: MIT Press.

McClurg, Scott D. 2003. "Social Networks and Political Participation: The Role of Social Interaction in Explaining Political Participation." *Political Research Quarterly* 56:449–64.

Meltzer, Allan H., and Scott F. Richard. 1981. "A Rational Theory of the Size of Government." *Journal of Political Economy* 89:914–27.

Mettler, Suzanne, and Joe Soss. 2004. "The Consequences of Public Policy for Democratic Citizenship: Bridging Policy Studies and Mass Politics." *Perspectives on Politics* 2 (5): 5–73.

Meyer, Stephen Grant. 2000. *As Long as They Don't Move Next Door: Segregation and Racial Conflict in American Neighborhoods*. New York: Rowman & Littlefield.

Miler, Kristina. 2010. *Constituency Representation in Congress: The View from Capitol Hill*. Cambridge: Cambridge University Press.

Miller, Arthur H., and Ola Listhaug. 1990. "Political Parties and Confidence in Government: A Comparison of Norway, Sweden and the United States." *British Journal of Political Science* 20:357–86.

Miller, Warren E., and Donald E. Stokes. 1963. "Constituency Representation in Congress." *American Political Science Review* 57:45–56.

Mitchell, Glenn E., and Christopher Wlezien. 1995. "The Impact of Legal Constraints on Voter Registration, Turnout, and the Composition of the American Electorate." *Political Behavior* 177:179–202.

Musterd, Sako, and Wim Ostendorf. 2013. *Urban Segregation and the Welfare State: Inequality and Exclusion in Western Cities*. New York: Routledge.

Mutz, Diana C. 2002. "The Consequences of Cross-Cutting Networks for Political Participation." *American Journal of Political Science* 46:838–55.

Nall, Clayton. 2015. "The Political Consequences of Spatial Policies: How Interstate Highways Facilitated Geographic Polarization." *Journal of Politics* 77:394–406.

Newman, Benjamin J. 2014. "My Poor Friend: Financial Distress in One's Social Network, the Perceived Power of the Rich, and Support for Redistribution." *Journal of Politics* 76:126–38.

Newman, Benjamin J., Christopher D. Johnston, and Patrick L. Lown. 2015. "False Consciousness or Class Awareness? Local Income Inequality, Personal Economic Position, and Belief in American Meritocracy." *American Journal of Political Science* 59:326–40.

Nicholson, Stephen P., and Gary M. Segura. 2012. "Who's the Party of the People? Economic Populism and the US Public's Beliefs about Political Parties." *Political Behavior* 34:369–89.

Nie, Norman H., Jane Junn, and Kenneth Stehlik-Barry. 1996. *Education and Democratic Citizenship in America*. Chicago: University of Chicago Press.

Noelle-Neumann, Elisabeth. 1993. *The Spiral of Silence*. Chicago: University of Chicago Press.

O'Brien, Robert M. 1990. "Estimating the Reliability of Aggregate-Level Variables Based on Individual-Level Characteristics." *Sociological Methods and Research* 18:473–504.

Oliver, J. Eric. 1999. "The Effects of Metropolitan Economic Segregation on Local Civic Participation." *American Journal of Political Science* 43:186–212.

Oorschot, Wim van, and Loek Halman. 2000. "Blame or Fate, Individual or Social?" *European Societies* 2:1–28.

Oxendine, Alina. 2012. "City Seclusion and Social Exclusion: How and Why Economic Disparities Harm Social Capital." In *Urban Social Capital: Civil Society and City Life*, ed. Joseph D. Lewandowski and Gregory W. Streich. New York: Ashgate.

Pacheco, Julianna Sandell. 2008. "Political Socialization in Context: The Effect of Political Competition on Youth Voter Turnout." *Political Behavior* 30:415–36.

Page, Benjamin, Larry Bartels, and Jason Seawright. 2011. "Interviewing Wealthy Americans." Working Paper, Institute for Policy Research, Northwestern University.

Page, Benjamin, Larry Bartels, and Jason Seawright. 2013. "Democracy and the Policy Preferences of Wealthy Americans." *Perspectives on Politics* 11:51–73.

Page, Benjamin I., and Lawrence R. Jacobs. 2009. *Class War? What Americans Really Think about Economic Inequality*. Chicago: University of Chicago Press.

Page, Benjamin, and Robert Shapiro. 1992. *The Rational Public: Fifty Years of Trends in Americans' Policy Preferences*. Chicago: University of Chicago Press.

Parker, Glenn R., and Roger H. Davidson. 1979. "Why Do Americans Love Their Congressmen So Much More Than Their Congress?" *Legislative Studies Quarterly* 4:53–61.

Peel, Roy Victor, and Thomas Claude Donnelly. 1935. *The 1932 Campaign: An Analysis*. New York: Farrar & Rinehart.

Petrova, Maria. 2008. "Inequality and Media Capture." *Journal of Public Economics* 92:183–212.

Pettigrew, Thomas F., and Linda R. Tropp. 2006. "A Meta-Analytic Test of Intergroup Contact Theory." *Journal of Personality and Social Psychology* 90:751–71.

Pierson, Paul. 1993. "When Effect Becomes Cause: Policy Feedback and Political Change." *World Politics* 45:595–628.

Pierson, Paul, and Theda Skocpol. 2007. *The Transformation of American Politics: Activist Government and the Rise of Conservatism*. Princeton: Princeton University Press.

Piketty, Thomas, and Emmanuel Saez. 2014. "Inequality in the Long Run." *Science* 344:838–43.

Piston, Spencer. 2014. "Sympathy for the Poor, Resentment of the Rich, and Their Political Consequences." PhD diss., University of Michigan.

Piven, Frances Fox, and Richard A. Cloward. 1988. *Why Americans Don't Vote*. New York: Pantheon.

Piven, Frances Fox, and Richard A. Cloward. 2000. *Why Americans Still Don't Vote: And Why Politicians Want It That Way*. Boston: Beacon Press.

Plutzer, Eric. 2002. "Becoming a Habitual Voter: Inertia, Resources, and Growth in Young Adulthood." *American Political Science Review* 96:41–56.

Poole, Keith T., and Howard Rosenthal. 2007. *Ideology and Congress*. New York: Transaction.

Popp, Elizabeth, and Thomas J. Rudolph. 2011. "A Tale of Two Ideologies: Explaining Public Support for Economic Interventions." *Journal of Politics* 73:808–20.

Powell, Lynda. 1982. "Issue Representation in Congress." *Journal of Politics* 44:658–78.

Radcliff, Benjamin, and Patricia Davis. 2000. "Labor Organization and Electoral Participation in Industrial Democracies." *American Journal of Political Science* 44:132–41.

Rigby, Elizabeth, and Gerald C. Wright. 2011. "Whose Statehouse Democracy?" In *Who Gets Represented?*, ed. Peter Enns and Christopher Wlezien. New York: Russell Sage Press.

Rigby, Elizabeth, and Gerald C. Wright. 2013. "Political Parties and Representation of the Poor in the American States." *American Journal of Political Science* 57:552–65.

Rogers, Jonathan. 2014. "A Communotropic Theory of Economic Voting." *Electoral Studies* 36:107–16.

Roosa, Mark W., Sarah Jones, Jenn-Yun Tein, and Willa Cree. 2003. "Prevention Science and Neighborhood Influences on Low-Income Children's Development: Theoretical and Methodological Issues." *American Journal of Community Psychology* 31:55–72.

Rosenstone, Steven J. 1982. "Economic Adversity and Voter Turnout." *American Journal of Political Science* 26:25–46.

Rosenstone, Steven J., and John Mark Hansen. 1993. *Mobilization, Participation, and Democracy in America*. New York: Longman.

Rosset, Jan, Nathalie Giger, and Julian Bernauer. 2013. "More Money, Fewer Problems? Cross-Level Effects of Economic Deprivation on Political Representation." *West European Politics* 36:817–35.

Rueda, David, Daniel Stegmueller, and Timo Idema. 2014. "The Effects of Income Expectations on Redistribution Preferences in Western Europe." Paper presented at the Annual Meeting of the American Political Science Association, Chicago, April 3–6.

Rusk, David. 1995. *Cities without Suburbs*. Washington, DC: Woodrow Wilson Press.

Sadin, Meredith. 2014. "Campaigning with Class: Ambivalent Stereotypes and Wealth in U.S. Elections." PhD diss., Princeton University.

Sampson, Robert J. 2003. "The Neighborhood Context of Well-Being." *Perspectives in Biology and Medicine* 46:53–64.

Sanders, Elizabeth. 1980. "On the Costs, Utilities, and Simple Joys of Voting." *Journal of Politics* 42:854–63.

Schattschneider, E. E. 1960. *The Semisovereign People*. New York: Holt, Rinehart and Winston.

Scheve, Kenneth, and David Stasavage. 2006. "Religion and Preferences for Social Insurance." *Quarterly Journal of Political Science* 1:255–86.

Schlozman, Key Lehman. 1984. "What Accent the Heavenly Chorus? Political Equality and the American Pressure System." *Journal of Politics* 46:1006–32.

Schlozman, Key Lehman, and John Tierney 1986. *Organized Interests and American Democracy*. New York: Harper and Row.

Schroeder, Matthew B. 2008. "Economic Inequality, Economic Segregation, and Political Participation." PhD diss., Pennsylvania State University.

Sears, David O., and Carolyn L. Funk. 1990. "The Limited Effect of Economic Self-Interest on the Political Attitudes of the Mass Public." *Journal of Behavioral Economics* 19:247–71.

Serra, George, and David Moon. 1994. "Casework, Issue Positions, and Voting in Congressional Elections: A District Analysis." *Journal of Politics* 56:200–213.

Sigelman, Lee. 1982. "The Nonvoting Voter in Voting Research." *American Journal of Political Science* 26:47–56.

Smets, Kaat, and Carolien van Ham. 2013. "The Embarrassment of Riches? A Meta-Analysis of Individual-Level Research on Voter Turnout." *Electoral Studies* 32:344–59.

Soder, Roger.1996. *Democracy, Education, and the Schools*. San Francisco: Jossey-Bass.

Solt, Frederick. 2008. "Economic Inequality and Democratic Political Engagement." *American Journal of Political Science* 52:48–60.

Solt, Frederick. 2010. "Does Economic Inequality Depress Electoral Participation? Testing the Schattschneider Hypothesis." *Political Behavior* 32:285–301.

Sombart, Werner. 1976. *Why Is There No Socialism in the United States?* New York: M. E. Sharpe.

Soroka, Stuart, and Christopher Wlezien. 2005. "Opinion–Policy Dynamics: Public Preferences and Public Expenditure in the U.K." *British Journal of Political Science* 35:665–89.

Soroka, Stuart, and Christopher Wlezien. 2008. "On the Limits to Inequality in Representation." *PS: Political Science and Politics* 41:319–27.

Soss, Joe, and Lawrence R. Jacobs. 2009. "The Place of Inequality: Non-participation in the American Polity." *Political Science Quarterly* 124:95–125.

Soroka, Stuart, and Christopher Wlezien. 2010. *Degrees of Democracy*. Cambridge: Cambridge University Press.

Stewart, Endya B., Eric A. Stewart, and Ronald L. Simons. 2007. "The Effect of Neighborhood Context on the College Aspirations of African American Adolescents." *American Educational Research Journal* 44:896–919.

Stimson, James. 1999. *Public Opinion in America*. Boulder, CO: Westview Press.

Stimson, James. 2011. "The Issues in Representation." In *Who Gets Represented?*, ed. Peter Enns and Christopher Wlezien, 347–60. New York: Russell Sage.

Stimson, James A. 2015. *Tides of Consent: How Public Opinion Shapes American Politics*. 2nd ed. Cambridge: Cambridge University Press.

Stoker, Laura, and M. Kent Jennings. 1995. "Life-Cycle Transitions and Political

Participation: The Case of Marriage." *American Political Science Review* 89:421–33.
Stonecash, Jeffrey M. 2000. *Class and Party in American Politics*. Boulder, CO: Westview Press.
Strömbäck, Jesper, and Daniela V. Dimitrova. 2006. "Political and Media Systems Matter: A Comparison of Election News Coverage in Sweden and the United States." *Harvard International Journal of Press/Politics* 11:131–47.
Sullivan, John L., and Eric M. Uslaner. 1978. "Congressional Behavior and Electoral Marginality." *American Journal of Political Science* 22:536–53.
Svallfors, Stefan. 2006. *The Moral Economy of Class: Class and Attitudes in Comparative Perspective*. Palo Alto, CA: Stanford University Press.
Tam Cho, Wendy K., James G. Gimpel, and Iris S. Hui. 2013. "Voter Migration and the Geographic Sorting of the American Electorate." *Annals of the Association of American Geographers* 103:856–70.
Tate, William F. 2008. "'Geography of Opportunity': Poverty, Place, and Educational Outcomes." *Educational Researcher* 37:397–411.
Tavares, António F., and Jered B. Carr. 2013. "So Close, Yet So Far Away? The Effects of City Size, Density, and Growth on Local Civic Participation." *Journal of Urban Affairs* 35:283–302.
Theriault, Sean M. 2008. *Party Polarization in Congress*. Cambridge: Cambridge University Press.
Tiebout, Charles M. 1956. "A Pure Theory of Local Expenditures." *Journal of Political Economy* 64:416–24.
Twyman, Joe. 2008. "Getting It Right: YouGov and Online Survey Research in Britain." *Journal of Elections, Public Opinion and Parties* 18:343–54.
Ura, Joseph Daniel and Christopher R. Ellis. 2008. "Income, Preferences, and the Dynamics of Policy Responsiveness" *PS: Political Science and Politics* 41:785–94.
Uslaner, Eric M., and Mitchell Brown. 2005. "Inequality, Trust, and Civic Engagement." *American Politics Research* 33:868–94.
Van der Waal, Jeroen, Peter Achterberg, and Dick Houtman. 2007. "Class Is Not Dead—It Has Been Buried Alive: Class Voting and Cultural Voting in Postwar Western Societies (1956–1990)." *Politics & Society* 35:403–26.
Vanneman, Reeve, and Fred C. Pampel. 1977. "The American Perception of Class and Status." *American Sociological Review* 42:422–37.
Vauclair, Christin-Melanie, and Ronald Fischer. 2011. "Do Cultural Values Predict Individuals' Moral Attitudes? A Cross-Cultural Multilevel Approach." *European Journal of Social Psychology* 41 (5): 645–57.
Verba, Sidney. 2003. "Would the Dream of Political Equality Turn Out to Be a Nightmare?" *Perspectives on Politics* 1:663–79.
Verba, Sidney, and Gary R. Orren. 1985. *Equality in America: The View from the Top*. Cambridge: Harvard University Press.
Verba, Sidney, Kay Lehman Schlozman, and Henry E. Brady. 1995. *Voice and Equality: Civic Voluntarism in American Politics*. Cambridge: Harvard University Press.
Walseth, Sam. 2013. "School Funding: Where We've Been and What's Next." Minnesota Rural Education Association. http://mnrea.org/fundingreport/
Walsh, Katherine Cramer. 2004. *Talking about Politics: Informal Groups and Social Identity in American Life*. Chicago: University of Chicago Press.

Walsh, Katherine Cramer. 2015. *The Politics of Resentment: Rural Consciousness in Wisconsin and the Rise of Scott Walker*. Cambridge: Cambridge University Press.

Walzer, Michael. 1983. *Spheres of Justice*. New York: Basic Books.

Weber, Max. 1930. *The Protestant Ethic and the Spirit of Capitalism*. New York: Scribners.

Wilkinson, Richard G., and Kate E. Pickett. 2006. "Income Inequality and Population Health: A Review and Explanation of the Evidence." *Social Science & Medicine* 62:1768–84.

Wallerstein, Michael, and Bruce Western. 2000. "Unions in Decline? What Has Changed and Why." *Annual Review of Political Science* 3: 355–77.

Wilson, William Julius. 2012. *The Truly Disadvantaged: The Inner City, the Underclass, and Public Policy*. Chicago: University of Chicago Press.

Winters, Jeffrey A., and Benjamin I. Page. 2009. "Oligarchy in the United States?" *Perspectives on Politics* 7:731–51.

Wlezien, Christopher. 1995. "The Public as Thermostat: Dynamics of Preferences for Spending." *American Journal of Political Science* 39:981–1000.

Wolfinger, Raymond E., and Steven J. Rosenstone. 1980. *Who Votes?* New Haven: Yale University Press.

Wolpert, Robin M., and James G. Gimpel. 1997. "Information, Recall, and Accountability: The Electorate's Response to the Clarence Thomas Nomination." *Legislative Studies Quarterly* 22:535–50.

Wright, Gerald C. 1978. "Candidates' Policy Positions and Voting in U.S. Congressional Elections." *Legislative Studies Quarterly* 3:445–64.

Yen, Irene H., and George A. Kaplan. 1999. "Neighborhood Social Environment and Risk of Death: Multilevel Evidence from the Alameda County Study." *American Journal of Epidemiology* 149:898–907.

Zaller, John. 1992. *The Nature and Origins of Mass Opinion*. Cambridge: Cambridge University Press.

Index

Printed and bound by CPI Group (UK) Ltd, Croydon, CR0 4YY
16/09/2026
14963491-0005